A Functional Perspective on
Language, Action, and Interpretation

Natural Language Processing

1

Mouton de Gruyter
Berlin · New York

A Functional Perspective on Language, Action, and Interpretation

An Initial Approach with a View to Computational Modeling

by
Erich Steiner

Mouton de Gruyter
Berlin · New York 1991

Mouton de Gruyter (formerly Mouton, The Hague)
is a Division of Walter de Gruyter & Co., Berlin.

⊗ Printed on acid-free paper which falls within the guidelines
of the ANSI to ensure permanence and durability.

Library of Congress Cataloging in Publication Data

Steiner, Erich.
A functional perspective on language, action, and interpretation ; an initial approach with a view to computational modeling / Erich Steiner.
p. cm. — (Natural language processing ; 1)
Includes bibliographical references and index.
ISBN 3-11-012379-7 (cloth : alk. paper)
1. Systemic grammar. 2. Children—Language. 3. Computational linguistics. I. Title. II. Series.
P149.S75 1991 91-33628
401'.41—dc20 CIP

Die Deutsche Bibliothek — Cataloging in Publication Data

Steiner, Erich:
A functional perspective on language, action, and interpretation : an initial approach with a view to computational modeling / Erich Steiner. — Berlin ; New York : Mouton de Gruyter, 1991
(Natural language processing ; 1)
ISBN 3-11-012379-7
NE: GT

Printing: Ratzlow Druck, Berlin. — Binding: Dieter Mikolai, Berlin.
Printed in Germany

Contents

Acknowledgements

An earlier version of this study was accepted as "Habilitationsschrift" at the "Philosophische Fakultät der Universität des Saarlandes" in February 1989.

I am grateful to the following colleagues, who have at various stages supported the present study by their critical comments:

Several earlier versions of chapters of this study were read and critically commented on by Paul Chilton (Warwick), Eirean Davies (London), Christa Hauenschild (Berlin), and R.H. Robins (London). During my term as Visiting Lecturer at RICE University, Houston/Texas, I profited from insightful discussions with Sydney Lamb and Peter Reich on topics of this study. Bill Mann, John Bateman , Bob Kasper, Christian Matthiessen, and Cecile Paris (ISI/USC Los Angeles) provided a very stimulating environment within which to argue within and about Systemic Linguistics during joint periods of work at the University of the Saarland in Saarbrücken, particularly within Eurotra-D, at the Gesellschaft für Mathematik und Datenverarbeitung in Darmstadt, and at the Information Sciences Institute of the University of Southern California in Marina del Rey. The person, though, to whom I owe probably most, as far as systemic theory is concerned, is Robin Fawcett, with whom I had the chance of working for a whole year, and who has never lost his influence on my linguistic thinking, to the extent that it is situated within Systemic Linguistics. I am drawing heavily on his work in chapter 3 of this study.

I am also very much indebted to my colleagues at Saarbrücken University, especially Peter Godglück and Annely Rothkegel, who, on many occasions, pressed me to clarify ideas connected with the theory of activity. Roger Charlton spent an extraordinary amount of his time correcting my English in some places and commenting on matters of content.

Finally, and most importantly, it is Peter Erdmann (Saarbrücken) who in many ways accompanied this study from its first ideas to its final form: He laid many of its foundations as one of my first teachers in linguistics, he prepared its way by being a constructive supervisor of earlier work, and he followed its development as a competent and productively critical colleague.

To the extent that the former manuscript typographically ever turned into a readable monograph, I would like to give the sole credit to Peggy Daut, who very skillfully produced a print-ready version out of a heap of files, originally edited in various different editors.

None of the above mentioned, though, can in any way be held responsible for weaknesses in the present study, especially because, more often than not, I have chosen paths of my own rather than follow the advice of my colleagues.

Chapter 1
Introduction

The present study, its particular goals and its structure, grew out of an interest in what may be broadly termed *functional linguistics*, its relationship to cognition, and in computational applications of such an approach. The interest in cognition as an element of human goal-directed action led to the cognitive interpretation of a certain type of functional grammar, and to the empirical investigation of some types of semantic complexity in English child language. The computational applications will be referred to more fully below and at various places within this study. Essentially, they consist in the implementation of a substantial part of the clause semantics used here in a machine translation system (EUROTRA-D, a multilingual machine translation project of the European community). The text grammar deriving from the theory of goal-directed action outlined here is formulated with an orientation towards computational text generation. Still, this study is mainly one in linguistics with much of the computational work being reported elsewhere (cf. Steiner, Schmidt & Zelinsky-Wibbelt 1988; Steiner 1986, 1989, 1990; Steiner & Winter 1987; Steiner & Winter-Thielen 1988; Bateman, Kasper, Schütz & Steiner 1989, 1990; Steiner et al. 1990).

Under a global perspective, our investigation has two goals:

The primary goal is a contribution to the further development of some aspects of the theory of *Systemic Linguistics*, also known as *Systemic Functional Grammar* (cf. Berry 1975, 1977; Butler 1985; Halliday 1985a; Halliday & Martin 1981; Halliday & Fawcett 1987; Kasper 1987; Patten 1988). I have described its history and its relevance for German linguistics extensively elsewhere (Steiner 1983).

The secondary goal is an investigation of certain phenomena of the language of English speaking children. In this investigation, we shall apply Systemic Linguistics in a version including the new developments which we have introduced, treating it as a hypothesis about cognitive processes in children's interactions, thus aiming at empirical evidence for the theoretical claims made under the primary goal.

What we shall have to say in this study, and the way how we shall say it, is formulated with these two goals in mind - and specifically not with any goals which would also be very legitimate, but are not on our agenda at the moment, such as goals derived from and situated within cognitive psychology or artificial intelligence. These remarks appear to be important, because with a study such as the present one, we are moving on the borderline between linguistics and several neighbouring disciplines, so that it becomes important to keep in mind where precisely we want to make a contribution - in other words, what is our focus and what is not.

As far as areas of development under the primary goal are concerned, we shall concentrate on two main aspects of the theory: we shall make a proposal for a certain view of the level of *context of situation*, a proposal which is new within Systemic Linguistics but which bears a very obvious relationship to work that has gone on before within the theory (cf. chapter 2). This will entail discussing some essentials of a grammar of human goal-directed action, regarding it as a cognitive model underlying the structure of this kind of action, and considering the representations generated by such a grammar as a type of knowledge representation. Secondly, we shall critically evaluate and, where necessary, modify certain core areas of the theory, mainly the semantics of transitivity, circumstances, time, logical connection, and aktionsart, and also the notion of *context dependency*, a frequently used key notion in Systemic Linguistics and in work in other theories (cf. chapter 3).

One of the basic views of Systemic Linguistics is that theory and practice, particularly in their development, should be interrelated in a kind of dialectical relationship: Theoretically developed notions have to be tested in practice, and the experience gained in this cycle of testing should reflect back on the development of the theory, after which another cycle starts. There is, in the systemic view, no strict separation between theory and practice, between *theoretical linguistics* and *applied linguistics*. This basic view has straightforward implications for our work here:

We shall set out (chapter 2.3.) by outlining a model of goal- directed action which gives structure to the level of *context of situation*. We shall then apply this model to different types of linguistic texts to explore some of the main characteristics of this framework in the practice of descriptive work (cf. 2.4.). It will be seen that this aspect of the current study covers, within a Systemic environment, many aspects that would in other theories be labelled *pragmatics*. Next, we shall use our theoretical claims about goal-directed action to generate a set of hypotheses concerning the structure of language in certain phases of action in texts taken from a study in English child language development (2.5.). These hypotheses provide another testing ground for the theory of goal-directed action.
Apart from this, testing our hypotheses will involve us in pursuing our secondary goal: in order to be able to test our hypotheses, we shall have to critically evaluate and also sometimes change some key areas of systemic semantics on clause level. This second cycle of testing will give us feed-back not only on the plausibility of the theory of goal-directed action, but also on systemic "core" semantics. In the process, we shall have to discuss critically several key notions in the area of English syntax and semantics in general.

It might be appropriate, at this point, to emphasize the increasingly important role which computational applications have for the development of Systemic Linguistics:

So far, computational applications of systemic linguistics to text generation and parsing have usually been based on the account that SFG gives for the clause, either in its functional syntax (Winograd 1972, 1983: 273ff.; McCord 1977; Davey 1978), or in semantics and syntax (Mann & Matthiessen 1985; Matthiessen 1987; Matthiessen & Bateman in press). There are also implementations of aspects of systemic semantics in interaction with a non-systemic syntax (Steiner et al. 1988; Sharp 1988; Heid, Rösner & Weck 1987; Yang. 1990). Increasingly, though, systemic applications in that area include the levels of *text* and *rhetorical structure* as knowledge representations (Bateman 1985, 1987, 1989; Bateman & Paris 1989; Houghton & Isard 1987; Mann & Thompson 1987a,b), and it is here that we want to make a theoretical contribution in chapters 2.3., 2.4, 2.6., and 3.2. mainly. So, while computational applications will not be foregrounded in this study, we intend to present some of the theoretical work which is necessary for an implementation of the models of *context* and *situation* developed in this study. These models will interface either with the clause semantics directly, or, at least for some types of texts, with an approach to text structure as developed in section 2.4.5. below. Recent formalizations of aspects of SFG have influenced our thinking in some chapters in obvious ways (cf. Patten & Ritchie 1987; Kasper 1987, 1988 a,b).

As we have said above, our secondary goal is the exploration of certain phenomena in English child language. In this connection, it would be appropriate to express our gratitutde to the former Polytechnic of Wales Child Language Development Project for making their entire extensive corpus available to us (for the written transcripts cf. Fawcett & Perkins 1980). The most interesting aspects of our work in this area are the following: We have to develop definitions and metrices for semantic complexity within the framework of Systemic Linguistics. Furthermore, we shall explore *phase of action* as an independent variable, a variable which has so far been relatively neglected in child language studies.

Finally, we would like to make some commments on the overall structure of our presentation:

Section 2 develops a framework for the representation of human goal-directed action, whereas section 3 tests hypotheses deriving from the theory underlying the framework developed in section 2. The introduction of the framework is attempted in a slightly unusual way, proceeding in three larger steps:

- Discussing the historical and theoretical background (2.1, 2.2.)
- Providing the conceptual backbone (2.3.)
- Developing details and topics for further research in application to texts (2.4.)

Section 2.6., then, has a special status linking the concepts developed in earlier sections to work in artificial intelligence. Chapter 3 treats the theory developed earlier as a source of hypotheses about certain types of semantic complexity in the language of children engaged in a certain type of goal-directed action.

To those readers who would be more interested in a presentation of the model developed here, and less in questions deriving from it, there is a straightforward way of getting an impression of the backbone of the model by reading sections 2.3., 2.4.5., and 2.6.7. only. Sections 2.4.5. and 2.6.7. , in particular, sketch a system of text generation which implements major aspects of our model. For more guidance into the structure of this study, we provide introductions to chapters and sections.

As far as our usage of the terms *Systemic Linguistics* and *Systemic Functional Grammar* is concerned, we shall use the term *Systemic Linguistics* for the overall theory, and the term *Systemic Functional Grammar* or the abbreviation SFG for the grammatical core of that theory.

As we said at the beginning of this section, the overriding goal of this study is the investigation and the further development of some aspects of the theory of Systemic Linguistics. Under this perspective, the empirical results of a pilot study which we shall obtain are only a by-product of our method. On the other hand, it is only through empirical results that a theory can be ultimately justified, and to this extent, the results are in no way unimportant, even if they are only the results of a pilot study and as such cannot claim full statistical significance.

In summary, then, we shall discuss the outline of a grammar of goal-directed action, we shall discuss the structural descriptions assigned by such a grammar to actions, regarding them as one type of *knowledge representation*, and we shall apply this framework to the generation of hypotheses guiding an exploratory investigation of some parameters of semantic complexity in English child language. The investigation itself will take us through discussions of several of the core-areas of current systemic semantics, and we will, at several places, have to suggest modifications of existing models.

Chapter 2
Goal-directed action as a structuring principle for the concept of "situation"

There are several reasons why linguists may be interested in the study of human activity in general:

For many linguists, the problem of *meaning* has become the focus of linguistics within, roughly, the last twenty years. At the same time, it has become more obvious that the understanding of the nature of meaning is impossible as long as linguistics confines itself strictly to the domain of linguistic form. In talking about meaning, we feel the constant need to refer to concepts like *context, situation,ongoing activity*, and the like. Yet, how can we make this reference in a controlled way?

One way is to start from "inside" linguistics, i.e. to investigate bundles of formal properties of language and from there to postulate semantic entities corresponding to these bundles. This happens, for example, when we define semantic cases in terms of patterns of syntactic realization. A strong version of such a view, usually associated with *functionalism* in linguistics, holds that to every formal distinction in the structure of language corresponds a difference in function, and therefore, in meaning.

Another way is to look outside linguistics for models in neighbouring disciplines which can give us an independent motivation for a linguistic semantics. This happens, for example, in the fields of cognitive psychology, neurolinguistics, artificial intelligence, and others.

We shall start by looking outside linguistics, because it is here that the approach we are adopting has done less work previously than in other parts of the overall model. The question of the formal motivation of our semantic entities, though, will always be with us, and it will even become our focus in later sections.

Given the theoretical background of Systemic Linguistics (cf. 2.1.), it is an obvious choice to start by looking in the direction of theories of human activity in general: Systemic Linguistics regards language as a particular form of human activity, and therefore, one should expect language to inherit the characteristic properties of human activity. We shall return to some of the issues raised here in a later section (cf. 2.6).

From these considerations, the general goal of chapter 2 emerges:

We are looking for theories of human activity, and human goal- directed action in particular, aiming at a relatively broad range of phenomena while at the same time offering the possiblity of integrating specifically linguistic descriptions within an

overall description of activity. Furthermore, we want a framework that offers the possibility of linking up in its terms and rules with the methodology of the specific school of linguistics from which our linguistic work is derived, which is that of Systemic Linguistics as developed in the work of Halliday, Fawcett, and others.
It would be unreasonable to assume that we can find such a framework in a ready-made form - rather, we shall have to learn from theories of human activity while at the same time working on the specific conceptual tools that we need. The result will be a framework for describing the structure of human actions of the type we are interested in. To what extent this framework is based on a "theory" in a stricter sense, should be evaluated afterwards. From the perspective of linguistics, we hope that this framework is interesting in so far as it makes predictions for the structure of language dependent on the phase of an action this language functions in (cf. 2.5.); it generates hypotheses which will be tested in the later parts of this study (chapter 3).
The structure of chapter 2 is as follows:

Section 2.1 briefly mentiones the main lines of development of the concepts of *situation* and *context* in Systemic Linguistics, thus looking at how these concepts are approached from the perspective of that particular school of linguistics.

Section 2.2 derives its main motivation from the general claim of Systemic Linguistics that using language is one type of activity in general. Starting from that premise, we shall be briefly looking at some representative frameworks which are concerned with human activity as such, gradually narrowing down our focus to human goal-directed action.

Section 2.3 explores the possibility that some of the essential structural properties of language may be structural properties of human actions in general. Conversely, the structural properties of activities and actions should also be structural properties of language. We shall outline a framework for human goal-directed actions which allows us to assign representations to sequences of behavioural units in a parallel way to that in which a grammar of a language assigns representations to sequences of phonemes. These representations will have an *action* and a *situation* interpretation.

Section 2.4 takes the preceding section one step further: we shall explore a number of questions following from the general approach developed in 2.3., and we shall be doing so in the course of detailed analyses of texts. 2.4.5. in particular will outline the form and content of an interface between analysis of goal-directed actions and linguistic analysis.

Section 2.5, then, derives some empirical claims about types of semantic complexity from the theory of goal-directed action developed previously. The theory, essentially a systemic reformulation of the Leont'evs' theory of human activity (cf. A. A. Leont'ev 1982; A. N. Leont'ev 1978, 1981; A. A. Leont'ev, A. N. Leont' ev, & E. G. Judin 1984), will thus be used for the generation of research hypotheses to be tested in chapter 3.

Section 2.6 will be concerned with the area of knowledge representation in artificial intelligence, relating techniques developed there to the representations for knowledge about goal-directed actions used in our present study.

During this whole study, and in chapter 2 in particular, the following basic assumptions should be kept in mind:

The structure of human activities, as it appears to us as external observers, is incomplete, fragmented to a considerable extent, exhibiting parallel executions, unaccountable sequences of behaviour - in short, it is much more chaotic than the framework which we shall be discussing might lead one to expect. Yet this must be expected to be the case with any complex system which is, at least in its implementation, at some level, usually some low level, a distributed and parallel system. We have four types of reasons, though, why we believe that it is legitimate to look at a model of goal-directed action on the level and in the way we do:

- The question of *levels* of description itself: The apparent chaos of phenomena on one level is translated into order on some other, often higher, level. There is nothing surprising or new in the fact that the relatively high degree of structuring on one level such as *actions* appears as chaos on a lower level such as *operations*, if the same notions of *order* are still applied.
- Our focus in this investigation is on prototypical goal-directed actions, at least in the more theoretical parts. This is in parallel to the fact that linguists often look at constructed, deliberately chosen sentence structures before confronting actual data. This is, in our perspective, a legitimate and even necessary abstraction, provided one does not forget what it is that is to be explained ultimately, namely the full range of data with all their deviations from preconceived norms.
- Throughout this study, we shall be concentrating on the *logical* structure of actions, rather than on the *temporal* structure. This is a rough parallel to investigating, in linguistics, constituency separated from linear precedence phenomena. And, as before, as long as it is clear in one's perspective that both accounts are ultimately needed, and as long as a place is assigned to both types of structure, the emphasis on logical structure is not one-sided.
- We shall not foreground much the parallel execution of actions, or parts of them, or the overlap and scrambling between the various parts, except where our data make that necessary.

In summary, then: we are looking into some theories of human activity, and more specifically, human goal-directed action. These theories, and the emerging descriptive framework, should be judged on their own grounds, yet our main interest lies in the fact that such a theory generates hypotheses concerning the structure of human language - hypotheses which, if the theory is sound, should provide fruitful guidelines for research in certain areas, such as linguistics or child language development.

2.1 The concepts of "situation" and "context" in Systemic Linguistics

The concepts of *context of situation*, *context of culture*, and *situation* in general are central organizing concepts of Systemic Linguistics. Frequently, and with some justification, it is this fact which is taken to be the most characteristic feature of the theory as a whole, which is why the German label for it is *Britischer Kontextualismus*. The literature on these concepts within Systemic Linguistics has become so extensive that it is no longer possible to give a comprehensive survey (cf. Halliday 1978, 1984, 1985a,b; Hasan 1985).
We shall very briefly trace the main lines of development here:

- Within Systemic Linguistics, there is one tradition which takes as input for models of the situation concepts from sociology (Firth 1950; Halliday 1974; Steiner 1985b: 217ff.). This line of thought very often has to face the difficulty that sociological concepts do not, as a rule, automatically give a very prominent place to language. It is therefore frequently combined with a certain input from semiotics.
- A second line of thought within Systemic Linguistics displays a strong orientation towards semiotics (Halliday 1984; Martin 1985; Thredgold et al. 1986). The tendency of semiotics to interpret social processes as processes of communication offers one possible approach to bridging the gap between sociology and Systemic Linguistics.
- A third line of thought tries to interpret Systemic Linguistics as an application of notions from *general systems theory* to the study of language (Lemke 1983, 1984, 1985). Whereas Lemke's work may not be the most influential of the lines which we are tracing here, it certainly offers the possibility of clarifying certain key concepts of a systemic theory of *situation*, a clarification which becomes increasingly important, as more and more people are trying to apply the theory.
- A fourth line of thought takes as input ideas from cognitive psychology and artificial intelligence (Fawcett 1980, 1988; Mann & Thompson 1986, 1987a,b; Bateman 1985; Matthiessen & Bateman in press; Patten 1988, and others).

It is mainly in the four directions mentioned that systemic linguists have been looking for further development and clarification of thoughts in the area of context and situation. Methodologically, the specifically *systemic* perspective within these developments is in large parts the application of system-structure-methodology. There is, however, a deeper principle: Systemic Linguistics at its base regards language as one form of human activity in general, and therefore, the search for models can be described as the search for a theory of human activity, and a theory for language as one particular form of this activity. In that context, our own attempts here at finding some sort of interface between theories of human activities and Systemic Linguistics looks like a plausible way to follow.

Let us add a brief remark here for the sake of terminological clarification: More philosophically oriented approaches usually assume a fundamental difference between the "semantic representation of a sentence", its "core meaning", and the "interpretation of an utterance" (cf. for example Sperber & Wilson 1986: 9ff.). Considered from the perspective of such an approach, we shall be investigating a framework for interpretation of what would essentially be the semantic representation of clauses. Systemic Linguistics does not accept the dichotomy between meaning and interpretation as fundamental: While considering the interpretation of an utterance and the representation of its meaning separately may be two valid strategies for highlighting two complementary aspects of meaning, sentences and representations are, historically and methodologically, abstractions made from utterances and their interpretation in some context of situation. Within Systemic Linguistics, there is thus no separate discipline of pragmatics because questions which are often conceived as forming the content of pragmatics are, to a large extent, fully integrated within the Systemic concept of linguistics. Whenever we shall make a link with "pragmatic issues" in the sections to follow, this basic orientation should be kept in mind.

2.2 Relevant developments in the investigation of goal-directed action

2.2.1 Goal-directed action as a field of research

This section does not aim at providing a comprehensive and detailed survey of theories of human activity in general and of theories of goal-directed action in particular. For treatments giving a fuller picture of these fields, the reader is referred to Cranach & Harré (1982), Sacerdoti (1975), Lepore & McLaughlin (1986), Hartung (1982), Lenk (1977-1981), and for a more historical treatment to Leont'ev (1982). Our own perspective in this study is shaped by our specifically linguistic interests in the phenomenon of human activity. The function of this rather general section 2.2.1. is to give the outlines of the context in which we will be selecting our particular model.

Why do researchers work on theories of human activity? Why is it not sufficient to divide the field of human activity up into its special applications and let the specialists in each field formulate theories of activity for just those fields? The answer to these questions is complex, so we shall at this point only give a general answer and then look at some points in more detail:

For a considerable time in the history of academic disciplines, there existed only fairly rudimentary and general views on what the nature and structure of human

activity is, mainly in the area of philosophy. Elaborate and more detailed models of human activity seem to be a product of the fairly recent past. In general, it is the growing complexity of human production and interaction which seems to demand more powerful theories. We shall survey two complementary areas for developments of theories of human activity, two areas which we shall keep distinct for reasons of clarity, yet which are not really separated from each other:
On the one hand, we shall briefly consider some fields of material production and of "practical" problems in modern societies. The effectiveness of theories of human activity in such fields has to be one major criterion of evaluation of any such theory. On the other hand, we shall look at developments within the overall field of "theory production", i.e. academic disciplines and the competition of opposing theories within these fields.
Both of these directions should be followed, because the particular developments on both the applied and the theoretical side have to be understood in the light of internal contradictions as well as in the light of contradictions between these two general aspects of social processes. Our own criteria for concentrating on certain theories rather than on others are, even if indirectly, derived from these considerations.

Looking at the more practical realm first, we see a necessity for theories of activity in cases of social conflict. In such cases, we need to know how these conflicts arise within the structure of activity, both on the individual level (cf. Eckensberger & Silbereisen 1980 for theories on the nature of moral dilemmas) and on the supra-individual level, as covered in standard theories in sociology, political science, and political economy. It should be obvious that work in these fields leads not only to the analysis, but also to the control of human behaviour.

A second class of problems can be seen in cases in which human activity breaks down on the individual level, as in cases of psychological or sensori-motor disturbances of activity. In such cases, therapeutic work is influenced by theories and models from neurophysiology and psychology explaining certain aspects of the structure of human activity on the individual level.

A third field where theories of human activity have come into focus is the organization of productive work activities. Part of that field is covered by what is known in German as *Arbeitslehre*, or *Arbeitspsychologie*, in French as *Psychologie du Travail*, in English as *Work Study*, and as *Operations Research* if we are dealing with man-machine systems. To the extent that the organization of production and the structure of our tools, such as modern computers, are becoming more and more complex, we seem to need a framework to organize man-machine systems in such a way as to ensure maximum productivity as well as the satisfaction of the needs of the people involved in the process of production.

Finally, and perhaps most importantly, more and more activities which were formerly considered as typically human, are becoming accessible to algorithmic processing and are thus "operationalized" in the sense to be specified in section 2.3.

later on. If previously specifically human activities are to be operationalized and carried out by machines, we need some fairly specific knowledge of at least certain aspects of the overall system of human activities if we want to model the process in such a way as to gain some degree of conscious control over it. This has led to the currently very active field of artificial intelligence, a field with which we shall have to deal in some detail later on.

This is all we want to say about theories of human activity arising from the practical sphere at this point. We shall now turn to the academic or theoretical field, because within this field, too, the need for theories of human activities is being felt, usually as a product of theoretical debates and contradictions - debates and contradictions, however, which certainly are not unrelated to the practical sphere.

Within the theoretical field, we shall outline six areas.

First, we shall have to consider the so called *problem solving paradigm* in the social sciences and the humanities. Beyond the empiricist-mentalist controversy, we can detect a clear tendency to take human activity as a basic concept, rather than taking either the internal aspects of it (*ideas*) or else the external aspects (*behaviour*) as basic. Regarding human activity as a non-dualistic phenomenon is a common tendency in, for example, *interactionism*, or the problem-solving paradigm in cognitive psychology and cognitive science (Miller, Galanter & Pribram 1960; Johnson-Laird 1983; Gentner & Stevens 1983) In our context, it is certainly a decisive feature of the problem-solving paradigm that those working within it try to unite external and internal processes in the analysis of human activity without abandoning the claim for the testability of their hypotheses. The problem-solving paradigm in its modern version is connected to the advent of computers on which certain so called "intelligent" types of behaviour can be modelled, i.e. concepts can be operationalized and hypotheses can be tested in a new way.

Second, within the study of the neurophysiology of the human brain, theories have evolved which make very interesting claims about the structure of human activity on the neuronal and motoric levels. Such theories (cf. Luria 1973; Pribram 1971; and in a very different tradition Rumelhart & McClelland & the PDP reserach group 1986, and others) were often developed in opposition to conceptions of relatively fixed *centres* in the human brain, some of them using the key concept of *systems of activity* within the higher nervous system. These systems are assumed to be mobile and flexible to a considerable extent. They are described in their ontogenetic and phylogenetic development. What is crucial in our context is that these systems of activity in the higher nervous system share many features of systems of activity on *higher* or more *outward* levels, language in particular. The concept of *activity* as a unifying concept is thus extended from the observable outer level to the neuro-physiological and psychological levels, which is one way of overcoming the old empiricist-mentalist controversy.

Third, there is a school of psychology represented in the works of Vygotsky, Rubinstein, A. N. Leont'ev, A. A. Leont'ev and others. From its roots in the 1920s, it has been a central tenet of this school of psychology that it would be fundamentally wrong to argue for either side in the empiricist-mentalist controversy, and that the dilemma of these two alternatives was that they both lead into a dead-end street for psychology. The organizing concept of Marxian psychology has always been not cognition or behaviour, but human activity uniting both internal and external aspects. Human activity is considered as being built up of certain systems (cf. section 2.3.) which are identical or at least parallel in many important aspects internally and externally. The mediating link between these two aspects of activity is language, the study of which has therefore always had an important place within this school of psychology. It seems to be well motivated that concepts from this school will have a decisive role to play in what we have to say in later parts of this study.

Fourth, we have *general systems theory* and its application to social and intra-human systems of activity (cf. Ackoff & Amery 1972; Pawelzig 1970; Lemke 1984). General systems theory is another possible answer to the empiricist-mentalist controversy in at least some respects. If general systems theory is applied to the decription and analysis of human activity, it will through its methodology lead to frameworks which incorporate both internal and external aspects of human activity. Also, and interestingly in our present context, it will make possible analysis not on one, but on several levels. Furthermore, systems in general systems theory, if they are systems on different levels, can be elements of each other without having any close parallels in their structures. This is important in the analysis of activity because it helps us to avoid the danger of reductionism. In some respects, Systemic Linguistics is an application of general systems theory to language.

Fifth, certain theories of action have been developed within philosophy (Davidson 1967; LePore & McLaughlin 1986; Vermazen & Hintikka 1985; Moore. 1986), especially in von Wright's well known work. Here, formal calculi were developed as essential parts of modal and deontic logic (von Wright 1972). As it turns out, the formal and abstract representation of *likelihood* and *obligation* seems to necessitate such calculi. At some places within this study, we shall make reference to ideas from this context.

Sixth, there is *ordinary language philosophy* as in Wittgenstein's later work and the related developments in *speech act theory* (Harras 1983; Ballmer & Brennenstuhl 1981 for work having a bearing on our study). Speech act theory tries to avoid the danger of mentalistic definitions of meaning on the one hand, and of narrowly behaviouristic definitions on the other, by taking as its starting point the conception of *what we do with language*. This has led to very elaborate classifications of human actions as far as they are realized linguistically. An interesting question for the framework which we shall suggest (cf. 2.3.) is where exactly speech acts come in.

Finally, there is linguistics. Linguistics has gone through the debate between mentalism and empiricism very extensively. From, say, Bloomfield to Chomsky to McCawley, Lakoff, and Langacker, we have gone one full circle from empiricism to mentalism, and back. Current state-of-the-art studies try to find out whether and exactly in what respects the discipline has made progress in the course of this debate in the 20th century. Part of this endeavour usually is the question why a whole discipline could fall into the traps of the extremes of mentalism and empiricism. As a way out for the future, it is usually suggested that language should now be taken in its many sided interconnections with all the other aspects of human activity. The current popularity of socio-linguistic, semiotic, pragmatic, and interactionist approaches to language bears ample evidence to this trend. Particularly within textlinguistics, concepts from theories of action have deeply influenced conceptions of *story structure* and, in general, content on the ideational plane (Beaugrande 1982; van Dijk 1976, 1979). Very few linguists, however, such as Firth, Pike, or Halliday, have consistently tried to develop a framework of human activity within which the description of language could be embedded. Halliday, in particular, has been trying for a considerable time now to put into practice the description and analysis of language as "what people do realized in what people mean realized in what people say" – an integrated description of non-linguistic, semantic, and lexico-grammatical activity.

> A few years ago it was commonplace for articles on language 'behaviour' to begin with a disparaging reference to the fact that linguists confine their attention to the language 'code'; and this limitation was accepted as a fact of life, rather than being seen for what it was - a phenomenon arising at a particular time and place in the history of the study of language, when 'code' and 'behaviour' had been rigorously held apart. In the past ten years, the two have been quietly merging again, and this has revitalized the concept of 'linguistics': the justification for having a discipline devoted to the study of an object 'language' is that only in such a context is the object seen simultaneously as system and process. (Halliday 1984: 3)

Systemic Linguistics has been working for some time now towards integrated descriptions of non-linguistic and linguistic activities. Halliday (1984) represents what is perhaps the most widely accepted approach at the moment. In our study, we shall make another attempt at precisely the interface between linguistic and non-linguistic human activity.

This brings to an end our survey of areas in which theories of human activities which seem to be relevant for our task have been developed. We have separated the entire field into a more "practical side" and a more "theoretical side" in this section. This separation is, of course, artificial: both spheres develop independently to some extent, yet ultimately there are strong interdependencies. For some theoretical field to flourish, there has to be some degree of support for research activities, and this support will normally come from more practical needs inside and outside the scientific community, industry in particular. On the other hand, if decisive improvements in the sphere of production and reproduction are to be achieved, there has to be theoretical progress which will, at least in the case of more complex issues, have to come through scientific theory-building and model construction in a broad sense.

In the following section, we shall narrow down our focus to theories which will provide the more immediate theoretical context for our own work.

2.2.2 Some theoretical frameworks

So far in section 2, we have surveyed areas, with a very broad perspective, where conceptions of human activities have been developed. We shall now narrow down the focus of our view to those conceptions which seem the most promising with respect to our aims.

Let us, at this point, make explicit our criteria for choosing among the various theories: we shall look in some detail at those theories

- which have undergone some testing in practice in the sense that they have been applied to the analysis and the systematic change of activities in some area, and
- which give a high degree of attention to the role of language within the structure of human activity, and
- which are *systemic* in their general orientation, i.e they use the notions of *system* and *structure* in a way parallel to Systemic Linguistics.

Given these criteria, the range of theories to be considered is narrowed down to basically two: A theory of activity developed within Russian psychology, on the one hand, and one of the theories labelled "theories of goal- directed action" in a representative survey (Cranach & Harré 1982), which can be found in the work of von Cranach and Harré in that same volume.

The theory of activity within Russian psychology, which is referred to above, has been developed in the writings of Vygotsky, A N. Leont'ev, and his son A. A. Leont'ev (Vygotski 1962, 1978; A. N. Leont'ev 1978, 1981; A. A. Leont'ev 1975, 1982). It has been tested for its implications for the sensori-motor and neurophysiological levels of activity (Luria 1973), and it was and is being applied to the analysis and therapy of aphasia in clinical applications of this research. As far as the higher levels of activity are concerned, it has been applied extensively to the analysis and organisation of productive work activities (Hacker 1976; Hacker 1982). An application to language teaching can be found in A. A. Leont'ev (1981), and a critical appraisal of that application in Rühl (1983). Furthermore, in the course of its development, the theory entered into a mutually beneficial process of comparison and critical discussion with one of the most influential Western conceptions of activity represented by the work in Miller, Galanter and Pribram (1960). As will be seen in the more detailed exposition of the theory, it has a truly central place for language, and it certainly is *systemic* in the sense required.

The second framework has a somewhat weaker record of application (Cranach 1982; Harré 1982; Cranach & Kalbermatten 1982), yet the research methods used are well developed, and the research is fairly extensive. It also does well on our other two criteria. Furthermore, von Cranach, in particular, pays considerable attention to language within his work. People working in this framework start from a relatively recent and comprehensive knowledge of modern theories of human activity which enables them to make progress in the area of methodology and to avoid certain weaknesses which sometimes result from a simple lack of knowledge of competing theories. Von Cranach's theory in particular does not seem to make claims which are essentially different from those of the Russian theory, yet in some aspects of research methodology and experimental techniques, he seems to be more explicit and precise.

These are the two approaches which we shall deal with here. There are two more approaches which at some stages seemed to offer themselves:

First, there is the work of Rehbein in linguistics (1979, 1976a, 1976b). His approach looks like a good candidate on the second of the criteria mentioned above, though not, as far as we can ascertain, on the other two. His theory of action is in some respects closely related to those represented by the Leont'evs or by Cranach and Harré. His analysis of the planning stages, especially, is more detailed than that of most other approaches. However, his approach is a single-level one as opposed to a multi-level one, which raises a number of fundamental problems in view of our orientation towards Systemic Linguistics. Therefore, we shall not keep it, at this stage, in the focus of our interest. It is necessary to mention, though, that within the research community it is generally known that multi-level approaches raise their own problems of definition and controlling of levels within analysis, and that it therefore is not entirely unmotivated for anyone to explore a single-level approach.

Second, there are models and theories of activity developed in the context of artificial intelligence and related fields. As we shall deal with these in more detail later (cf. 2.6.), we shall say nothing more at this point.

Let us start, then, by outlining the theory of activity that is to be found in the writings of the Leont'evs mentioned above. We shall give a first outline here, in order to offer a general impression of its structure, and we shall refer to it in more detail in section 2.3. In this section, we shall begin to distinguish, by capital spelling, the technical use of certain terms. We shall make explicit our rules for doing so in 2.3. The notion of *activity* that we shall be using is restricted to activity instantiated by, or *filled*, in our later terminology, by consciously planned actions initially. Only when it is *operationalized* will it be transferred to activities which are not consciously planned, thereby losing its initially defining characteristic. In the following exposition of the first outlines of the theory, we shall be using the term *realize* in its non-technical sense. Technical usage will be introduced explicitly later on.

The theory operates with three ranks of structure within the overall structure of activity on the individual level - the ranks of ACTIVITY, ACTION, and OPERATION. From here on, we shall distinguish the technical use of words for units of activities and for phases of actions by spelling in small capitals.

ACTIVITIES are units of human behaviour, described and perceived on a general level, answering peoples cultural and/or physiological needs. ACTIVITIES are aroused by needs and have objectives which will satisfy those needs. The ACTIVITY ceases with the satisfaction of the needs which gave rise to it. ACTIVITIES, then, are units of behaviour like eating, sleeping, being together with people, working, playing etc. When we say that the level or rank of ACTIVITY is a relatively general one, we mean that here behaviour is seen directly in relationship to a need, i.e. it will, as a rule, be highly complex.

Looking more closely at the entire phenomenon of human activity, we find that an ACTIVITY is realized by one or more ACTIONS, and, conversely, that one ACTION can be the realization of quite different ACTIVITIES. For this type of relationship, we shall use the technical term *filling* from the next section onwards. An ACTION is defined by its conscious purpose or goal, designed to partly satisfy the need which gave rise to the ACTIVITY that it realizes. The conjunction of all the goals of the ACTIONS realizing an ACTIVITY under given environmental conditions will provide a sufficient condition for the achievement of the objective of the ACTIVITY. The relationships between these goals can be those of conjunction, disjunction, negation, and condition, and possibly even others, but we shall return to this question later. In fact, it is precisely the ascription of such logical relationships to goals of a series of ACTIONS which make these appear as ACTIONS belonging either to superordinate ACTIONS or else to an ACTIVITY. In this sense, the analysis of any ACTION is a process of interpretation.

ACTIONS, in this framework, are composed of four major phases, or elements, as we shall call them later:

- MOTIVATION, where a course of ACTIONS is invoked in relation to the need of the ACTIVITY;
- PLANNING, where a programme for the ACTION is developed, alternative hypotheses are evaluated and related to their probable results if put into action;
- EXECUTION, where the ACTION is actually carried out;
- EVALUATION, where the outcome of the ACTION is evaluated against the original plan, and where the EXECUTION is checked. In the case of failure, the whole ACTION may be re-entered from there.

Each of these elements of an ACTION is in turn realized by units of activity from one rank below: OPERATIONS. These are units of activity defined by the task which helps towards the achievement of the goal of the ACTION which the

OPERATION realizes in any given instance and in any given SITUATION. When we describe a particular individual in the course of an ACTIVITY, the OPERATIONS filling MOTIVATION, PLANNING and EVALUATION will typically, but not necessarily, be internal OPERATIONS, whereas OPERATIONS filling EXECUTION will be external, except in cases of cognitive ACTIONS. OPERATIONS are thus the lowest units in this framework and do not have a structure on this level of the theory. They do, however, have a structure in terms of the sensori-motor organisation of human activities, as analyzed in detail in neurophysiology.

In describing an ACTIVITY, we do not necessarily go "straight down the line" in the following sense: elements on the rank of ACTION can be filled by units from the same rank in the case of complex or otherwise difficult ACTIVITIES. Especially in the PLANNING phase, whole sequences of ACTIONS may be planned, and later executed, and this EXECUTION may be conjunctive, conditional, embedded, recursive, or otherwise complex. The question behind this kind of organisation is that of the temporal and logical sequence of ACTIONS, and we shall spell out in more detail later, what this question implies for certain necessary mechanisms within the theory.

ACTIVITIES as a whole can be internal or external, as well as linguistic or non-linguistic. This does not imply that the ACTIONS realizing each sub-type do all have to be of the same type: an internal ACTIVITY, like problem solving, for example, may require that there be a whole ACTION realizing the PLANNING phase of an ACTION *solving problem x*, and this PLANNING phase may very well require an external realization in, say, writing.

This brings our first exposition of the theory of activity of the Leont'evs to an end. In another cycle of work on this theory, we shall go deeper into certain crucial questions (cf. 2.3.). A few comments, though, should be made at this point:

Our presentation here is already an interpretation for several reasons. First, there are difficulties with terminology, especially concerning key terms like *activity, action, operation* and some others. The available English and German translations are inconsistent in this respect, and we have done our best to avoid these inconsistencies. Consulting the Russian originals has only been possible in a limited number of cases.

Second, coming from the background of Systemic Linguistics, we have imposed a certain conceptual grid on the theory, which may not correspond to the original authors intentions. Broadly speaking, the framework we are dealing with here certainly is *systemic*, cf. A. N. Leont'ev 1978: 74:

> Thus a systemic study of human activity must also be an analysis according to levels. It is just such an analysis that will make it possible to overcome the opposition of the physiological, and the sociological, as well as the reduction of any one of these to another.

Yet, even if the approach of the Leont'evs is broadly systemic, it does not adopt the full systemic methodology in its original version. The terms *filling, compo-*

nence, exponence, realization, for example, have a tightly defined meaning within Systemic Linguistics (Fawcett 1974-76: 7ff.). There is a certain danger that these terms in their precise technical meaning are transferred to the analysis of activity at too early a stage, thus distorting aspects of the original theory. To explain this problem in some more detail:

Filling is used in Systemic Linguistics for grammatical units of one rank filling elements of structure of units of some higher rank. *Componence* is used for the unit-element relationship, e.g. for the relationship between clause and subject. *Exponence* is used for the relationship of lexical items to the grammatical elements of structure which they expound. *Realization* is used for the relationship between grammatical items and the semantic structures which they realize. That is to say, *componence* and *filling* are intra-level relationships, *exponence* is a relationship between two levels of form, and *realization* is the relationship between the interlevel *semantics* and the levels of *grammar* and *lexis*.

The same problem can be seen in the terms *rank* and *level*: In Systemic Linguistics, *rank* is used for the hierarchy of units within a given level, whereas the term *level* itself refers to standard strata in linguistics like phonology, grammar, lexis, semantics.

The Leont'evs use the term *level* to refer to behaviour regarded as ACTIVITY or ACTION or OPERATION, as different from a consideration of human activity on the, say, neurophysiological level. There could be further levels in their sense, presumably neurochemical and neurophysical on the one hand, and sociological on the other. With our own background in Systemic Linguistics, we shall refer to the relationship between ACTIVITY, ACTION, and OPERATION as one of *rank*, and to the relationship between this stratum and others, like the sociological, as one of *level*. The underlying assumption justifying this methodological decision is that human activity as a general phenomenon has a certain structure, and that language is just one particular sub-type of human activity which inherits this structure.

In what way, then, does language enter into the process of human activity as seen within the present framework? In giving a first answer to this question, we shall follow A.A.Leont'ev.1982:76ff. Language may, in the first place, come in during the operational phase of an ACTION, thus filling an element of the ACTION without having itself the status and structure of an ACTION. The same assumption holds for any OPERATION. In such a case, the utterance will not have any phase of conscious planning.

In the second place, language may enter into the structure of an ACTION at the rank of ACTION, in which case it will go through the full process of generating an ACTION. The specific stages in the case of language would seem to be:

- System of motives: Here the motivation of the utterance takes place in so far as it involves orientation towards the needs of the ACTIVITY and towards the specific SITUATION of the utterance.
- The communicative intention is built up.

- An internal programme is generated, using the code of "personal senses", to quote Leont'ev, who at this point is somewhat difficult to understand (A. A. Leont'ev 1982: 76ff.).
- The internal programme is realized (executed) in two phases: semantic and grammatical, where the execution is probably never sequential.
- Phonetic execution
- Evaluation

These assumed phases of the execution of a linguistic ACTION are nothing but the general phases of the EXECUTION of any ACTION, only in their specifically linguistic form. Grammatical and phonetic EXECUTION, it should be said, will hardly ever take place at the rank of ACTION, but rather as an OPERATION.

Within the framework of ideas sketched here, a certain dialectical characteristic of language is captured: Language is, on the one hand, part of human ACTIONS in the sense of being an instrument, functioning as an OPERATION. On the other hand, language itself may be an ACTION, and as such exhibits the same general structural characteristics as any other form of human ACTION - it can be said to reflect the structure of human activity.

We shall, at this point, not give a full example of an analysis, because this will be done extensively in later sections. A general motivation for assuming ranks within human activity will suffice here:

If one thinks of how to describe driving a car, for example, one immediately faces the difficulty of the level, or rather rank, on which to organize such a description. Should one talk about units of behaviour like *opening the car, starting, accelerating, slowing down, getting somewhere*? Or, alternatively, should one move on a rank which involves talking about *moving your arms forward, gripping the s-teering wheel, lowering your right hand, grasping the gear lever, moving your arms forward..* etc? Or, to go to the other extreme, should one only talk about *moving, driving...*? Seen from different perspectives, all of these descriptions, and many others , would seem to refer to the same phenomenon, and, what is more, each of them might be an adequate descripton for a given purpose and under a given set of circumstances. It is questions such as these which underly our attempts in the following section at making more precise what we mean by ranks and levels. In artificial intelligence, questions such as those just raised are sometimes addressed under the label of *granularity of knowledge representation.*

In the following, we shall have a closer look at the theories of activity by Cranach, Harré, and Kalbermatten. Harré's chapter on theoretical preliminaries to the study of action (Cranach & Harré 1982) states the requirements that any theory of activity has to meet. Against this background, ideas such as those of Cranach and Kalbermatten are to be seen. Cranach's approach, like that of the Leont'evs, is a three-level approach, incorporating the analysis of goal-directed action on the levels shown in Table 1 (Cranach 1982: 37ff.; Cranach & Kalbermatten 1982: 115ff.).

Table 1: Levels of action

LEVEL	DEFINITION
Act	Social
Strategic Level	Functional
Operational Level	Structural

Theses levels can be compared, though not equated, with those of Harré (1982: 2ff.) and those of the Leont'evs. Cranach states that his levels are the same as those of Harré, yet they may not be so entirely, at least as far as the notion of *act* is concerned. The differences from the Leont'evs are more obvious, even if there seem to be two variants of these differences. According to Cranach (1982: 37ff.), the categories of the two approaches would seem to be related in the way shown in Table 2.

Table 2. Comparison of levels

Cranach	Leont'ev
Act	Activity
Action	Action
Operation	Operation

In this relationship, the correspondence between *act* and *activity* is doubtful, yet the remaining two pairs seem to be very close conceptually.
According to Cranach and Kalbermatten (1982), the relationship is slightly different, as shown in Table 3.

Table 3. Comparison of levels

Cranach/Kalbermatten	Leont'ev
Act	Action
Strategic Level	Action/Operation
Operational Level	Operation

Whether or not Cranach and Kalbermatten's strategic level corresponds to an action, depends on whether the unit of behaviour is consciously planned. Also, some of the behavioural units described by the authors on the operational level may even be on the sensori-motor level, and in that case would fall outside the theory of activity by the Leont'evs. Cranach and Kalbermatten's categorization in some more detail looks like this:

Acts, according to their framework, are sequences of activity such as the following (Cranach & Kalbermatten 1982: 126ff.):

- Going to a restaurant to eat a meal

- Staying at home and eating a cold meal
- Fight between children in a kindergarten for the possession of toys.

The units on the next level below, the strategic level, are called *action steps*, examples of which are given as follows:

Categories of non-verbal behaviour:	Categories of verbal behaviour:
1. Turn towards (TT)	24. Claim (C)
2. Turn to partner (TTP)	25. Request (RQ)
3. Turn to object (TTO)	26. Command (CO)
4. Turn away (TA)	27. Protest (PR)
and many others	and many others.

On the next level downwards, we get the structural units of behaviour realizing each action step. Examples are given as follows (Cranach & Kalbermatten 1982: 131f.):
Action step *grasp/take away*:
Hand position in relation to body:

Height:	horizontal position:
- hand over head	- hand before body
- hand level top head	- hand behind body
- hand level to shoulders	- hand right side of body
- hand level to trunk	- hand left side of body
- etc.	- etc.

As we can see, the operations named here are just some of all the operations realizing the action step *grasp/take away*, which, in turn, is only one action step out of a long catalogue of action steps realizing the act *fight for the possession of toys*. The sheer complexity might be taken as an indication that the description as illustrated here has jumped the boundary between two levels. To give a parallel from linguistics:
It is possible to write a linguistic grammar for the generation of language, starting from sentences and going down to phonemes, or, at least, morphemes. If, however, someone tried to include the structure of *phones* within that same grammar involving their execution in terms of the sensori-motor and neurophysiologtical events, s/he would commit a theoretical error in jumping levels without reflecting this in his/her methodology. This theoretical error would also lead to such a degree of complexity that the endeavour would become a practical impossibility. Given the present state of knowledge as far as theories of activity are concerned, we cannot be sure that the parallel actually holds, but there are indications that it does.

This is as far as we shall go in this section, the aim of which was to sketch the two most promising theories from our perspective. Both of them have certain weaknesses, and they do not categorize the phenomenon which they are trying to handle in exactly the same way. In what follows, we shall rely mainly on the theory of the Leont'evs, but we shall at many points bear in mind the requirements and some central principles of the theories of Cranach, Harré, and Kalbermatten.

The next section will, in another cycle of working on our framework, develop the theory of activity to the point where it becomes applicable to linguistic texts and to the kind of activities which we shall have to analyze in the empirical parts of our work.

2.3 A "Systemic" framework for the analysis of goal-directed action

2.3.1 Introductory remarks

The roots of the framework developed here are to be found in their original form in A. A. Leont'ev (1975, 1981, 1982), in A. N. Leont'ev (1978, 1981), and in Leont'ev, Leont'ev and Judin (1984). In what we shall suggest here, it undergoes substantial re-interpretation.

Let us start with a general motivation for pursuing a stratified approach rather than a single level one: The description of human behaviour on a hierarchy of levels has a simple and to some extent useful analogue in the structure of computational processes. Moving from hardware through machine code, assembler languages, and compilers to high level programming languages is in a rough way like moving from the human "hardware" at the, say, electrophysical level (to assume a somewhat arbitrary starting point) to electrochemistry, neurology, neurophysiology, physiology, psychology to the outer manifestations of activities (operations, actions, activities) in the individual, and on to the social level of organization (sociology, economics, anthropology, political science etc.). The particular level of individual activity in our current theory is again internally stratified into ranks, and if it is at this level that we are entering language, it would not be surprising to find that language, as one form of action inherits the general structural properties of activity. At each of these ranks, we could then expect the phenomena of recursion, embedding, and rankshift, as well as the relationships of delicacy and exponence (Halliday 1961), where the last would be an inter-level relationship.

The particular number of ranks or levels which one assumes is not only founded in the nature of the phenomenon described, but it is at least as much a consequence of the purpose of description. As is generally the case in general systems theory, the number and types of levels are not a priori given. On the other hand, certain characteristics of a certain level may even be ontogenetically and/or phylogenetically expressed in man's physiological make up, as, for example, neurophysiological correlates of *consciousness* in the human brain, in so far as they exist (Luria 1973: 187ff.).

Bearing these remarks in mind, we shall in the following sections investigate the notions of *level* and *rank* in more detail, reserving the discussion of additional scales and categories of the model for section 2.4. After introducing *level* and *rank* as technical terms, we shall identify sources of *rankshift* and *re-entry*, turning then to a discussion of the place of language in the strcuture of activity. Having thus considered the *dynamic aspect* of activity, we shall outline a simple notion of *situation* which complements the dynamic perspective on activity as a more static counterpart. Representations of activities and situations in this model are two ways of representing knowledge about human goal-directed action, derived from viewing what is essentially the same phenomenon from two different perspectives. Following these remarks, we shall enter into a brief and introductory discussion of formalization of the model presented earlier, and finally, we shall give a rapid overview of those concepts of Systemic Linguistics which are necessary for an understanding of the terminology used in the linguistic analyses throughout sections 2.4 and chapter 3. In the course of the present section, we shall introduce certain key terms which we shall then distinguish in their technical use by capital spelling. These key terms will refer to units of action, phases of actions and to the situation in which actions are embedded.

2.3.2 Levels

To describe the phenomenon of human activity in one go is an impossibly complex task as soon as we look at the many different levels of generality on which such a description could be made.

One might want to describe and analyze, for example, the behaviour of the whole human race, or that of nations, or that of institutions within a state, or, again, the behaviour of classes within a society as well as that of groups of people in which you are interested for certain reasons. All this, in fact, is done by different disciplines.

Then again, we may be interested in the individual, in his or her activities in so far as they derive from needs like production and reproduction, exchange of goods and services, or exchange of messages, as well as the satisfaction of hunger, thirst, and other biological needs. If we enter the overall system of activities at this point, we shall soon find that even within individual activities, there seem to be different degrees of generality, abstraction and, partly, size, as measured by length of time and/or complexity of organization.

Therefore, we seem to be faced with the necessity of setting up different ranks of description within the level of activity, for example those introduced in section 2.2.2.. In our particular approach, this yields ACTIVITIES, ACTIONS, and OPERATIONS.

On yet another level, we might choose to move "into" the organism and describe the activity on that level: the sensori-motor organization of activity (co-operations of muscles, tendons, joints etc.), the neurophysiological organization (the structure of the nervous system, the establishment and working of neurophysiological systems in the cortex and other areas of the human nervous system), and even the organisation of activity on the neurochemical and neurophysical levels. Part of all this is summarized in Table 4.

Table 4: Levels of actitivity

LEVEL	ACTIVITY OF	EXAMPLE
Social	nations, states, institutions, social classes, groups	wage disputes between employers and employees
Individual	individual human beings including external and internal activities	Individual X's work activities in his/her job,
Intra-Individual	The physiological and neurological systems of an individual	The working systems of language in the cerebral cortex

In the sense indicated in Table 4, and in the sense discussed in the previous section, i.e. Systemic usage, we shall henceforth use the term *level.*

In narrowing down our focus to the analysis and to the description of activity on the individual level, it may seem as if we have conceived of the activity of the individual as something that is isolated from the social on the one side and from the physiological on the other. This is not the case: Individual activity in all the aspects that we shall have to deal with has its source in the social, in the organization of productive work and social relations. From there derive needs and objectives, as well as the instruments and conditions of human activity. Also, on the other hand, there is no human activity which does not require realization on the levels "further down" in the sense of Table 4, and these physiological and neurological patterns of organization and their potential for activity also set boundaries for the structure of human activity, even if these boundaries are far more open to change and extension than is often assumed by nativists.

2.3.3 Ranks

Within the structure of activity on the individual level, we shall distinguish three ranks: ACTIVITY, ACTION, OPERATION. Henceforth, in referring to these ranks, we shall use capitals, whereas, if we use any of these words in a non-technical sense, we shall use lower case spelling.

Rank: ACTIVITY

ACTIVITY is a type of human behaviour which is aroused by a cultural and/or physiological need, expressed as a state of the individual in relation to his/her environment. We shall call an ACTIVITY *successful* only if the execution of the ACTIVITY is a sufficient condition for the reaching of another state of the individual in relationship to his/her environment, a state which we shall call "objective". The *objective* is a projected, i.e. subjective state as long as it is not reached. From this it follows, that the objective of an ACTIVITY does not necessarily have to be reached. The reaching of the objective constitutes the *satisfaction* of the need and the ACTIVITY ceases in this case.
At this stage, we do not postulate a structure for ACTIVITIES, that is to say, we do not give a specific set of functional elements out of which ACTIVITIES are compounded. We shall only assume that such elements, for which we may use variables at this stage, are filled by one or more ACTIONS, i.e. units from one rank below. The relationship between elements of ACTIVITIES and ACTIONS is thus one of *filling* (cf. Figure 1), that between ACTION and ACTIVITY one of *constituency*. There is no limitation on the number of branches in Figure 1 below precisely

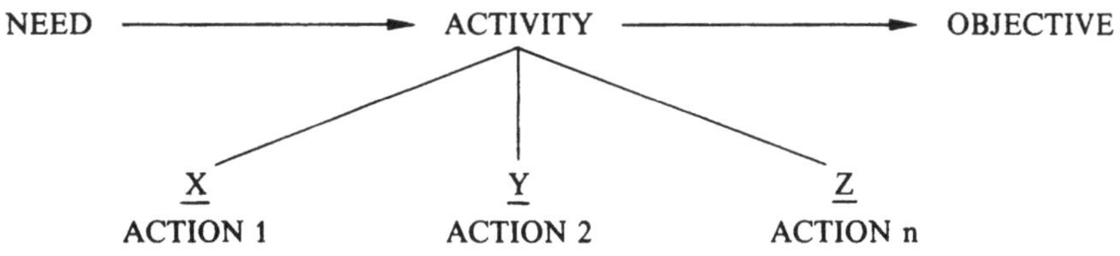

Figure 1. The rank of activity

because we do not specify here the set of elements of ACTIVITIES. Also, a certain ACTIVITY may consist of different ACTIONS depending on the situation in which it is executed. A given ACTION, in turn, can be a constituent of different ACTIVITIES depending on the situation. The question of possible classes of ACTIONS depending on certain types of ACTIVITIES and/or on structural places in ACTIVITIES can, at this stage, only be raised in a non-technical sense. In analogy to modern functional grammars, ACTIVITY and ACTION are units (structures) of a certain category, which have *elements* or *functions*, and these, in turn, are filled by units of a given category. This use of *features* to model these relationships is further discussed in section 2.3.7 below.

In Figure 1, we use branching for the relationship of *componence* and horizontal lines for the relationship of *filling*, which are not usually kept apart in this way in an ordinary constituent structure grammar. *Componence*, it should be said here, is formally similar to the *unit-function* relationship in syntax (e.g. *Subject-of*, *Object-of*, etc.), while all the elements on one functional level in a tree (sisters), i.e.

those immediately above horizontal lines in the representation, have a dependency relationship in Systemic syntax. *Filling* is the relationship between *functions* and *forms*, i.e. phrasal categories, or lexical categories (cf. Butler 1985: 14ff. and 114ff., Fawcett 1974-76, Hudson 1976: 22ff., and for a formalization of this area of Systemic syntax Patten & Ritchie 1987: 280ff.). We would like to draw attention to the fact, though, that at this stage it would be premature to import all the formal principles of syntax into our rules and representations for ACTIONS. In particular, we shall not, at this point, discuss the relationships between structural configurations and functions, which are different from those of a purely configurational approach, nor shall we impose constraints on *head-dependent* relationships.

Rank: ACTION

An ACTION is a unit of human activity to which we attribute a goal, formulated as a state of affairs. If an ACTIVITY is filled by one ACTION, which is a marginal case, then the goal of the ACTION must be a sufficient condition for the reaching of the objective. If an ACTIVITY is filled by more than one ACTION, the goals taken together must provide a sufficient condition for the reaching of the objective in a given situation (for the concept of *situation* cf. below).

The unit of ACTION is compounded of the following elements: *Motivation, Planning, Execution, Evaluation*. These will typically be filled by OPERATIONS, units from again one rank below, as shown in Figure 2 (except for cases of rankshift and embedding, cf. 2.3.4.).

OPERATIONS can be internal or external to the organism. On the level of individual ACTIVITY, internal OPERATIONS are normally the so-called cognitive OPERATIONS. All OPERATIONS have an internal realization (in the technical sense) on the neurophysiological level and the levels further down, yet this is not a cri-

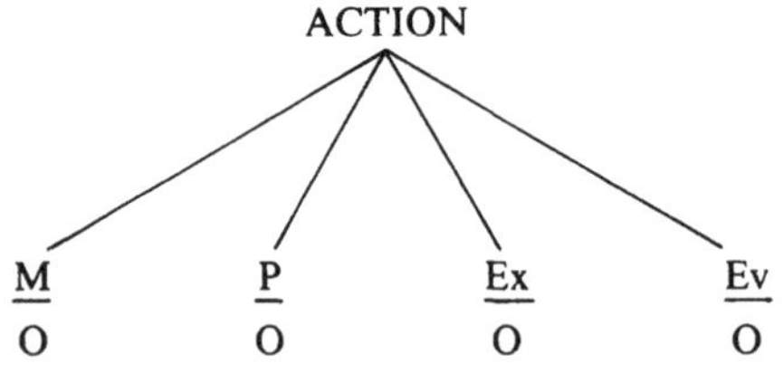

M = Motivation
P = Planning
Ex = Execution
Ev = Evaluation

Figure 2. The rank of action

terion for the classification into *external vs. internal* on the level we are currently concerned with. An ACTION is called *external* if its characteristic OPERATIONS under EXECUTION are external, and *internal* otherwise. Also, ACTIONS as well as OPERATIONS can be linguistic or non-linguistic (cf. Figure 3).

The notation in Figure 3 is standard Systemic notation, as, for example, in Halliday (1967-68) and Fawcett (1980). Curly brackets symbolize conjunction, square brackets exclusive disjunction.

Rank: OPERATION

OPERATIONS are units of activity filling elements of structure of ACTIONS. An OPERATION is interpreted as having a task formulated as a state of affairs. The tasks of all the OPERATIONS filling the elements of an ACTION together form a sufficient condition for the attainment of the state described as the goal of the ACTION of which they fill the elements.

The setting up of the unit of OPERATION is partly motivated by the ascription of *consciousness* to a sequence of human activity in the following way: ACTIONS are characterized by a planning stage which is conscious, i.e. the agent can report on it. OPERATIONS do not have a conscious planning stage.

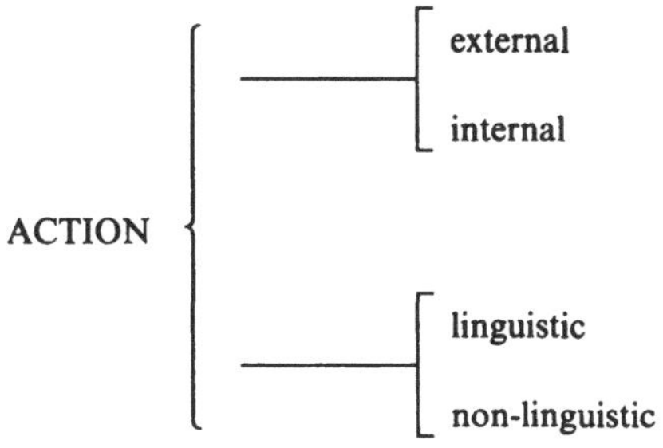

Feature	Sample Realization
external/linguistic	speaking, writing ...
external/non-linguistic	non-linguistic ACTIONS
internal/linguistic	"thinking" in the code of language
internal/non-linguistic	"thinking" in non-linguistic codes

Figure 3. Types of action

They will normally have a stage of *programming* on the neurophysiological level, yet without consciousness involved. All this implies that ACTIONS can be transferred into OPERATIONS as a consequence of *facilitation* or practice. OPERATIONS, on the other hand, can be raised to the rank of an ACTION if they are consciously planned, for example in a situation with certain conditions making conscious attention necessary because of factors that make an OPERATION difficult, which happens when there are certain obstacles to be overcome for the OPERATION to be executed sucessfully. OPERATIONS, like ACTIONS, can be external or internal, linguistic or non-linguistic.

A few remarks are in place here concerning the use of the concept of a *conscious planning stage*:

The term as used here is restricted to the element of *planning* within an ACTION. It does not refer to all forms of consciousness and/or intentionality in human ACTIONS. For example, an agent may be aware of some behaviour, that he/she did something, and whether or not he/she was successful. This form of awareness or consciousness in itself does not define an ACTION in our sense. Furthermore, processes of monitoring by themselves do not automatically make a sequence of behavioural movements an ACTION. There is another problematical aspect to the term: How do we test whether in a given phase of an ACTION we have a case of conscious planning?

In the first place, as an interpreter of another person's behaviour, we ascribe consciousness or the absence of it to whatever sequence of events we are observing, and to that extent, our analysis of activity represents the psychological reality of the observer. On the other hand, there is at least some evidence from the neurophysiology of the human brain that consciousness and conscious planning in particular have certain functional and even structural correlates, i.e. the presence or absence of conscious planning can be ascertained independently of the process of interpretation by the analyst of activity. Luria (1973: 198f.) makes the following observations:

> The frontal lobes...therefore constitute an apparatus with the function of forming stable plans and intentions capable of controlling the subject's subsequent conscious behaviour. Observations on patients with sufficiently large lesions of the frontal lobes give clear evidence of this role....
> Disturbances of the function of the frontal lobes may lead to the disintegration of complex programmes of activity and to their ready replacement either by simpler and more basic forms of behaviour, or by the repetition of inert stereotypes, neither relevant to the situation nor logical in character.

This is not to say that *consciousness* as a concept within a theory of activity could be defined by notions from a level further down. However, some degree of motivation which is independent of the level one is currently concerned with, or even independent of one's own discipline is usually considered desirable and important for the assessment of the explanatory value of any theory.

Finally, the notion of *consciousness* we are assuming here is neither that of a *complete consciousness*, nor that of a *true consciousness*: If some agent has a conscious representation of his/her plans, motivations and so on, this consciousness only "illuminates" a small area of all the factors leading him/her to action. In other words: quite possibly, a substantial share of the motivations and even plans for an action remain unconscious. Furthermore, the conscious representation of elements of an action for an agent may be an outright misrepresentation of why and how s/he acts the way s/he does. This can often be brought out in an analysis of causes and effectes of some goal-directed-action, which then contracdicts the consciousness if the agent.

In laying out our framework so far, certain key notions of Systemic theory have not been explained, or rather not been applied to the analysis of activity. These notions are: Class, System, Delicacy, and Exponence, as defined in Halliday (1961). We shall introduce these categories where and when it is necessary. In the present context, they would introduce additional descriptive power without justification, some of which will be developed in the actual analyses to be presented later (2.4.). Section 2.8 gives a brief overall introduction into some necessary Systemic terminology.

Figure 4 gives us an impression of what the overall analysis of ACTIVITY looks like within the framework just outlined.

It may be necessary to stress here that Figure 4 does not imply that there is only one OPERATION realizing each element of ACTION. Otherwise, it should be fairly simple and self-explanatory in the context of what we have said so far.

2.3.4 Rankshift and re-entry

In the analysis of an ACTION, we will frequently find cases in which an element of an ACTION is not filled by an OPERATION or several OPERATIONS, but by one or

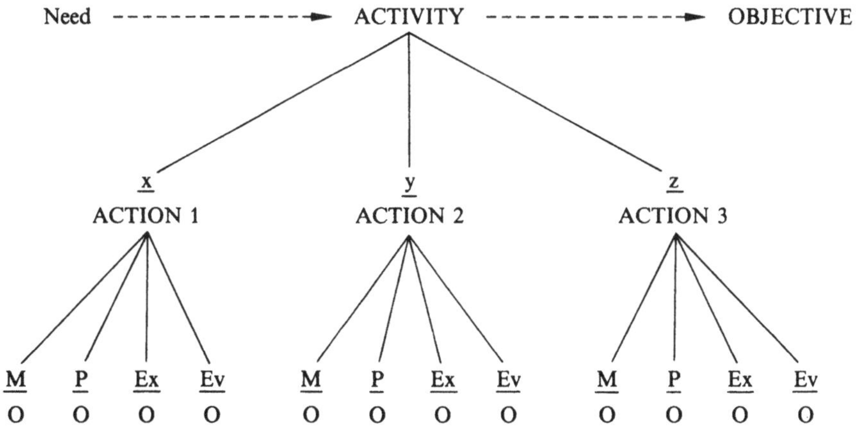

Figure 4. The structure of activities

more ACTIONS instead. This phenomenon may be called *rankshift* in analogy to the same phenomenon in the grammar of natural languages (cf. Halliday 1961; Butler 1985: 18ff; Patten & Ritchie 1987). Formally, rankshift is just non-immediate recursion of a category. Thus, we are adopting a somewhat more general definition of rankshift than Halliday (1961), taking into account criticisms of the more restricted usage of the term (cf. for one version of such criticisms Huddleston 1988). What are the main sources of rankshift in this sense?

Perhaps the main source is to be found in the planning phase of an ACTION. In planning, an agent may only be concerned with planning one ACTION, having only one goal. However, the planning phase of a given ACTION may be concerned with the creation of sub-goals, and in these cases, from this planning phase sub-ACTIONS will have to be entered. The creation of the sub-goals will then fill the planning phase of the superordinate ACTION, possibly along with a projection of the whole course of the embedded ACTIONS. The execution phase of the superordinate ACTION will then contain the execution phases of its sub-ACTIONS in co-ordination or in various types of internal sub-ordination. *Contain* is meant here in a logical rather than in a temporal sense (cf. 2.4.4. for a more formal discussion). This phenomenon would be *embedding* rather than *rankshift* in terms of Halliday (1985a).

Another source of rankshift is to be expected at the rank of OPERATIONS: Whenever the actual carrying through of an OPERATION meets with unforeseen difficulties, a re-entry at ACTION can be expected, i.e. what would normally have been an OPERATION not requiring conscious planning may at a given point and under given circumstances require conscious planning.

Rankshift in the sense just described is possible at any rank. In general, we may expect that the better planned an ACTION is, the fewer cases of rankshift at the rank of OPERATION have to be expected. Obviously, this last remark in no way applies to rankshift at the rank of ACTION.

There is another phenomenon, connected to the one just mentioned: that of re-entry after evaluation. The evaluation phase of an ACTION consists of a comparison between the goal as the projected outcome of an ACTION and the actual result. If the actual result is not sufficiently similar to the projected outcome to count as achievement of the goal in the given situation, then the whole ACTION may be re-entered. Re-entry may again take place at different points: If the source of the failure is seen by the agent to lie in the execution phase, then the ACTION will be re-entered at execution with possibly one or more OPERATIONS now being raised to the status of ACTION. If, on the other hand, the source of the failure is seen in either the planning or the motivation stage of the former ACTION, then the re-entry may have to take place at these points: there will have to be new and to some extent different phases of motivation and/or planning. Of course, re-entry may lead to nothing but a repetition of the former ACTION, possibly in the hope that something in the situation has changed which will now permit success of the formerly unsuccessful ACTION.

We will not discuss here the problems of the temporal sequence of (elements of) rankshifted ACTIONS. Given a certain degree of complexity of organization, planning may lead to certain ACTIONS being suspended until (parts of) others are finished. That also implies that at least the execution of more than one ACTION can take place at the same time, either in parallel with each other, or through multi-functionality of one sequence of OPERATIONS. Multi-functionality is an interesting aspect of more complex ACTIONS. To give one example: In writing a pre-registration for a conference one may pursue the goal of getting registered. Yet, sending in such a pre-registration may also serve as one element of an ACTION such as *store and keep track of conference x*, i.e., one may, at the same time, pursue the goal of getting further news about the conference without having to keep records in one's own diary.

We shall not, at this point, go into the whole complex issue of *monitoring*. The execution of any ACTION is monitored all the time, corrections on the rank of OPERATION are made constantly and re-entry may easily take place before the entire ACTION is finished. Insightful discussion on these issue which have a direct bearing on what we have said so far can be found in Cranach 1982, and in Cranach/Kalbermatten. 1982.

Most of the questions touched upon here will be taken up again, and in more detail, in the course of the application of the framework in later chapters. In the following section, we shall turn to the place of language within the overall analysis of activity as described here.

2.3.5 The place of language in the structure of activity

It is now time to specify more precisely than before how language enters into the overall structure of human ACTIVITY. To make this rather complex issue somewhat more transparent, we shall consider the following two aspects separately, which, it is felt, cover the two basic directions in which the interaction of language and ACTIVITY in general can be approached in our context:

- Language and its different levels as activity
  The guiding question here is: When the potential of language on its various levels and ranks is realized, does this take the form of ACTIVITIES, ACTIONS, or OPERATIONS?
- Language and its different levels and ranks within activity
  The guiding question here is: At which points within the overall structure of any ACTIVITY can the compounding and the filling structures be linguistic structures, and, subsequently, linguistic structures and events on what linguistic level?

It can be seen that each of these two questions naturally and inevitably leads to the other, thus revealing the dialectical relationship between these two aspects of human language (cf. Nuyts 1989: 92 for a brief discussion of the same question in the context of the functionality of language).

Before going into these questions, we should remind ourselves what type of representation of the *linguistic potential* is used in Systemic Linguistics (cf. also 2.3.8 below): The linguistic potential of the semantics of natural language is represented in system networks the features of which are realized on various ranks, such as text, clause, group/phrase, word. The linguistic potential of the form of natural language is represented either in system networks for cohesion, grammar, lexis, and possibly phonology, or else in *starting structures*, in the work of Fawcett in particular. We shall use such networks and their associated realizations frequently in later sections, so that we shall not give further examples here.

2.3.5.1 Language and its different levels as activity Assuming for the time being that the processes modelled in systemic system networks symbolize semiotic and psychological processes, do these processes occur as OPERATIONS, ACTIONS, or ACTIVITIES? In different words: At which levels of language does conscious planning take place, and when this happens, what are the categories and rules of planning?

Given our framework as developed so far, this would seem to be largely an empirical question, i.e. the theory which we have outlined does not impose any constraints on the possiblities as such. As far as non-conscious planning and/or programming take place, psycholinguistic evidence points to its occurrence on all levels (cf. Clark & Clark 1977: 223ff.). In an examination of the limiting cases of linguistic structures, let us consider the text level first. The formal aspects of this level are captured in Systemic Linguistics through the concept of *cohesion* (Halliday & Hasan 1976). The aspect of meaning would seem to require separate treatments for text types, such as *story structures* (Beaugrande 1982: 383ff.; Colby 1982: 463ff.). It is intuitively plausible to assume planning on text level, and here rather on the level of meaning than on the level of form. Yet, even a relatively large-scale structure like a story can be operationalized, as in the case of narratives which are regularly delivered in a ritual context, such as Bible texts. In such a case, planning would be substituted by programming. This kind of phenomenon certainly is not the rule, but it is possible within the constraints of our theory.

For the sake of illustration, let us move to the other extreme of the linguistic spectrum, to phonological form. There are instances in which even that level is raised from its unmarked status as a set of OPERATIONS to ACTIONS. This is the case when someone is writing a piece of poetry which requires conscious consideration of patterns of verse structure. Similarly, it is part of the essence of learning a foreign language, at least as an adult, that processes which are not subject to conscious attention and planning in the mother tongue regularly become ACTIONS, at least as long as they are not operationalized, i.e. until some degree of fluency in the foreign language is attained.

If what we have just said is correct, then conscious planning can take place on any level. In other words, the actualization of the linguistic potential can take place in the form of ACTIONS on any level, even if some of these cases require unusual conditions. There are, of course, the typical cases, and they would seem to be those where planning takes place on the level of meaning, either as realized in the text, or else as realized in the clause (Clark & Clark 1977: 223ff.). Consequently, the semantic networks which can be made conscious relatively easily are those creating text coherence and/or clause structure. In principle, this is true of all *functional components* (cf. Halliday 1985a: 32ff.), yet there may be certain preferences for the ideational and the interpersonal components. It should also be said that the lexical item probably plays a very important role in this connection, yet is relatively neglected within Systemic Linguistics as well as in many other contemporary linguistic theories.

Another obvious question in this context is the following: How does the notion of a *speech act* fit into the framework which we are discussing? To answer this question, let us remind ourselves of a few basic distinctions which are drawn in standard speech act theory. A speaker will perform the following types of speech acts (cf. Searle 1969):

- the locutionary act: the act of producing phonetic, lexical, and grammatical structures as such;
- the propositional act: the act(s) of referring to the world and of making predications about states of affairs in this world;
- the illocutionary act: the ACTION or OPERATION which is performed in making an utterance;
- the perlocutionary act: the (intended, in the case of an ACTION,) effect of the utterance.

The locutionary act will, under usual circumstances, take the form of OPERATIONS, except in cases such as language learning. To put this into a more systemic perspective, realization in grammar and phonology will normally not be subject to conscious planning. The locutionary act is symbolized within Systemic Linguistics in system networks of form. Propositional acts are symbolized in the process of selections from semantic system networks, and therefore will be consciously planned frequently, especially on text level. The semantic systems symbolizing the potential for propositional acts are prototypically those of the experiential and logical components. Illocutionary acts, being by definition largely restricted to realization in the clause, may, but need not be conscious. If a linguistic ACTION is defined as in our study, then, by definition the propositional and/or the illocutionary act must be conscious, or else their correlates on text level. Finally, perlocutionary acts: They are meant to cover the *intended effect* of the utterance. This formulation implies that we are leaving the linguistic system at this point. A linguistic utterance in a framework such as the one we are investigating here, can either be a realization of, or an instrument in a human ACTION. If as it is the second, the perlocutionary acts simply are the goals of the agent, in so far as they are pursued through the utterance. Perlocutionary acts, it is true, fall outside *core linguistics*, yet they have a very natural place within a perspective on language as a form of human activity.

In a discussion of speech acts, one should be aware of the fact that even such basic notions as we have been discussing are not uncontroversial, especially as far as the distinction between illocutionary and perlocutionary acts is concerned. The theory of ACTIVITY makes a theoretical distinction here, which, however, is probably open to a similar controversy as the one within speech act theory.

2.3.5.2 Language and its different levels within activity. Can language be analyzed on the rank of ACTIVITY directly? In other words, are there needs which directly and predominantly lead to linguistic communication and can be satisfied through it? This touches the problem of the classification of ACTIVITIES, a problem which cannot be solved on the rank we are working on currently, just as one cannot classify sentence types "from above", i.e. not structurally, in a classical scale-and-category-grammar (cf. Halliday 1961; Postal 1967). Classes of ACTIVITY have to be established as functional classes against theories from political economy, sociology, and psychology. Assuming for the time being a broad classification into types like *productive, aesthetic, interactive...* (A. A. Leont'ev 1982: 135ff.), *communicative* would be a sub-type under *interactive*, and linguistic communication would certainly be analyzable on the rank of ACTIVITY, i.e. in its relation to needs and objectives. It should be emphasized again that every ACTIVITY goes through the inevitable processes of being compounded of elements, being filled by ACTIONS, being realized physiologically (to change levels) etc., just as a sentence can always be analyzed into groups, words etc., and is always realized phonologically. But just in the same way as the assumption of a *nominal group* does not necessarily imply the assumption of some *nominal sentence*, the assumption of linguistic ACTIONS does not imply the assumption of linguistic ACTIVITIES.

So, while the theory of ACTIVITY makes no claims about functional classes of ACTIVITIES (in a technical sense), it has more to say about linguistic ACTIONS. Language may come into any activity at the rank of ACTION. It may come in as an ACTION in itself (linguistic ACTIONS), or as part of the *situation* (instrument etc., cf. below), in which case the whole potential of recursion and embedding arises. We will only discuss the case of language as an ACTION here, knowing that ACTION is recursive and that the remarks we are making apply to any cycle of application subsequent to the primary cycle, with possibly some additional constraints on later cycles, which, however, must be the subject of later work.

In the case we are discussing here, the agent will, in producing linguistic utterances, go through the full cycle of MOTIVATION, PLANNING, EXECUTION, EVALUATION. The execution phase, in particular, will be filled linguistically, in a broad sense, in its OPERATIONS. The other elements can be filled linguistically or non-linguistically. During the planning stage, the agent will work consciously and, in most cases, "internally", on semantic categories and rules, on text level in the unmarked cases. For the time being, we assume for the semantic representation of texts conjunctions of proposition-like structures with possibly some additional labelling. The closest candidate for some text-types is a representation as in *Rhetorical Structure Theory* (Mann & Thompson 1987a,b), which is specifically developed against the theoretical background of Systemic Linguistics. Also, a text may or may not consist of more than one sentence.

Planning may occur at a lower rank, particularly at the rank of the clause, and in these cases the agent generates and/or activates categories and rules corresponding to semantic system networks at clause rank. In these cases, the ACTION at clause rank will often be a rankshifted ACTION, i.e. planning on the rank/level of *text* has already taken place. The phenomenon of a badly structured text would often seem to be describable as a lack of planning on text level.

Finally, language may come in at the rank of OPERATION, in which case there will be no phase of conscious planning. The OPERATION may fill linguistic or non-linguistic ACTIONS, as well as internal and external elements of each type of ACTION. Now, in spite of the lack of planning, linguistic OPERATIONS still have meaning, because language encodes meaning, and this meaning is realized every time that the linguistic potential is actualized. Whether or not there can be meaning for the agent if his/her behaviour is unconscious, is a different matter.
Because of the absence of planning, the linguistic realizations of OPERATIONS are rather short and often formulaic, except for cases of long bits of language memorized in advance and delivered without *thinking*, and a few other cases.

Let us finish this section with a set of prototypical examples of realizations of language at the various ranks which we have been considering (cf. Table 5).

2.3.6 The concept of "Situation"

At various points in our discussion of ACTIONS so far, we have used the term *situation*, assuming something like its everyday meaning. We shall now try to elaborate more closely what we mean by *situation* and what the role of this concept is in the analysis of ACTIONS (cf. Steiner 1985 b, 1988 b,c for earlier thoughts along the lines to be taken in the following). An extensive application of the concept of *situation* in the analysis of a text is demonstrated in section 2.4.5, where some details of analysis are discussed. Furthermore, we shall henceforth use capital spelling for SITUATION as a technical term, as well as for the situational roles introduced in this section.

Table 5. Linguistic realizations

Rank	Typical linguistic realizations
ACTIVITY	Instances of *phatic communion*, gossipping etc.
ACTION	To tell someone about an incident To promise something To tell someone that... To make a plan
OPERATION (filling elements of non-linguistic ACTIONS)	
MOTIVATION	*Now, let's see, I'd rather not, but I have to ...*
PLANNING	Talking aloud to oneself during planning
EXECUTION	*Now, Come on, Right, Left*
EVALUATION	*Great, Missed it*

There are two possible extreme interpretations of the term SITUATION within the present context:

An extremely "materialist" position, one describable as "mechanical materialis-m" in philosophical terms, would maintain that a SITUATION is anything that is empirically and physically given in the environment in which an ACTION is taking place. Such a position neglects the subjective factor deriving from the presence of a human agent. On the practical side, it leads to the difficulty of deciding in a non-arbitrary way what to include in a description of a SITUATION. A SITUATION is not just "given", it is, to some extent, constructed by the agent, in particular by his/her goals and his/her perception, which is in various ways dependent on goals. Also, under such an approach, it would seem difficult to maintain the notion of *levels* in the analysis of ACTIVITY.

An extremely "subjectivist" position, on the other hand, might hold that a SITU-ATION encompasses everything and anything that a given individual thinks it does. This approach, too, leads to serious difficulties: If a SITUATION as a concept is only generated within the mind of individuals, how can we arrive at something like "mutual knowledge", on which alone co-operative ACTIVITY can be based. Furthermore, how do we decide in a principled way between competing descrip-tions of one SITUATION? Finally, a SITUATION may contain elements influencing the course of an ACTION without being consciously represented in the mind of an agent.

In our account to be put forward here, we shall try to take account of both the objective and the subjective aspect: We insist, on the one hand, that the *slots* in our framework of SITUATION are filled by objects and processes which can be identified in a controlled way, even if it is only through the effects they are having on factors of the SITUATION, like, for example, internal and external ACTIONS themselves, which can enter into different slots of our situational framework. On the other hand, we have to be aware of the fact that the constituents of our SITUATION do not exist in their specific quality independently of human ACTIONS: Some physical object becomes an *instrument* only if human ACTIVITY, in an historical and/or immediate sense, is presupposed. An agent does not exist, except in purely physical terms, in the absence of a goal, of plans, and ways to relate these to each other. Some *thing* becomes a *product* with all its qualities only within the structure of human ACTIVITY. In that sense also, the terms we are using to analyze a SITUATION form a system.

We shall now list the set of SITUATIONAL roles which we use to describe a SITUATION, along with standard questions for coders to identify these roles (cf. Table 6).

Table 6. Situational roles

QUESTION	SITUATIONAL ROLE
Who + predicate under PROCESS?	AGENT
What does AGENT do to the (entry under) MATERIALS?	PROCESS
Who/what is affected and/or changed by (entry under) PROCESS?	MATERIALS
What or whom does AGENT use to (entry under) PROCESS?	INSTRUMENT
What does the actualized (entry under) PROCESS lead to?	PRODUCT

The representation of a SITUATION can, and frequently will, contain more information than just the tokens filling our types listed under SITUATIONAL role. This information will normally be given in the form of propositions relating to the elements filling those slots. *States*, of course, will quite often themselves be the result of previous ACTIONS and /or events. Indeed, a serious methodological problem associated with our way of describing a SITUATION is that of determining

- which exactly are the propositions relating to our SITUATION, as given, say, in a text;
- precisely how do we extract from these propositions the elements filling our categorial slots, and how do we decide which structures provide additional information.

At this point, it might well be asked whether our categories for describing a SITUATION should not include the categories of TIME of ACTION and SPACE of ACTION. The answer is that, indeed, they do in those cases in which we are analyzing an *individual* rather than a *generic* SITUATION (cf. von Wright 1972: 39ff. on this question, as well as Barwise & Perry 1983: 55ff.).

What is the status of the categories which we are using to represent a SITUATION, if we compare them to the *participant roles* and the *features* of the model of linguistic semantics which we shall be using in our linguistic analyses (cf. Fawcett 1980; Halliday 1985a: 101ff.; Steiner et al. 1988), or to *deep cases* (Fillmore 1968, 1977; Polenz 1985) or *thematic roles* (Jackendoff 1983, 1987; Bresnan 1982)? Several of the terms for SITUATIONAL roles, which we have introduced, turn up again as transitivity functions in Systemic analyses of clauses. Are we not just reduplicating features (predicate types) and functions (participant roles) in rather an unprincipled way?

The answer is that we are not: AGENTS and AFFECTEDS, for example, on the semantic level of a linguistic semantics are not one-to-one realizations of, say, AGENTS and MATERIALS in a SITUATION, to which they refer. On this question, there is interesting psycholinguistic evidence (cf. de Zwaart 1973, and others). Also, it is obvious that we can encode one and the same SITUATION in linguistically very different ways on the level of semantics, cf.(1):

(1) *This knife cuts old bread very well.*

In (1), according to our analysis, we have a linguistic AGENT for what is, in terms of the SITUATION, an INSTRUMENT. Also, cf.(2):

(2) *A stream came rushing down from the mountain.*

Here we have a semantic AGENT-ATTRIBUANT (cf. section 3.4. for a detailed exposition of the SFG approach to semantic roles) for what is, in terms of the SITUATION, some other role, or, as an isolated sentence, not part of an ACTION at all. To illustrate the same point from the opposite direction, let us briefly consider possible linguistic realizations of the situational role of PRODUCT: A PRODUCT may be realized in a congruent way as the transitivity function *Effected*, cf. (3):

(3) *John built a house.*

However, it may also be derived from a *relational predicate* as in (4):

(4) *X carries Y to Z.*

The PRODUCT here is not a single transitivity feature, but a whole proposition like *Y is at the location* Z. More precisely, the PRODUCT is not part of the transitivity representation of the sentence at all, but part of the inferences drawn by some hearer in the process of interpreting the sentence. These inferences are linguistically triggered by an *Aktionsart* feature (cf. 3.10 below).

Let us consider the example of a *mental process* predicate like (5):

(5) *X observes Y.*

In this case, the PRODUCT is a proposition like *X has some knowledge of Y*, and part of the interpretation rather than the semantic representation of the sentence. Finally, there is the case of *communication* predicates like (6):

(6) *X tells Y a story.*

In such a case, the PRODUCT would seem to be realized as something approaching the perlocutionary effect of the utterance, rather than any transitivity feature of the clause itself.

From the examples above, it is evident that the situational role PRODUCT behaves very differently in its realizations in the basic clause types *action, mental process, communication,* and *relation.* What we have illustrated here with respect to the situational role of PRODUCT is true of all the situational roles we have given above.

There are other fundamental reasons for having a level of SITUATION different from that of linguistic semantics. The description of a SITUATION will often consist of more than one clause, whereas the linguistic semantics which we shall be using to analyze clauses is restricted to the clause by definition. What we are calling a SITUATION is more like a *frame* (Minsky 1975), and our ACTION is more like a *script* (Schank & Abelson 1976).

While accepting all these reasons for having two distinct levels in the way just indicated, one must be aware that there are, at least, two major methodological problems associated with two such levels of SITUATION and transitivity of the clause. These problems are those of the identification of categories on the one hand, and the problem of formulating realizational rules from the SITUATIONAL level to the semantic level on the other.

Let us discuss the problem of the identification of categories in analysis first: Generalizing from what we have said so far, there seem to be at least two types of reasons for postulating two distinct levels of SITUATIONAL categories and of categories of clause semantics respectively. One reason is a philosophical one: If there is a world outside us, and if there are ways of getting access to this world in the form of knowledge which is not just an arbitrary symbolic representation of some sort, then there are entities and processes in this world which are in some sort of correspondence *to the categories of our representation, otherwise our representation would not represent any information with a truth value. Only the requirement of some kind of isomorphism between pairs of representations permits the recognition of *meaning* and *truth*, or the lack of them. Even leaving aside consideration of some *world* outside an organism, one has to concede the plausibility of the existence of non-linguistic codes of perception and cognition: If these codes exist, and if representations using these codes convey in some way the same information as the linguistic code, then it would seem to be counterintuitive to assume only a linguistic representation of our knowledge - even if the expression of our knowledge uses the linguistic code predominantly.

The second type of reason, not unconnected the one just given, is derived from examples like those in (1) and (2) above: If it is possible for us to make statements about differences between representations on different levels (as between the transitivity of a clause and the SITUATION it encodes), then there has to exist at least one level of representation which is different from the one in which our propositions are encoded. This level, it should be said at once, cannot be syntax, because syntax, clause semantics and the representation of SITUATIONS can be shown to vary independently.

Still, the problem remains of how to identify categories on each level. For the identification of syntactic categories, well-known batteries of tests have been developed, which have led to a high degree of operationalization and standardization. For the identification of semantic functions like participant roles or semantic cases, we also have whole batteries of tests, which carry their own problems with them in so far as they are not independent either of syntactic categories or of SITUATIONAL categories. For the identification of SITUATIONAL categories, all that we seem to have is our knowledge of the world, knowledge which can only be tested and modified by human ACTIVITY itself. More detailed methods of identification of SITUATIONAL categories will be discussed in the course of our sample analyses in the following sections.

Let us now turn to the problem of formulating realizational rules from SITUATIONAL categories to the level of linguistic semantics. There are two strategies of overcoming this problem, both of which are, as yet, far from perfect.

According to one strategy, SITUATIONAL categories are more or less straightforwardly mirrored in structures of clause semantics. Variants of this strategy are often to be found in work in artificial intelligence (cf. Hoeppner 1982, and many others). This would seem to imply that there is not really a necessity for two distinct levels, at least for those areas where a one-to-one correspondence is assumed. In view of what we have said about the necessity of having two distinct levels of representation for the SITUATION and for linguistic semantics, transitivity in particular, this strategy is not open to us.

The other strategy is that SITUATIONAL categories are, indeed, not straightforwardly mirrored in categories of linguistic semantics (cf. Winograd 1983: 312). The problem then is that of formulating realizational rules representing a state of knowledge that is more workable than the general statement as such. Yet, in principle, there seems to be no limit to the number of different ways in which our experince can be encoded linguistically . Take an example where, say, a demonstrator is beaten by the police in a violent demonstration. This SITUATION could be encoded linguistically in very different ways, as is shown by the following examples:

(7) *Terry got licked by the cops last Friday.*
(8) *Terry took a battering in the demo.*

(9) *In view of the circumstances, the officers decided that the necessary steps had to be taken.*
(10) *An officer beat up a demonstrator.*
(11) *The batons of the police began their work on Terry.*
(12) *Terry was beaten by the police on Friday.*

In a general way, (7) to (12) may be taken to refer to the same SITUATION if we assume just a truth-value oriented semantics. What matters in our context is not so much the choice of wording, but rather the semantic structures of the sentences above in terms of participant roles, thematic structure, information distribution, and interpersonal meaning. The question is whether and how we can formulate rules from the SITUATIONAL level to the linguistic level which limit the options a speaker has in some useful way. The possibility usually tried within Systemic Linguistics is that of working with the notion of *register* (cf. Ghadessy 1988; Halliday & Hasan 1980; Hasan 1977), but much remains to be done in this area if we want to go beyond merely statistical correlations. A particularly promising approach in our context would seem to be the elaboration of an *upper model* as yet another level of abstraction from linguistic semantics, but related to it in a principled and constrained way (cf. Matthiessen. 1987; Bateman, Kasper, Moore & Whitney. 1989). First attempts at elaborating an approach along the lines suggested here in a computational context have clearly shown the potential, but also the difficulties associated with finding the constraints mentioned above (cf. Bateman & Kasper & Schütz & Steiner. 1989, 1990; Bateman 1989; Schütz 1989).

The concept of SITUATION which we have illustrated in this section, is certainly difficult to integrate into a theory in such a way as not to raise more problems than it solves. We have tried to pin down the areas of difficulty in this section. We have also tried to show that the concept of SITUATION is essential to a semantic theory that tries to link a theory of human activity with linguistic semantics. The questions which have been raised in this context will again turn up in the course of the analyses to be given in later sections. The solutions which will be suggested there should be seen against the background of the discussion of this section.

2.3.7 Some remarks on formalization

In this section, we address, in a discussion of a relevant notational system, some issues of representation and, ultimately, of formalization. Our remarks here apply only to representations of goal-directed actions, for which we shall briefly discuss a form of representation (cf. Mellish & Evans 1989: 233ff. for a discussion of related problems in the context of natural language generation). About representations for SITUATIONS, not much will be said here, except that they can be represented as classical *frames*. We thus intend to give a minimal frame of reference for discussions in this section, but also for our analyses in 2.4. and in 3.2., all of which contain clarifications of key notions beyond the basic suggestions made in 2.3.

The following notation can be used for the expression of some essential aspects of the framework for analyzing ACTIVITY suggested in this study. The notation is basically that of *Functional Grammars* (Kay 1985: 255ff.; Winograd 1983: 328f-f.; and others). Systemic Functional Grammar (SFG) belongs into the family of functional grammars, both in its general orientation (Kay 1985: 251ff.), and in its formalizations (cf. Patten & Ritchie 1987; Kasper 1987, 1988 a,b; Winograd.1983: 328ff; Cummings 1987). Kasper (1987: 42ff.) argues that a formalism of Systemic Functional Grammar is essentially that of Functional Unification Grammar if we add two major extensions:

- designated attributes, to enforce frequent two way dependencies between SFG features
- selection conditions corresponding to complex input conditions of systems in SFG, which correspond to complex boolean expressions.

The second extension significantly improves the efficiency of an implementation of functional unification grammar, as shown by Kasper. The existing SFG formulations, on the other hand, are improved in the area of discontinuous constituents by the functional unification grammar multi-functional analysis plus the PATTERN attribute which can express discontinuity of functions , and in the area of feature percolation, where traditional SFG appears to be weak in tools for feature propagation other than top down propagation.

It is not surprising that there is so much similarity between functional unification grammar and SFG, at least on a general level as expressed by the formalism, because Kay developed his framework partly as a response to Halliday's ideas (Kasper 1987: 33), which is very clear from statements such as the following (Kay 1985: 252f.):

> 'In practice, I take it that the factors that govern the production of sentences typically come from a great variety of different sources, logical, textual, interpersonal, and so forth. In general, each of these, taken by itself, underdetermines what comes out. When they jointly overdetermine it, there must be priorities enabling a choice to be made among the demands of the different sources. When they jointly underdetermine the outcome, the theory must provide defaults and unmarked cases. The point is that we must be prepared to take seriously the claim that langugae in general, and individual utterances in particular, fill many different functions and that these all affect the theory, even at the syntactic level.'

We think that there are questions concerning theoretical notions beyond those raised by Kasper which merit further thoughts on extensions to unification-based formalisms (cf. our comments below on the conflation of theoretical notions in functional notations), yet these clearly open up areas of further development for functional grammars, rather than providing any sort of argument against such a development. Figure 5 is an illustration of our arguments.

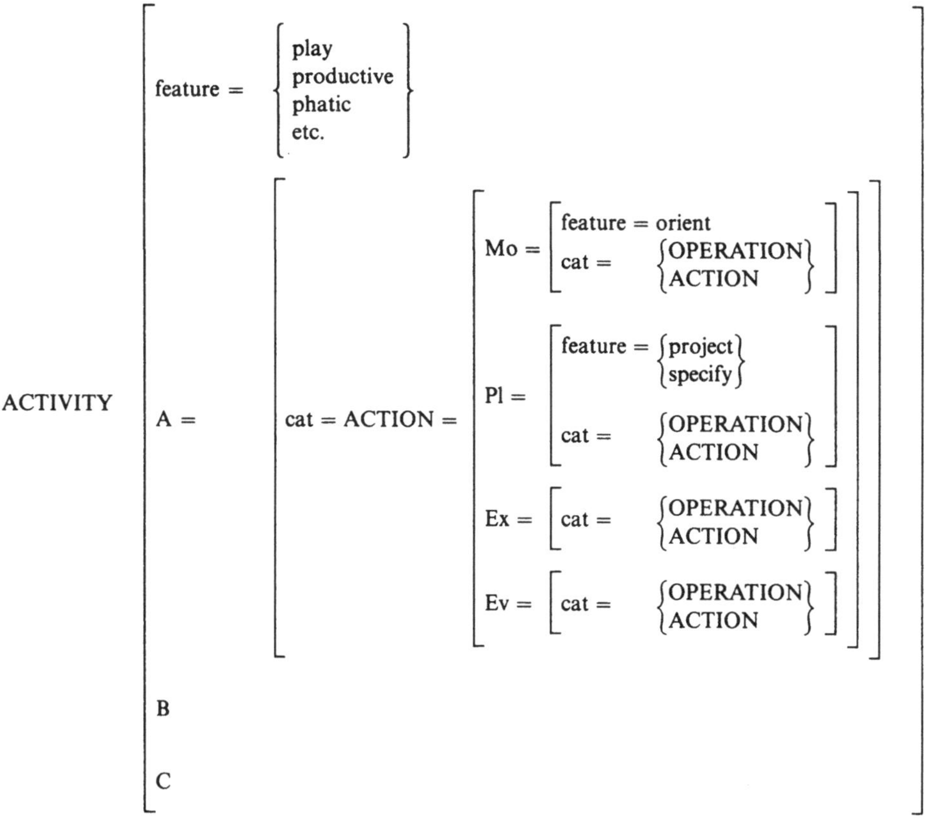

Figure 5. An analysis of activity in a functional notation.
A,B,C stand for elements of ACTIVITIES. We are using the following additional abbreviations: Mo=MOTIVATION, Pl=PLANNING, Ex=EXECUTION, Ev=EVALUATION

Figure 5 conflates in its notation the theoretical notions of *constituency* and *function*, as is well known for functional grammars in general (Winograd 1983: 329). The " = " and/or bracketing are also used to express the notions of *feature of* and *lexical realization of*. More specifically, and with special reference to SFG, the notions of *filling, componence, exponence* are expressed by the same notation. Below we shall give an example of each:

Constituency/Filling:	A = [cat=ACTION], where A is some element of ACTIVITY structure filled by an ACTION.
Function/Componence :	ACTION = [Mo=[...]], where ACTION is a unit on some rank and Mo is one of its elements.
Feature of :	Pl = [feature=project], where Pl is a subcategorized element of the unit ACTION

Exponence/lexical realization is not directly covered here. As discussed in several places in section 3, the expounding elements in our version are either clauses or *rhetorical structures*. The ordering relations in traditional SFG realizational rules expressed by *order at front* and similar operators, can be captured by the PATTERN attribute. Compared to the trees we used as representations earlier on in this section, the *cat* feature marks the horizontal lines between elements and units. The temporal structure of ACTIONS is an interesting issue which we can only refer to briefly here: Initially, we assume that the temporal sequence of units of ACTION at some rank is a function of the temporal sequence of elements of that units daughters on lower ranks (cf. Pollard & Sag. 1987 chapter 7, who use this approach for an account of word-order phenomena in languages). Yet, just as in the case of language, the precise nature of this function is not clear at the moment, and therefore one uses relevant constraints that are known to investigate what this function will be ultimately. However, as we shall indicate in various places, temporal order cannot simply be assumed to operate on units on one rank: We expect ordering statements to operate on units from different ranks relative to each other, comparable to *extraction* phenomena across levels in language, and we expect frequent *scrambling* or discontinuity (cf. 2.4.4. and 3.2. for some discussion of these questions). The theoretical notions which we are using in our notation in Figure 5 are introduced earlier in section 2.3.

2.3.8 Some core notions of Systemic Functional Grammar

The purpose of this brief section is not an introduction into Systemic Functional Grammar (SFG), and much less an introduction into the whole of Systemic Linguistics. What we want to do here is to prepare ourselves for some of the terminology used in the linguistic parts of the analyses presented in the sections to follow.

Introductions to SFG are available in many places. Halliday (1961) and (1967-68) contain the original formulations. Fawcett (1980) and (1987) represent an important variant of SFG, and it is this variant that we rely most heavily on in most places. Steiner (1983) presents an introduction in German, and overviews from a computational perspective are given in Kasper (1987); Patten (1988); and Winograd (1983).

Systemic Functional Grammar is the grammatical core of the theory of Systemic Linguistics. In SFG, each linguistic unit is classified in terms of a set of features. Combinations of these features specify the formal properties of units in terms of morpho-syntactic properties, linear precedence relationships between its constituents and their parts, the functions of these constituents, control and raising properties, lexical insertion etc. The features which are possible for a given unit, i.e. the *potential*, are represented in the form of a *system network*. A path through a system network yields a *selection expression*, which is the *actual*. The process triggered by a selection expression is called *realization*, of which there are again several sub-types according to the various types of structural properties of linguistic units. A system network, together with other system networks, makes up a *functional component* of the grammar, such as the experiential, logical, thematic, or interpersonal components. Each functional component typically determines a particular type of linguistic structure, such as constituency, dependency, linear precedence, intonation and stress. As a notational convention, we shall write selectional expressions such as [mood, interrogative, polarity] in square brackets.

As compared to other widely used linguistic frameworks, the idea of subcategorizing units of linguistic structure by sets of features is quite common nowadays, although it should be said in this context that SFG elaborated this idea long before most other approaches did. What may be fairly unique to Systemic Grammar, on the other hand, is the range of features considered, together with the principle of clustering sets of features into networks and components which together determine the structure of a unit.

The term *semantic* is used in SFG in two different ways: In the version following from Fawcett (1980), which is the one predominantly followed in our third chapter, features in system networks are referred to as *semantic features*. In a more Hallidayan version of SFG, they would be referred to as *lexico-grammatical features*. The way we shall be using features, networks and selection expressions in this study is as follows: whenever we discuss linguistic units, such as clauses or words or phrases, we shall want to classify them, especially in the case of the empirical studies in chapter 3. This classification will be done in terms of the features made available in system networks. However, even for readers unfamiliar with the systemic literture, the use of features should be largely self-explanatory, because by far most of them designate linguistic properties which are discussed in other linguistic theories as well, so that, even if one has difficulties understanding all of the implications of a particular linguistic analysis suggested here against the background of SFG, it should be possible to follow the general linguistic arguments which we shall be making. We shall also take care to provide discussion linking up SFG concepts with concepts from other theories where this seems desirable.

The following examples illustrate in a simple way the key terms of Systemic Linguistics introduced here:

Linguistic *units* correspond to constituents on various levels posited by other theories. Grammatical units are thus *clause complex, clause, phrase, group, word, morpheme*. Each unit is *classified* in terms of a set of features. A clause, for example, will have features such as [agent-centred, active, non-modalized] and many others - in short, all the features which control its formal properties. A feature [agent-centred], for example, will constrain its head verb to be of a certain class, and it will constrain the role of *Agent* to be assigned to its Subject role if at the same time the *voice* feature is [active]. All the possible features for a given unit constitute the *potential* of that unit. For example, if we assume that in English the number system for *nominal groups* has only the potential of *singular, plural*, then this is the potential for that type of unit in a grammar of English. If our small system network says that *number* for the nominal group in English is thus constrained, and that number has to be strictly one or the other, *singular, plural* are the only two terms in the *number* system, and they are in a disjoint relationship, shown by square brackets in *system networks* such as we shall be using them in chapter 3 (for example in Figure 25, section 3.4) and elsewhere. Any *selection expression* from our small number system has only one feature, but usually system networks are more complex and so are selection expressions. A system network, for example, which says for some language that *number* of nominal groups is always either [singular] or [non-singular], and [non-singular] is always either [plural] or [dual], admits the following selection expressions: [singular], [non-singular, dual], [non-singular, plural]. Any such selection expression, or *path* through a system network is an *actualization* of the *potential* of the language. Features of the type just illustrated have one or more of a small number of different consequences, the most important of which in our context is *realization*. The feature [plural] for nominal groups of English, for example, will in most cases trigger *s* - affixation on head nouns. A feature such as *unmarked information* on clause rank will assign primary stress to the rightmost fully lexical item, and through it to phrases, etc. A feature such as [active] on clauses will cause a certain participant role to be conflated with Subject. Features and realization statements are in very complex disjunctive and conjunctive relationships in any grammar fragment of even moderate coverage.

Next, let us illustrate the notion of a *functional component*: A Systemic analysis postulates that the structure of any linguistic unit is the product of various functions of that unit along different dimensions. These different functions of linguistic units are "crystallized" in different *functional components* of a language. A sentence and clause, such as one of our sample sentences from 2.4.1. *I'll shoot that cat on sight*, will be classified as [action, agent-centred, +affected, overt affected] in terms of *transitivity*, as [+circumstance] in terms of *circumstances*, as [statement, indicative] in terms of *mood*, and as [theme-on-first-inherent-role] in terms of *theme*. Transitivity and circumstance are *ideational*, more specifically, *experiential* features, mood features are *interpersonal*, and theme features are *textual*. Each of the components *ideational, interpersonal, textual* make their own specific contribution to the overall structure of the clause: The *selection expression* [action, agent-centred, +affected, overt affected] classifies the clause as one that has a main verb of the class [action, agent-centred], the second *participant role* of the verb is an *Affected*, it is *overt*, and it is conflated with the direct Object, if the clause is in active voice. Thus, *experiential features* control constituency. The other sub-type of *ideational* features are *logical* features, in terms of which our sample sentence has a very simple structure, not being tactically linked to any other clause. In terms of *logical interdependency*, there is only one head at clause rank. Any *embedded* or *projected* clauses would be modifiers, yet modifiers of very different types. The *interpersonal features* [statement, indicative] classify the clause as one that has a Subject, which precedes the *Finite* element and and as a clause which will have falling intonation on its tonic element, if the *information distribution* is [unmarked] and *modality* is [non-modalized]. Interpersonal meaning, then, accounts for part of the contituent structure, some syntactic functions, and some aspects of intonation, in interaction with textual and ideational information, as illustrated by the conditions which we have informally attached to our remarks on realization. Finally, [theme-on-first-inherent-role] specifies that the *Theme* role will be conflated with the *Agent* role, so that the Agent will appear leftmost in terms of linear precedence.

Our illustrations for some key terms of Systemic Linguistics should in no way be understood as attempts at full analyses: They are meant as illustrations, and nothing but that. Fuller analyses are given in our discussions in 2.4.1–2.4.3, and even more so and with some linguistic discussions in sections within chapter 3.

The second level on which our terminology has to be understandable is the level on which we discuss how features of some linguistic model, or the equivalent of features in other theories, are interfaced with an analysis of goal-directed action, and again we shall try to make sure that this is brought out very clearly whenever it becomes relevant.

We thus hope to keep this study reasonably independent of standard introductions into Systemic Grammar. Quite clearly, though, as with any reasonably complex set of ideas, so in the case of SFG readers willing to go into many of the detailed implications of what is presented here for the theory as such will at some stage want to consult the standard literature, unless they bring some background of their own to this study.

2.4 Sample analyses

In this section, we shall give four sample analyses illustrating the framework which we outlined in 2.3. In doing so, we shall try to demonstrate some detailed analyses, investigating in detail strengths and weaknesses of the framework. Also, we shall try to deal with different types of ACTION and different types of text, which only share the characteristic that they are part of and/or realize some goal-directed

ACTION. Section 2.4.5. is of particular significance, in that it contains a model of the interface between analyses of goal-directed actions and linguistic analyses.

The analyses in this section will not only be used for the sake of demonstration: at various points in the exposition of the overall framework we have formulated questions arising from the theory or pointing towards issues that are in need of further clarification. Many of these issues will be taken up in the present section, and solutions to open questions are proposed in the appropriate places. While we could have chosen to handle all of these theoretical and methodological questions in the theoretical section 2.3., it seemed more appropriate to handle questions from a certain degree of specifity onwards in the course of analyses. To present all of these questions "in advance" would run counter to the philosophy of science of Systemic Linguistics, which has as one of its fundamental characteristics the recognition of an interaction between theory and practice, which suggests an interactive and cyclical, rather than a purely deductive way of presenting a set of ideas.

In section 2.4.5., we shall try to prepare the ground for a first fomalization of the interface between representations of goal-directed-actions and linguistic representations on text level, rather than clause level.

2.4.1 The analysis of a story

In the following, we present the lyrics of an American folk ballad which we shall then go on to analyze (cf. Steiner 1988d for an earlier version of this analysis). The numbering in the left hand margin refers to clauses in the text with embedded clauses, projected clauses, and adverbial clauses counted separately.

The Cat

Verse 1	
1	Old Mr. Johnson had troubles of his own.
2,3	He had a big yellow cat that wouldn't leave his home.
4,5	He tried and he tried to give that cat away,*
6,7	and he gave it to a man who was going far away.
Chorus	
8	And the cat came back the very next day.
9,10,11	The cat came back, you know,** he thought he was a gonner
12,13	The cat came back, he just couldn't stay away...
Verse 2	
14	So, he gave it to a boy with a five dollar note.
15,16,17	Said: "Take it down to the river, take it out in a boat!"
18,19	He tied a weight around its neck, must have weighed a pound.
20,21	Now they're searching the river for the poor boy that's drowned.

Chorus	
Verse 3	
22,23	Then the man around the corner said "I'll shoot that cat on sight."
24	And he loaded up his shotgun with nails and dynamite.
25,26	He waited and he waited* for that cat to come around.
27,28	But ninety-seven pieces of that man was all we found.
Chorus	
Verse 4	
29	The A-bomb fell, just the other day.
30	The H-bomb fell in the very same way.
31,32,33	England was gone, and France was gone, and even the good old USA.
34	The whole world was demolished on that day.
Chorus	

* The repetitions here are not counted as separate clauses.

** *You know* is not counted as a separate clause, because its discourse function is different from that of the remaining clauses

Concentrating on the story told in the text, we can see that it derives its characteristic features from the conflict between two ACTIVITIES driving the story to its climax (cf. Tables 7 and 8).

Table 7. Activity 1

NEED 1	ACTIVITY 1	OBJECTIVE 1
Untroubled state of mind. If disturbed (by presence of cat) $\Longrightarrow$	remove disturbance	Removal of disturbance; satisfaction of NEED 1

Table 8. Activity 2

NEED 2	ACTIVITY 2	OBJECTIVE 2
Untroubled state of mind; if disturbed, (by absence from home) $\Longrightarrow$	remove disturbance	removal of disturbance Satisfaction of NEED 2

On this general level already, we can see the source of conflict, which does not lie in the NEEDS, ACTIVITIES, and OBJECTIVES as such, but in the fact that what

disturbs the satisfaction of NEED 1, in this particular SITUATION (cf. below), is exactly the state of affairs constituting the satifaction of NEED 2: The cat's being in the vicinity of Mr. Johnson, or at least of his home. Both ACTIVITIES provide the entry conditions for ACTIONS which are followed through in the course of the text. *Entry condition*, it should be said here, is a structural condition, and has nothing to do with temporal sequence: The ACTIONS to be analyzed below are not in any temporal sense the consequence of ACTIVITIES 1 and 2, but their constituents. This relationship holds true for any analysis of ACTIVITIES, and is thus part of the theory rather than an accidental property of the particular ACTIVITIES which we are analyzing here.
The first ACTION would be the one in Table 9.

Table 9. Action 1

From ACTIVITY 1:

ACTION 1 Remove cat		GOAL cat be far away	
MOTIVATION	PLANNING	EXECUTION	EVALUATION
perceiving troubles= cat	not in text; to be inferred	give cat to man (...)	not in text; to be inferred

We shall not analyze *He tried and he tried to give the cat away* as a separate ACTION here; it can be interpreted as describing ACTIVITY 1, just like our ACTION 1. Notice that this analysis brings out an interesting ambiguity in the interpretation of this part of the story: Either *He tried and he tried...* is a sequence of events different from those in ACTION 1, or else, and this is our interpretation, ACTION 1 is just part of the sequence of events described in clauses 4,5 of our story, just like the state of affairs *he had a big yellow cat...* is part of *Mr Johnson had troubles of his own*. The notion of *part of* is further explicated below (2.4.4.).

We are not being told anything about the OPERATIONS carried out, because, in the opinion of the author, these are not relevant for the interpretation of the story as it is being told.

There is an interesting structural property of ACTIONS which we can see in ACTION 1: embedding. "Interpreting" an ACTION means, among other things, expecting the EXECUTION to provide a sufficient condition for the reaching of the state of affairs described under GOAL. The GOAL, together with the MOTIVATION, provides the reason for the EXECUTION. This, however, is not the case here at first sight. So, either we have to consider ACTION 1 as badly planned, or else we have to look out for embedded ACTIONS which might provide the missing link in a chain of cause and effect. Indeed, looking at verse 1 of our story we can find the embedded ACTION we are looking for: The linguistic reflection of EXECUTION of

ACTION 1 (6,7) contains an embedded clause which tells us that the "receiver" of the cat is himself an argument in an embedded proposition in the following way (in a somewhat loose notation):

(Johnson$_x$ CAUSE (man$_a$ POSSESS cat$_b$)Y) AND
(man$_a$ CAUSE (man$_a$ DISTANT FROM X)Z),

where the entire proposition after AND can be embedded after *man$_a$* in the first line of the expression. In other words, *Mr. Johnson* performs ACTION 1 by involving in his EXECUTION another person who will function as an AGENT in yet another ACTION, and these two ACTIONS together will provide the sufficient condition for the GOAL of ACTION 1. We shall discuss a different type of embedding in our analyses of ACTIONS 3.1.-3.3. below.

What is still lacking as an element of ACTION 1 is the EVALUATION. Again, there is none directly given in the text, but it clearly is to be inferred from what we are told about ACTION 2: only if we infer a *failed* EVALUATION of ACTION 1 do we get the necessary entry condition for ACTION 3 later on.

Admittedly, given a certain reading of the story, we do not entirely have to infer the EVALUATION of ACTION 1: In the refrain, we find the line *He thought he was a gonner*. If we took the first *he* in this line to refer through anaphoric reference to *Mr.Johnson*, and the second *he* to *the cat*, then this line would reflect the EVALUATION phase of ACTION 1. As the analysis of cohesion and thematic progression shows, there are no compelling reasons for preferring such a reading over a reading in which both instances of *he* refer to the cat. It is this second reading which we shall assume here, and accordingly, there is no linguistic reflection of the EVALUATION phase of ACTION 1 in the text.
We shall now proceed to the analysis of ACTION 2 (Table 10).

Table 10. Action 2

From ACTIVITY 2:

ACTION 2 come back to Johnson		GOAL (cat) be close to Johnson	
MOTIVATION	PLANNING	EXECUTION	EVALUATION
can't stay away	not in text; to be inferred	cat comes back	not in text; probably *successful*

The cat's ACTION is not narrated in any great detail, the only important effect being that it is successful, which leads us, in the *Situation of Utterance* (Davies 1979: 57ff), to infer a *successful* evaluation by the cat as well. Note that there is a basic difference between the EVALUATION of the listener/reader of the story, which is an EVALUATION of ACTION 2 by a person different from the AGENT of that ACTION and in a different SITUATION (*Situation of Utterance* of the text), and the EVALUATION of ACTION 2 by its own AGENT, which is not reported in the story, and which the listener/reader can only infer to have taken place in the *Situation of Performance*. The difference between the *Situation of Utterance* and the *Situation of Performance* is also evident in the fact that one ACTION (2) is encoded three times, where the encoding expresses certain rhetorical strategies in the Situation of Utterance, i.e. ACTION 2 in the Situation of Performance is encoded in three ACTIONS or OPERATIONS in the Situation of Utterance.

After ACTION 2 has been carried out, then, the old conflict between ACTIVITIES 1 and 2, deriving from the particular constellations of NEEDS and OBJECTIVES in this SITUATION, is in full force again, permitting re-entry into the cycle of ACTION and counterACTION (cf. Tables 11-15).

The text in this case also explicitly narrates the wording realizing the second OPERATION under EXECUTION of 3.2. as *Take it out in a boat*. This OPERATION would have to be analyzed in a parallel way to the one above.

In our analysis of 3.2, we have assumed that what is consciously planned is, roughly, the propositional content of the utterance and its illocutionary force, whereas the particular semantic options, as well as the wording and the intonation structure of the utterance are not consciously planned and monitored so that these are analyzed on the rank of OPERATION. This may well be the unmarked case in the production of speech in the genre we are dealing with here, but certainly not the only one admitted by the theory: In writing a paper, for example, or in preparing a speech for a public occasion the AGENT will quite frequently have to deal with semantic options and even with the actual wording on the rank of ACTION. In this case, the semantic options in the ideational, interpersonal, and textual components and/or the realizational statements would have to be raised to the rank of ACTION. Let us have a look at ACTION 3.3 next (Table 15).

In ACTIONS 3.1 to 3.3, we find a type of embedding of ACTIONS which is different from the type of embedding in ACTION 1: In ACTION 1, further ACTIONS are embedded as expected ACTIONS of AGENTS realized as arguments or participant roles under GOAL of ACTION 1, their AGENT not being identical with the AGENT of the superordinate ACTION. In ACTION 3, the agents of superordinate and subordinate ACTIONS are identical. In a more formal sense, while both kinds of recursion of the ACTION symbol are cases of indirect domination by the topmost ACTION symbol, they are still different in that the number and kind of intervening levels in a tree of the ACTION are different. At the moment, when we do not aim at a full formalization of our theory, these considerations may be of secondary importance. They should be made explicit, though, because they indicate ways of further research.

Table 11. Action 3

From ACTIVITY 1

ACTION 3 kill cat		GOAL cat be dead	
MOTIVATION	PLANNING	EXECUTION	EVALUATION
not in text; to be inferred	to be inferred: create sub-ACTIONS 3.1.-3.3.	filled by 3.1.-3.3.	indirect, cf. lines 20,21 of the text: failed

Table 12. Action 3.1

From EXECUTION 3

ACTION 3.1 give cat to boy		GOAL boy possess cat (boy=AGENT in some further ACTION X=cause cat to be in water)	
MOTIVATION	PLANNING	EXECUTION	EVALUATION
not in text; to be inferred	not in text; to be inferred	Johnson gives cat to boy	not in text; to be inferred: *successful*

Table 13. Action 3.2

From EXECUTION 3

ACTION 3.2 cause boy to take cat out on water (and do ACTION X= boy cause cat to be in water?)		GOAL boy take cat out on water (and do ACTION X?)	
MOTIVATION	PLANNING	EXECUTION	EVALUATION
not in text; to be inferred	not in text; to be inferred: command boy to do GOAL 3.2. and pay boy	utterance: lines 16,17 and pay boy	not in text; to be inferred

Table 14. Execution 3.2

OPERATION, from EXECUTION 3.2.: enter linguistic system*	
Functional Component	Selection Expression
Interpersonal	[command, imperative jussive, no politeness formula...]
Ideational	[locational, third party agent, change, +accompanyment...]
Textual	[Theme not realized, unmarked information focus...]
Feature	**Realization**
[command,imperative]	0 at S(ubject)
[no politeness formula]	0 at n (=number of corresponding place in starting structure of the clause
[locational]	enter lexical networks at [locational]
[third party agent]	agent at S(ubject)=0
[change, + accompanyment]	continue in lexical network to specified system
[theme not realized]	0 at S(ubject)
[unmarked information focus]	stress on last fully lexical item
Realization: *Take it out on the river*	
Features selected from networks appear in square brackets.	

*In the realizational part, we have omitted the statement of conditional features in order to avoid unnecessary complications in this presentation. Details and system networks are from Fawcett (1980).

Table 15. Action 3.3

From EXECUTION 3

ACTION 3.3. add weight to cat		GOAL cat be so heavy as to go under	
MOTIVATION	PLANNING	EXECUTION	EVALUATION
not in text; to be inferred	not in text; to be inferred	tie weight around cat's neck	not in text; to be inferred: *successful*

Note that there is an ambiguity as to the referent of the AGENT of ACTION 3.3 between *the boy* and *Mr. Johnson*. Furthermore, we will not discuss here the question of the actual temporal sequence of ACTIONS and elements, yet we should take note of one question connected with embedding: The PLANNING stages of 3.1-3.3 could already be realized within the PLANNING stage of the superordinate ACTION

3, rather than in their unmarked place in the sequence of elements of the embedded ACTIONS. This, however, is entirely an empirical question for any single ACTION under description. We do have to make sure, though, that our model provides for these possibilities, which the present model, indeed, does. Also, the GOALS of ACTIONS 3.1-3.3 will have been created as part of the PLANNING of ACTION 3, because it is this very fact that makes them subordinate to ACTION 3.

Back to our story now, where ACTION 3 is again followed by ACTION 2 (refrain), leading to another re-entry.

In this case, there is, of course, the question of whether we still have an entry from ACTIVITY 1: The AGENT has changed to *the man around the corner*, and the listener/reader is free to infer that either there is a new ACTIVITY 3 with a new AGENT, which would have to have many features in common with ACTIVITY 1, or else that Mr.Johnson is using the *the man around the corner* as an INSTRUMENT in the course of ACTIVITY 1. This ambiguity is part of our story, which continues as shown in Table 16.

In Table 16, as before, we have not given the full selection expression necessary for generating the clause, but only enough features to illustrate the analysis.

We have analyzed OPERATIONS here only in so far as they are narrated in the text. Necessarily, in the *world* in which the ACTIONS described happened there must have been OPERATIONS filling all the phases of the ACTION. It is only because they are not reflected in our text that we shall not analyze them. Indeed, it would seem to be a likely feature of many genres, such as that of *story*, that the texts will basically reflect the ACTION rank of behaviour.

In order to arrive at a possible interpretation of the story, we must assume that some ACTION 4.3, that of shooting the cat, must at least have been planned, because of the incomplete relationship of 4.1. and 4.2. to the goal of ACTION 4 (cf. Tables 17 and 18). Nothing else is known about this ACTION, except that it may have had as an unplanned consequence *but 97 pieces of that man was all we found.* No analysis of 4.3 is attempted here, because its whole structure would have to be inferred, and it is another inherent aspect of this kind of story that the individual listener/reader is left free to make his/her own inferences.

Table 16. Action 4

From ACTIVITY 1 :

ACTION 4 kill cat		GOAL cat be dead	
MOTIVATION	PLANNING	EXECUTION	EVALUATION
not in text; to be inferred	see OPERATION	go to ACTIONS 4.1.-4.3	not in text; to be inferred: *not successful*

Table 16 (cont.).

OPERATION, from PLANNING 4: enter linguistic system	
Functional Component	Selection Expression
interpersonal	[statement, indicative, modalized...]
ideational	[action, agent-centred, +affected, overt affected, circumstance,...]
textual	[theme first inherent role, ...]
Feature	Realization
[statement,indicative]	S(ubject) precedes V(erb)
[modalized]	lexical item at place M in the starting structure of the clause
[action, agent-centred]	enter lexical networks at specified points
[+affected, +overt affected]	affected at S(ubject) or C(omplement) in clause structure
[theme first inherent role]	agent at (S)ubject, active voice
Realization: *I'll shoot that cat on sight.*	

Table 17. Action 4.1

From EXECUTION 4

ACTION 4.1 load gun		GOAL gun be loaded	
MOTIVATION	PLANNING	EXECUTION	EVALUATION
not in text; to be inferred	not in text; to be inferred	load up gun	not in text; to be inferred: *successful*

Table 18. Action 4.2

From EXECUTION 4

ACTION 4.2 wait for cat		GOAL be close to cat	
MOTIVATION	PLANNING	EXECUTION	EVALUATION
not in text; to be inferred	not in text; to be inferred	wait for cat	not in text; to be inferred

The final sentence of verse 3 leads us to the conclusion that the EVALUATION of ACTION 4 cannot have been anything but *unsuccessful*, if there ever was an AGENT left to carry out this EVALUATION.

The following repetition of ACTION 2 leads on to the climax of the story in verse 4. Here we run into some interesting difficulties: Firstly, there is no AGENT mentioned in our text, which means that we may either infer Mr. Johnson to be the ultimate AGENT, or else we may decide that we simply do not know the AGENT. If we choose the latter, we run into a further complication, which is that we do not find any NEED or OBJECTIVE mentioned for some assumed new ACTIVITY. In that case, we have to interpret it as an ACTIVITY and as ACTIONS with all but the EXECUTIONS unknown, or else not as an ACTIVITY at all, but as an event, or a series of events happening without agency, much like a natural disaster. Both interpretations are valid, with the second one being weaker in the sense that less structure in terms of our theory of ACTIVITY has to be inferred. It would simply mean attributing less coherence to the story than under the first interpretation which would assume Mr. Johnson as an AGENT for the ACTIONS of verse 4. If we choose the event-interpretation, verse 4 is nothing but a scenario, a SITUATION, which seems to put an end to our endless re-entry of the ACTION grammar. To everyone's surprise, though, ACTION 2 does recur, in spite of the SITUATION created in verse 4, and with all possible AGENTS of further ACTIONS against our cat being eliminated. That makes our cat a symbol of power and perseverance, and, at the same time, it makes human efforts a symbol of futility.

If the primary purpose of our analysis of this story were the discussion of certain structural properties of stories, then this would be the place to enter this discussion. Topics for discussion would have to be the obvious domination of the element EXECUTION in our story, complexity in terms of different types of embedding in the story structure as such, the rank at which the story predominantly encodes the ACTIONS (ACTION, rather than ACTIVITY or OPERATION), the restriction of the plot to the individual level of human ACTIVITY etc. Further areas of research generated by such an analysis would be the investigation of delicacy, rank and exponence of encoding itself, unit/element relationships, and other questions which are an immediate consequence of the scale-and-category model which we have been using. However, our primary purpose here is to investigate the method of analysis itself, rather than its potential for generating interesting and testable research hypotheses. Therefore, we shall now move to the second major aspect of analysis: The SITUATION.

So far, we have been looking at the dynamic aspect of what is going on in our story, at ACTIVITIES, ACTIONS, and OPERATIONS. We have been operating with units that are states and processes (NEED, ACTION etc), or mental images of states and processes (GOAL). If we are looking at the ACTIVITIES going on, as if they were frozen for a moment, we get what is known as a SITUATION, that category so essential for the meaning of any linguistic utterance, and, indeed, human behaviour in general. The SITUATION, the background to ACTIVITIES, can be seen as a matrix, with the following slots to be filled in every given instance: AGENT, PROCESS, MATERIALS, INSTRUMENTS, PRODUCT (cf. section 2.3.6.). Thus, ACTIVITY and SITUATION are nothing but two aspects of the same reality, looked at from different angles. How, then, can this notion of SITUATION be applied to the analysis of our story? We give an analysis in tabular form in Figure 6.

Figure 6.

Verse 1

AGENT	PROCESS	MATERIALS
Mr. Johnson (state 1: Johnson is in trouble) (state 2: Johnson posses cat); state 2 cause state 1	change possession/ location of cat	location/ possession of cat
INSTRUMENTS	PRODUCT	
man a (a= agent of ACTION n=a go far away)	cat belong to man a AND location of cat unchanged	

Refrain

AGENT	PROCESS	MATERIALS
cat	change location of cat	location of cat
INSTRUMENTS	PRODUCT	
- - -	cat be with Johnson ⇒ states 1,2	

Verse 2

AGENT	PROCESS	MATERIALS
Mr. Johnson	attempt (kill cat)	cat
Mr. Johnson	change location possession of cat	location of cat
Mr. Johnson	cause ACTION m = boy take cat out on water (=ACTION x)	boy, location of cat cat
Mr. Johnson	add weight 1 to cat	(weight 2 of) cat

INSTRUMENTS	PRODUCT	
boy (=AGENT of ACTION x)	boy is dead	
- - -	cat be with boy	
weight 1	cat is heavy	

Verse 3

AGENT	PROCESS	MATERIALS
Man b around the	attempt (kill cat)	cat
Man b	load gun	gun, nails, dynamite
Man b	wait	man b
Man b	shoot	cat

INSTRUMENTS	PRODUCT	
gun	? man b drowned	
	gun is loaded	
	?	
	?	

Verse 4

AGENT	PROCESS	MATERIALS
not given	drop	bombs
not given	demolish	world

INSTRUMENTS	PRODUCT	
	England, France, USA are gone	
bombs	world is demolished	

Figure 6. Situational analysis of the cat story

We have already shown in 2.3.6. that the categories of the SITUATIONAL level are not isomorphic to the categories known from clause semantics. This is perhaps most clearly evident if we look at the entries under INSTRUMENTS in our SITUATIONAL analysis, none of which is encoded as the CIRCUMSTANTIAL role of INSTRUMENT at clause level.

Another question in this context is that of whether our SITUATIONAL analysis does not simply reproduce the semantic structure of a *paragraph*, *span* (cf. Grimes 1975), or *phase* (cf. Gregory 1985). The answer would is dependent on how precisely one arrives at the semantic structure of such larger units. There would seem to be two basic possibilities:

- We arrive at the semantic structure of a paragraph by amalgamating the results of the analyses of its clauses, i.e. participant roles, themes, rhemes, given/new information units, sense relations etc. However, if we are correct in our assumption that SITUATIONAL categories and categories of the ideational structure of clauses are not isomorphic, then there is every reason to assume that the result of an amalgamation of the semantic structures at clause level will not be equal to our SITUATIONAL analysis. On this assumption, then, the SITUATIONAL analysis uses categories belonging to a level of reality different from, though related to, language. Categories of the SITUATIONAL analysis would then have to be seen as being encoded in the semantics of the clause and in the semantics of the paragraph, as well as in grammar and lexis. On which level the actual conscious planning of the AGENT takes place in a given case is a question of the exact point of entry of the linguistic ACTION/OPERATION into the overall structure of ACTIVITY.
- We may arrive at the semantic structure of paragraphs, spans, phases, or even stories, by postulating a level of semantic structure, ideational in particular, above the clause, which uses categories which are not derived from the semantic structure of clauses, nor simply the result of a SITUATIONAL analysis as sketched here (cf. the contributions in Coots 1982). The crucial question then would seem to be whether these are not describing generalized SITUATIONS, just as the semantics of clauses can be viewed as a highly generalized potential for the encoding of SITUATIONS on a level/rank below text structure.

Both approaches which we have been discussing would lead to the conclusion that the semantic structure of texts and the SITUATIONAL structures are not the same. We are choosing here the second of these alternatives, but we would like to stress that we are talking about an area which is open to discussion inside and outside of Systemic Linguistics.

This brings the analysis of our story to an end. The next step would have to be that of a detailed linguistic analysis with a subsequent correlation of results. We shall not, in the present section, have the space to go into this (cf. Steiner 1988 d for an attempt in this direction). Our main purpose here has been to exemplify the method deriving from the theory of ACTIVITY outlined in earlier sections. A secondary purpose has been to explore strengths and weaknesses of the framework, as far as it exists at this time, in order to open up the way for future research and change.

2.4.2 The analysis of a complex internal action

The series of ACTIONS which we are going to look at in this section is given in the text reproduced below following some introductory comments. It should be observed that in this section, we are not analyzing the ACTION of speaking or writing this text, which would be the ACTION that this text realizes. Instead, we are going to analyze the ACTIONS narrated i.e. encoded and reflected in this text. This is worth emphasizing at the outset because every goal-directed utterance has this twofold quality, namely that of realizing an ACTION and, on the other hand, that of reflecting an ACTION, event, or state of affairs.

The text we are going to look at is taken from work on the psychological study of human action and decision making in the context of individual and social conflict (cf. Eckensberger & Silbereisen 1980: 70; Eckensberger & Burgard 1985). The translation of the text is my own. The final sentences *After being deeply immersed in thought for a considerable time, he is heard to sigh "She's got to be alive. So I'll take it."* have been added to the original to give us a chance of looking more closely at the role of language in the analysis of this particular ACTION. An earlier version of this analysis appears in Steiner 1988 b.

> A woman is suffering from a fatal disease. There is only a single certain medicine that can save her. This medicine, however, is so expensive that no health insurance will pay for it. In their own town, there is a chemist's shop that has the medicine, yet the chemist only wants to release the medicine if he gets his price. Heinz, the husband of the doomed woman, has tried everything possible to raise the money for the medicine, yet, as it turns out, whatever he may do, he will never be able to raise the money.
>
> Because Heinz's wife will definitely die if she does not get the medicine, and because Heinz is in no way able to pay for the medicine, he is now thinking about whether he should not break into the chemist's shop to steal the medicine.
>
> After being deeply immersed in thought for a considerable time, he is heard to sigh:" She's got to be alive. So I'll take it."

In our analysis, we shall only remain on the rank of ACTIVITY for a very short time. On this rank, we are faced with a difficulty which is typical of a multi-level approach to the analysis of human behaviour, the difficulty of deciding on what level of generality to formulate descriptions of ACTIVITIES, ACTIONS, or OPERATIONS. Are there, for example, general human ACTIVITIES like *preserving (helping, maintaining...) the people one loves*, or *making money*? If so, then we could certainly classify Heinz's ACTIONS as an instance of the first class of ACTIVITIES, and those of the chemist as instances of the second. It would also be possible to formulate corresponding human needs, although somewhat controversial needs in the case of *making money*, and objectives. It is not clear at the moment, however, what precisely distinguishes an ACTIVITY from an ACTION, except that ACTIVITIES in general would seem to be on a higher level of generality. This is a difficulty within the present approach which emerges all the more clearly the more extensive the experience with the analysis of ACTIVITY becomes. We can list certain properties which ACTIVITIES, or rather, linguistic references to them, appear to have, and which can be used as guidelines in descriptive work:

ACTIVITIES are not situated in specific place and time, that is to say, they are conceived of as *general*, rather than as *specific* SITUATIONS. Linguistic references to them will not have time - Adjuncts or place - Adjuncts. Furthermore, linguistic references to ACTIVITIES, rather than ACTIONS or OPERATIONS, will not contain Adjuncts expressing manner, purpose, cause, condition, or concession. In fact, they will, as a rule, not contain any Adjuncts. This is, of course, a straightforward consequence of the theoretical status of ACTIVITIES in the present framework: they are not directly related to conscious goals, whereas the ACTIONS filling them are, and they are on the highest rank within our grammar of ACTION, which implies that they abstract away precisely from those factors expressed in Adjuncts. A further characteristic of linguistic references to ACTIVITIES seems to be that referring expressions in them, e.g. NPs, will frequently have a general rather than a specific lexical item as head (Halliday & Hasan 1976: 274ff.), where, of course, this rule applies to the Subject NP in a much more limited way than to the rest of positions in the clause. Finally, linguistic references to ACTIVITIES will frequently not contain a syntactic Object, as we intend to illustrate in the following pairs, where the first element would be coded by us as referring to an ACTIVITY, whereas the second elements of the pairs would much more likely refer to some (underspecified) ACTION: *to play vs. to play chess, to eat vs. to eat some meat, to work vs. to work on one's house*. Again, this characteristic may be seen as connceted to the fact that ACTIVITIES are not defined as such through their relationship to some conscious goal, nor to some PRODUCT in SITUATIONAL terms. However, it should be pointed out here that the realization relationship between GOALS and PRODUCTS on the one hand, and syntactic Objects on the other is very far from one to one.

Because of the nature of our particular example, the interest of which derives not from the question of whether or not we can draw the line between ACTIVITIES and ACTIONS perfectly clearly, but rather from a particular way of sequencing and embedding ACTIONS, we shall turn to the analysis of ACTIONS immediately. The following informal ACTION-graph (cf. Figure 7) is meant as a guide to help us follow through the structure of ACTIONS narrated in this text. In this graph, levels with numerals symbolize ACTIONS, intermediate levels symbolize elements of ACTIONS.

In this particular type of problem solving story, the graph represents temporal sequence, as well as the part-whole relationship. Of course, if the action graph included the non-realized EXECUTION and EVALUATION phases of ACTIONS 1

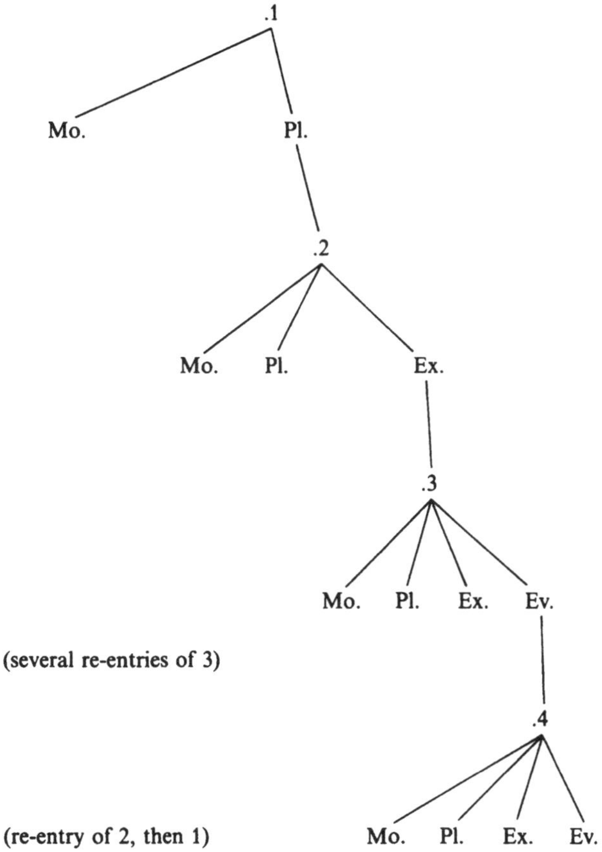

Figure 7. Action graph

and 2, it would no longer directly represent temporal sequence in this way. The general relationship between constituency and between linear sequence (temporal order) is this:

If some ACTION$_n$ is part of some ACTION$_{n-1}$, then n may start at the same time, or later, than n-1, and it must terminate before, or at the same time as ACTION$_{n-1}$ (cf. 2.4.4. for more thoughts on this). Quite naturally, then, in cases where we have recursive application of the ACTION embedding in a part-of relationship, certain parts of the top-to-bottom sequence in representations express temporal sequence at the same time. Otherwise, our representations are essentially constituent structure representations and thus may abstract away considerably from temporal sequence (for a related, yet not identical notion of an ACTION graph cf. Mellish & Evans 1989: 234).

In the following analyses, we shall in each case begin with an analysis of the SITUATION followed by an analysis of the particular ACTION taking place in this SITUATION. Neither ACTION, nor SITUATION, however, take absolute precedence, or could stand on their own: The SITUATION is only created by the ACTION, in that the categories are relative (an AGENT, for example, is always the AGENT of the particular ACTION we are describing at that moment), and, vice versa, an ACTION cannot take place outside a SITUATION. The following abbreviations are used:

A	=	Agent	Mo	=	Motivation
Pr	=	Process	Pl	=	Planning
Ma	=	Materials	Ex	=	Execution
In	=	Instruments	Ev	=	Evaluation
Pt	=	Product			

A comment is necessary on the language which we shall be using in the slots of our SITUATIONAL and ACTION descriptions: This language is just slightly abbreviated everyday language. It does not seem necessary, nor justified, at this stage to use a formal language, like, for example, predicate calculus, modal logic, or deontic logic. In a superficial way, one could certainly attempt such a reformulation, for example for some kind of knowledge base organized along the lines of SITUATION and ACTION frames, but at the same time, we might lose some of the aspects of information conveyed by everyday language, such as that encoded in semi-auxiliaries, modality-Adjuncts, questions, commands, and other natural language devices. Until we know exactly which aspects of this information we need, i.e. until the time when we can reduce the language we are using in a controlled way, we will continue to use everyday language with all its vagueness.

We shall now carry out an analysis of the SITUATIONS and ACTIONS which are essential in the process of understanding the text given above.

Table 19 is the analysis of a presupposed ACTION 1: The ACTION of healing Heinz's wife has to be suspended until the lacking element of SITUATION 1 is provided, which is the medicine. Let us make a comment here on the planning phase of ACTION 1: As we have analyzed it here, the AGENT decides within the planning phase that the first thing necessary is that Heinz provides the all important medicine, and that only afterwards can ACTION 1 continue. According to our analysis, the agent of ACTION 1 does not yet plan ahead how to proceed further in ACTION 1. This is not a question of principle, but a factual question. Both possibilities exist in the structure of human ACTIONS. In any case, all of the following ACTIONS are entered directly or indirectly from the planning phase of ACTION 1, as shown in our ACTION-graph.

The entire sequence of ACTIONS is run almost like a push-down-storage device: ACTION_n is interrupted and stored "below" ACTION_{n+1}, to be taken up again later

Table 19. Situation 1

<table>
<tr><td>A</td><td>Pr</td><td>Ma</td><td>In</td><td>Pt</td></tr>
<tr><td>Someone</td><td>attempt to heal wife$_b$</td><td>wife$_b$</td><td>medicine$_a$ (necessary)</td><td>suspended</td></tr>
<tr><td colspan="3">ACTION 1: Someone heal wife$_b$</td><td colspan="2">GOAL: Wife$_b$ be alive</td></tr>
<tr><td>Mo</td><td colspan="2">Pl</td><td>Ex</td><td>Ev</td></tr>
<tr><td>inferred:
orientation
in SITUATION 1
becoming
conscious of
need for
ACTIVITY</td><td colspan="2">inferred:

when Ev 2 =
successful,
go to ACTION 1</td><td>suspended
go to ACTION 2,</td><td>suspended</td></tr>
</table>

on the path "backwards". The exception here is ACTION 3, which would be omitted in a presumed complete backwards run of the entire sequence of ACTIONS because of the decision reached in ACTION 4. We shall see the details of this as we proceed in our analysis of ACTIONS (cf. Table 20-22).

Table 20. Situation 2

<table>
<tr><td>A</td><td>Pr</td><td>Ma</td><td>In</td><td>Pt</td></tr>
<tr><td>Heinz</td><td>attempt to get medicine</td><td>location/ possession of medicine</td><td>(large sum of) money</td><td>suspended</td></tr>
<tr><td>ACTION 2:</td><td>Heinz attempt to get medicine</td><td>GOAL 2:</td><td colspan="2">Heinz possess medicine AND go to ACTION 1</td></tr>
<tr><td>Mo</td><td>Pl</td><td>Ex</td><td colspan="2">Ev</td></tr>
<tr><td>inferred:
orientation
in SITUATION 2
effectiveness
of NEED 1</td><td>inferred</td><td>go to chemist;
find out price;
break</td><td colspan="2">inferred: *failed*
go to ACTION 3;
when Ev3=
successful go
to ACTION 2.
Cause of failure:
lack of instrument</td></tr>
</table>

Table 21. Situation 3

A	Pr	Ma	In	Pt
Heinz	attempt to get large sum of money	location/ possession of money	diverse, not specified	no change of Ma

ACTION 3: (from Ev2)	Heinz attempt to get money	GOAL 3:	Heinz possess money AND go to ACTION 2

Mo	Pl	Ex	Ev
inferred: orientation in SITUATION 3; effectiveness of NEED 1	inferred	diverse	*failed*;cause of failure= lack of adequate In. go to ACTION 4

Table 22. Situation 4

A	Pr	Ma	In	Pt
Heinz	project & evaluate possible ACTIONS 5,6	mental images & internal states of A	(partly) language	decisions on future ACTIONS

ACTION 4: (from Ev.3)	Heinz project and evaluate possible courses of ACTIONS	GOAL 4:	Decision on future courses of ACTION

Mo	Pl	Ex	Ev
inferred: orientation in SITUATION 4 effectiveness of NEED 1	inferred	projection 1, projection 2 evaluation of products in projections 1,2 & decision on further ACTIONS go to OPERATIONS 1-3	inferred: *successful*

Before we go on to analyze OPERATIONS 1-3, a short comment on the status of these OPERATIONS is necessary: In the actual course of ACTION 4, it is quite possible that these processes will take the form of embedded ACTIONS rather than OPERATIONS. This would again seem to be a factual question. The criterion, let us remember, is that of whether or not these processes are processes for the AGENT, involving conscious planning. According to our present analysis, Heinz would report on these in a form like the following: "I first thought what the death of my wife would mean to me, and then, what stealing the medicine would imply. After that, it was clear that I would steal it." Heinz would remember the PLANNING and the EXECUTION, i.e. what he did, though not how he did it, that is to say, the actual content of the OPERATIONS which we shall analyze below. This difference is partly reflected in the linguistic distinction between *reported* and *direct* speech: A direct speech quote of some linguistic utterance will normally indicate that it was executed as a linguistic ACTION from the perspective of the AGENT. Observe that such a direct quote would be a sufficient, but not a necessary condition for some utterance to count as an ACTION.

OPERATION 1 in Table 23 contains a projection of SIT 5 (internal, possibly non-linguistic code), and is entered from EX 4:

Table 23. Situation 5

A	Pr	Ma	In	Pt
Heinz	steal medicine	location/ possession of medicine	force	Heinz possess medicine & go to ACTION 1

In cases such as SITUATION 5 under PRODUCT, it becomes evident that it is, indeed, necessary to distinguish between the PRODUCT as the result of the ACTION to the extent that it is intended, i.e. in its relationship to GOAL, and the CONSEQUENCE of an ACTION, which is what follows from the ACTION logically (and/or temporally?). In SIT 5, for example, one of the consequences of Heinz's ACTION might be that the chemist is worried because someone has broken into his/her shop. In our framework, though, this is a consequence, but not a product, because it was not part of the GOAL of the ACTION. Whether or not one adds a CONSEQUENCE slot to the description of a SITUATION is, at this stage, a question of the purpose for which one is undertaking the description in the first place. The same applies for possible categories of *reason/cause*, which form a *subjective/objective* pair like *product/consequence*, and which could be added to the description of a SITUATION in this framework if the nature of the analysis demands it.

An interesting parallel in speech act theory is the nature of the *perlocutionary* act, and the connnected question to what extent it has to be intentional and/or conscious. For linguistic ACTIONS, not every perlocutionary effect is a PRODUCT, whereas PRODUCTS in this class of ACTIONS would always seem to be some perlocutionary effect. Linguistic ACTIONS, it is becoming more and more obvious, are in more than one way just a sub-type of ACTIONS in general, even if they have a particularly intricate structure.

Another question in this context is how we relate an encoding like *breaking the law* to our encoding of *process*, which is *steal medicine*: What are our criteria for choosing a certain degree of generality?

The answer is that too general a wording would destroy the systematic relationships within the description of our SITUATION. *Stealing the medicine* can be related to the *materials* in our SITUATION, but *breaking the law* would be too general. In a way, *steal medicine* in the context of our ACTION is an instance of *breaking the law*, but only in a social order in which this kind of change of possession counts as stealing. Our distinction here is not that between *socially meaningful* and *physical*: both *steal medicine* and *break law* are socially meaningful. A "purely physical" description would be an OPERATIONAL description in our framework. What is less obvious at the moment is, whether we have a case here of the ACTIVITY-ACTION distinction: There would not appear to be an obvious way of relating either of these sentences directly to physiological and/or cultural needs. Accordingly, one may even have to assume different degrees of generality within the rank of ACTION.

OPERATION 2 in Table 24 contains the projection of SIT 6 (internal, possibly non-linguistic code), and is entered from Ex 4:

Table 24. Situation 6

A	Pr	Ma	In	Pt
Heinz	omit ACTION 5	location/ possession of medicine	0	Heinz does not POSSESS medicine; ACTION 1 is *unsuccessful*

It must be added that the inevitable consequence would be that Heinz's wife dies. As Heinz is aware of this fact, the question is whether the wife's death would not even become a product of his possible ACTION 6 - an important moral and legal question, which we will not go into here. ACTION 6, obviously, is a "negative" ACTION, which is realized by omitting certain OPERATIONS and ACTIONS, but omitting them consciously and wilfully. This kind of negative ACTION is well known within the logic of ACTION (cf. von Wright 1972).

OPERATION 3 in Table 25 contains the EVALUATION of the PRODUCTS of SIT 5,6 and a decision on further ACTIONS. Quite importantly for our analysis, this OPERATION is realized linguistically and externally.

The clause produced by the process of semantic choice and syntactic realization as indicated above would be: *She's got to be alive*. Table 26 shows the generation of clause 2 of OPERATION 3.

Concerning our treatment of the generation of the two clauses in Tables 25 and 26, it should be noted that we have only presented a selection of choices from the semantic networks, i.e. a partial feature description of the sentence. The complete selectional expressions would take up considerably more space. Also, we have omitted here the formalization of selection and realization, which depends on the formalism one chooses but adds nothing, in our context, to a linguistic understand-

Table 25. Operation 3, clause 1.

Functional component	Selection expression
ideational: transitivity	[relational, attributive,simple attribuant...]
interpersonal: modality	[modalized,necessity...]
textual: theme	[Subject theme 1st inherent role]

Feature	Realization
relational	verb of class linking verb, or some stronger lexicalization
attributive	identifier at C
simple attribuant	first inherent role NOT agent or 3rd party agent
modalized	re-enter for adjunct OR clause OR modal operator at place O(m) in starting structure of the clause
necessity*	modal operator realized by *must* or *(have)got to*
Subject theme 1st inherent role	attribuant at S

**necessity* is not either deontic or epistemic. The realization is: *She's got to be alive.*

ing. Formalized versions of selection and realization are discussed extensively in the literature on computational implementations of Systemic Linguistics.

This is as far as we shall go in the analysis of our Heinz-story. To lead us back to our original motivation for undertaking the analysis, let us point out exactly which linguistic features of the texts are (partly) explained by an analysis such as the one we have undertaken here. For the time being, we shall concentrate on grammatical and lexical structure, including cohesion, of our two sentences *She's got to be alive. So I'll take it..*

First, there is the question of which is the antecedent of the lexical item *she*. Going back in the text to the first Nominal Group to which *she* could be related through agreement and anaphoric reference, we have to go back 8 clauses until we eventually find *she*, and then *Heinz's wife*. This, however, is accidental, and a corresponding rule would lead us to unacceptable results in many cases, as anaphoric reference may extend back beyond the first possible candidate. To determine the most plausible antecedent, it seems unavoidable to have a level of either *story structure*, or ACTION structure for the ACTIONS reflected in the text. Only then does it become evident that our agent Heinz is still operating (ACTION 4) in an ACTION which has been entered, ultimately, from ACTION 1 which has *wife* as an entry under MATERIALS, in view of which fact it is plausible (not, however, necessary) that *she* refers to *wife*. It is extremely counterintuitive to assume that

Table 26. Operation 3, clause 2

Functional component	Selection expression
ideational: transitivity	[relational, locational, 3rd party agent, covert location...]
ideational: time	[SITUATION [fut]] (cf.3.8)
interpersonal: mood	[declarative, indicative...]
textual: theme	[subject theme on first inherent role, marked theme on logical relationship...]
logical	[paratactic link, consecutive...]

Feature	Realization
relational, locational	locational verb
3rd party agent	go to sub-network of locational
covert location	0 at C,n in clause structure
SIT[fut]	*will* at O*
indicative	S precedes Operator in clause structure
Subject theme on 1st inherent role	3rd party agent at S
marked theme on logical relationship	linker at place Y in starting structure of the clause
paratactic link, consecutive	*so* or *therefore*

**will* can also be generated through the modality-network.
The realized clause is: *So I'll take it*

the listener/reader of such a story stores the wording of the text in memory for a span long enough to cover such cases of reference across a long textual distance. The level of ACTION structure thus could provide an explanation for preferences in certain strategies for resolving anaphoric reference (cf. Grosz & Sidner 1985, 1986; Pause 1988).

The same principle would seem to apply to the tracing of the antecedent of the pronoun *it*: The uttering of the clause *So I'll take it* is separated in time and space from a textual mention of the antecedent *medicine*, and in interpreting this clause, we do need an account of the structure of Heinz's ACTIONS if we want to find out about the antecedent.

Next, let us consider the case of the lexical item *will*: The item *will* can be a realization of features from the time-network within transitivity and/or of features from the modality-network within the interpersonal component. In the first case, it will realize the meaning of *later than the time of speaking on an assumed time line*: SIT[fut], in the second case it is an expression of intention within modality. Frequently, both meanings are jointly realized, at least in English. In interpeting the clause, however, we need a context of situation to determine whether there is one dominant meaning in any given instance, and which it is. This context is provided here by our analysis of ACTION.

Let us move on to the necessary disambiguation of the lexical item *take*: Part of the disambiguation takes place through an analysis of the syntactic and semantic context of the verb in terms of valency-bound clause elements and participant roles. Yet, what syntactic or clause-semantic evidence do we have to determine that Heinz is not talking about swallowing the medicine himself, rather than taking it away from the chemist? Again, unless we incorporate into our analysis some representation such as the one derived from our ACTION analysis, there can be no successful disambiguation.

A parallel case can be seen in the item *got to*, which is ambiguous between the readings of *obligation, high probability*, and *necessary for the speaker*, all of which are classical sub-types of modality. Again, there is not sufficient information in the purely linguistic context to make the disambiguation possible.

The decisive question concerning these examples is not so much whether or not one needs some representation of the kind we are advocating here in our analysis of ACTION- that much seems to be widely acknowledged nowadays, even if there are competing frameworks. From the point of view of linguistic methodology, the question rather is what the additional insights are for the analyst. There is, obviously, a world of a difference between speculating about some mental representation which humans might or might not generate in the process of understanding, and between the operationalization of some framework for analysis to a degree sufficient for the purpose of linguistic analysis. Our discussions here can be seen as an attempt to move towards that latter goal.

2.4.3 The analysis of children's activity in a play session

In Appendix 1, we have reproduced the transcript of a recording of ten minutes of a play session of three children playing with *Lego* (cf. Fawcett & Perkins 1980. Vol.4: 12 A Boys). The present section will give an analysis of the activity of the children in this situation. We shall thereby try to illustrate the framework in its application to an example of human interactive ACTIVITY, rather than focussing on individual ACTIONS (2.4.2.) or on an ACTION - counterACTION pattern (2.4.1.). In doing so, we shall, just as in the preceding examples of analyses, always pursue the secondary goal of bringing up questions of methodology where this seems appropriate, thus preparing the ground for some theoretical issues in the section to follow (cf. for an earlier version of this analysis Steiner 1988 c).

In the analysis of our children's play session, we shall concentrate on the following aspects:

- the structure of the ongoing ACTIONS in general

- the relatively detailed analysis of MOTIVATION and PLANNING phases of the superordinate ACTION.

A detailed analysis on the rank of ACTIVITY will not be attempted here. The general ACTIVITY in which the children are engaged could be classified as *playing*.

Table 27 contains an analysis of SITUATION 1.

Table 27. Situation 1

Agent	Process	Materials	Instrument	Product
children A.W. P.G. S.M.	building	*Lego* pieces	not in text	not finished during time of recording

No further comments need to be made at this point, except that the classification of the *Lego* pieces under the situational category of MATERIAL is not entirely without reservation: Using the tests we have given in section 2.3.6., we can see that the *Lego* pieces satisfy the test for MATERIALS, but possibly also the test for INSTRUMENTS. Observe that testing with prepositions does not help in this matter, cf.:

(13) *They are building a house with/from Lego pieces.*

In the first place, both prepositions are possible, possibly depending somewhat on the presence of the item *pieces* in the case of *from*. In the second place, *with* is notoriously ambiguous when it comes to finding out semantic roles on the basis of prepositions. More basically still, these tests seem to apply only to the classification of semantic roles, which we assume not to be isomorphic to the cognitive and perceptive categories in which we process and perceive information about the world. Accordingly, and as stated in our outline of the analysis of the category of SITUATION (2.3.6.), the analysis here is based on world knowledge.
The ACTION being carried out in SITUATION 1 is the one shown in Table 28.

The further analysis on the rank of ACTION consists of

a. specifying embedded ACTIONS of ACTION 1; this we shall do immediately;
b. specifying the elements of the ACTIONS; this we shall do after a., but only for the elements Mo and Pl of ACTION 1, because these are sufficient for illustrating the points we want to make in this section.

Table 28. Action 1

ACTION 1:		GOAL 1: A house	
Mo	Pl	Ex	Ev
1. Orientation in SITUATION 1 2. Orientation with respect to needs/ wishes of ACTIVITY	1. Project image of result 2. Project step 1: *making outside* 3. Specify product in more detail 4. Specify step 1 further; go to ACTION 1.1	1. ACTION 1.1 2. ACTION 1.2 3. ACTION 1.3 4. ACTION 1.4 interrupt	not carried out during time of recording

The embedded ACTIONS within ACTION 1 are those shown in Tables 29-32.

Table 29. Action 1.1

ACTION 1.1	GOAL 1.1
Agent build and insert door	Door be in house

The PLANNING phase of ACTION 1.1 is to be located in line 25 of p.1, its EVALUATION phase in lines 20ff of p.4 of the transcript (cf. Appendix 1).

Table 30. Action 1.2

ACTION 1.2	GOAL 1.2
Children build the walls	Walls be in house

The PLANNING phase of ACTION 1.2 is realized in line 23 of p.4 of the transcript, the EVALUATION on p.6, line 8.

Table 31. Action 1.3

ACTION 1.3	GOAL 1.3
Children build interiors	Interiors be in house

The PLANNING of ACTION 1.3 is to be found in lines 17ff. on p.6, and certain sub-phases of PLANNING even later on p.7. The children are then side-tracked into

ACTION 1.4 (p.8, lines 5ff.), in the sense that ACTION 1.3. is never completely executed and evaluated.

Table 32. Action 1.4

ACTION 1.4 Children build windows and shutters	GOAL 1.4 Windows and shutters be in house

We can see the realization of the PLANNING phase of ACTION 1.4 on p.8, lines 5ff, the realization of the EVALUATION at the bottom of page 8.

In the minutes which follow, the children are engaged in PLANNING and partly executing other ACTIONS relating to building a house, which they perceive as still related to ACTION 1 (cf.p.8, line 26,27), yet which are not completed within the time of recording. There is a certain time, from which onwards the children seem to be leaving ACTION 1, but only superficially so: At a certain stage, they engage in a discourse about people whom they know but who are not related to their ongoing ACTION 1 (p.10, lines 7ff). At the same time, however, they are continuing their house building, so that what we have at this place is not an entirely unrelated ACTION, but rather an instance of purely communicative ACTIVITY interspersed with ongoing ACTIONS. Whether or not this communicative ACTIVITY (*Verkehrstätigkeit*) is subordinated to goals of some ACTION unrelated to the ongoing ACTION cannot be ascertained on the basis of our transcript alone. As it is, we may interpret this communicative ACTIVITY as having a function within the ongoing ACTION, which is that of maintaining a friendly and cooperative atmosphere within the working group. The only alternative within the present framework would be that of finding another ACTION (future, present, or past), within which the conversation could be interpreted as filling a structural place (element).

Next, the children begin with what we shall analyze here as ACTION 2, which is closely related to ACTION 1 and its sub-ACTIONS (cf. Table 33).

Table 33. Action 2

ACTION 2 Children build people	GOAL 2 There be people

PLANNING and EVALUATION phases of ACTION 2 are to be found on p.11 of our transcript, which then breaks off shortly after the beginning of another bit of communicative ACTIVITY (bottom p.11).

As in the other analyses which we have carried out there are several points which would seem to require closer attention. Of these, we shall only mention one at this point:

The PLANNING of ACTION 1 and the EXECUTION of ACTION 1.1, and even some preliminary OPERATIONS of ACTION 1.2 seem to run parallel at certain moments.

A.W. of our group is obviously working on his suggested step 1 (cf. PLANNING of ACTION 1) while the rest of the group is still mainly engaged in PLANNING ACTION 1. Also, ACTION 1.1 and ACTION 1.2 obviously overlap to some extent, partly for the very simple reason that you cannot have a door in a house with nothing around it. This feature of the ACTIONS analyzed here points to the question of temporal and logical sequence of ACTIONS and elements of ACTIONS. For example, if an ACTIONn is logically presupposed by an ACTIONn+1, this does not imply that all the elements of ACTIONn have to be executed prior to all the elements of ACTIONn+1. Another typical source of overlap is to be found in errors of performance: An agent may, for example, start with an ACTIONn+1 and realize only later that ACTIONn should have been executed earlier.

Let us concentrate now on the closer examination of the MOTIVATION and PLANNING phases of ACTION 1. Two reservations have to be made at the outset:

- We shall continue to treat *the children* as the collective agent of the ACTIONS under description. The alternative, on a general level, would be that of analyzing the ACTIONS of each agent separately with an extra component for co-ordinating these individual ACTIONS. In the final analysis, and for some purposes, this may, indeed, be necessary. As, however, it would involve the application of some additional analytical apparatus, and because it does not seem to be necessary to illustrate the points we wish to make here, we shall choose the option of working with a collective agent in our analysis.
- At the points in our analysis where language comes in, it will be necessary in the end to have a discourse grammar in addition to a clause grammar (cf. Wells, Montgomery & McLure 1979 for a directly compatible Systemic approach). For our present purposes, we shall not apply such a grammar. Note, again, that it is not necessary to have an extra component for speech acts within his approach, because the corresponding linguistic phenomena are included in Systemic semantics as *Illocutionary Force Networks* (Fawcett 1980: 103).

We shall now focus on major aspects of the MOTIVATION and PLANNING phases of ACTION 1 (cf. Table 34).

With respect to this analysis, we should make it clear that our steps under MOTIVATION and PLANNING here are, from the point of view of the theory, secondary elements of ACTION structure. They are not OPERATIONS, that is to say, there is no change in rank, but only one in delicacy.

Table 35 shows the projection of step 1 *making outside*, which is done by entering the linguistic code. Networks and features, as in the other examples, are those in Fawcett (1980).

Two questions concerning methodology we shall briefly discuss here, because they will not be dealt with in the following section:

- Completeness and comprehensiveness of analysis: ACTION 1, as we have analyzed it here, is that of building a house. This ACTION is given to us only

Table 34. Motivation and planning of action 1

MOTIVATION (lines 1-6)	PLANNING (lines 7-25)
1. Orientation in SITUATION 1; go to OPERATIONS: linguistic: lines 5,6 non-linguistic: to be inferred 2. Orientation with respect to needs and wishes; go to OPERATIONS: linguistic: lines 2-4 non-linguistic: to be inferred	1. Project image of result; go to OPERATION (line 4) 2. Project step 1 *making outside* (line 7) 3. Specify product in more detail (line 14-17) 4. Specify step 1 further (line 25) go to ACTION 1.1.

in the recordings on tape and in the transcripts. Obviously, we do not have any immediate access to the internal ACTIONS and OPERATIONS on the one hand, and to the non-linguistic external ACTIONS on the other. In the case of internal ACTIONS and OPERATIONS, though, we have more data than is obvious at first sight: Relying on evidence from psycholinguistics, we can infer the propositional and possibly even the overall semantic planning of utterances as internal activities, either on the rank of ACTION or of OPERATION. In our analysis, we have assumed that they take the form of OPERATIONS. What else there may have been of internal activities is, of course, not accessible to us.

More superficially, quite a number of utterances remain unanalyzed in this section. However, this is only due to our particular focus of interest here. In general, of course, the whole material has to be accounted for at each level and each rank of analysis, just as in linguistic analysis.

- ACTION and OPERATION: The relationship between ACTIONS and OPERATIONS must be made clearer, or, more specifically, the criteria for assigning a given sequence of behaviour to one or the other. In our analyses, we have been relying on our assumptions about whether or not a given sequence, the PLANNING phases in particular, are conscious, like the planning of a sentence or some piece of text. One criterion for this is whether or not the agent can report on it. This can be tested, and has been tested in several cases, and yet there are methodological problems involved, like the problem of memory: When, for example, we are looking at how the children report on what they did in the course of their play session (cf. the published transcripts of these interviews after each play session), we find our analyses only partly corroborated. Yet, it is in no way obvious to what extent a lack of memory is the reason for this, because a PLANNING phase which was conscious at the time it was carried out, may still be forgotten afterwards. It is partly

Table 35. Projection of step 1.

Functional component	Selection expression
experiential transitivity	[action, agent-centred, plus other inherent roles, +effected]
circumstance	[time,when]
negativity Polarity	[affirmative]
logical relationships internal complexity	[enough]
interactional illocutionary force	[directive, simple, mild]
modality modal	[not modalized]
thematic subject theme	[first inherent role]
informational information focus	[new information point, re-enter, marked focus, on 2nd role, unmarked focus]
Feature	**Realization**
[action, agent-centred]	lexical items: (make, build, produce, construct...)
[effected]	Agent precedes Effected in case of unmarked subject theme
[time, when]	Time Adverbial (*first*)
[affirmative]	0 at O^n
[directive,simple]	0 at S
[mild]	tone 3
[new information point, re-enter]	create two information units
[marked focus on 2nd role]	primary stress on Effected
[unmarked focus]	primary stress on Time

Realization: *Well//just make the outside/first* (Appendix 1, p.1). The system networks producing only unmarked options are left out here, and so are conditional features. O and S under *Realization* stand for the positions of *Operator* and *Subject* in clause structure. Selection expressions appear in square brackets. Clause functions are distinguished by capital spelling of their first letter.

methodological problems like these which motivate a testing of hypotheses such as we shall undertake it in section 3. If our framework generates hypotheses for the structure of language which can be tested independently, i.e. in the linguistic material, and if these hypotheses are confirmed, then we have some motivation for the entire theory of activity from linguistics.
For the time being, we assume that PLANNING on the level of the system networks for the clause will usually be operational, which is to say that, in terms of our theory, it is programming rather than planning. Non-linguistic OPERATIONS are of the type we have illustrated from the work of Cranach and Kalbermatten in section 2.2.2.

The representation in Figure 8 is the product of our analysis of ACTION 1 as we have undertaken it in this section.

Some characterstics of the representation in Figure 8 should be mentioned, all of which derive from the model of ACTIVITY which we have been discussing:

In the case of elements of ACTION, we are using secondary, i.e. more delicate elements for MOTIVATION and PLANNING. This is not the same as using an additional level in our tree, which would correspond to a change in rank.

ACTIONS 1.1.-1.4. in Figure 8 *fill* the EXECUTION 1 in conjunction. The vertical line in this part of the representation does not really form part of the representation; it is for graphical reasons only that we had to "lower" this conjunction. Observe that, in planning ACTIONS at least, there can be any of the logical connectors between such embedded ACTIONS, as well as any depth of internal embedding, i.e. recursion of the category ACTION in the application of the grammar.

Project2 and *specify2* serve as pointers to certain elements of embedded ACTIONS, as shown in the representation. Yet, they are not merely pointers, but in having that function, they are already part of the PLANNING phases which they point to, and their OPERATIONS already fill part of those PLANNING phases. Our tree diagramm basically expresses temporal sequence of the starting points of the elements in its left-to-right ordering, whereas it expresses logical sequence in its labels for primary elements of structure. It does not express the temporal sequence, i.e. linear precedence, beyond the starting points. The full amount of scrambling and interleaving between functions is hidden. There are obvious parallels in linguistic grammars, and certain lines of theoretical elaboration suggest themselves: deep structure vs. surface structure, constituent structure vs. functional structure, constituent structure vs. dependency structure, or syntactic vs. semantic structure. Obviously, within a Systemic approach, it is the last line of development which one will try to follow. At this particular stage, though, it would seem premature to formalize a relationship which is not entirely within our grasp theoretically. The starting point for a formalization here is Patten & Ritchie (1987). Relevant thoughts on the question of linear precedence phenomena in languages can be found in Pollard & Sag (1987: chapter 7).

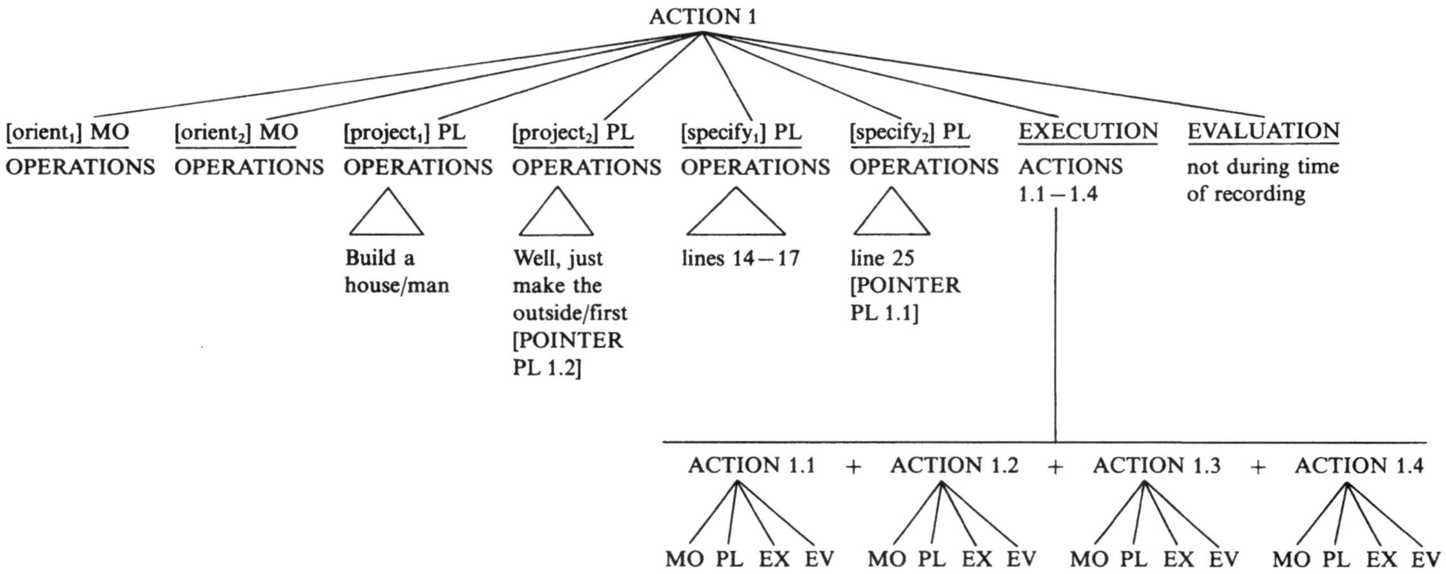

Figure 8. Action 1 of a play session

This brings to an end our illustrative analyses of some samples of interaction of children in a play session. Just as in the analyses in sections 2.4.1. and 2.4.2., our purpose has been to illustrate the analysis of human activities in some representative forms within the framework that we have suggested. In section 2.4.1., we also indicated the type of hypotheses which the theory generates for ACTION structures of a certain genre. These hypotheses will not be pursued any further in the present context, but they might serve as an interesting motivation for independent work at some later stage. In section 3 we shall be investigating certain predictions which the theory makes with respect to the linguistic structure of texts in terms of Systemic Linguistics, and it is this investigation which provides one motivation for setting up the whole framework as we have been doing so far. All the methodological discussions, especially their range and depth, should be seen against the background of this motivation. The following section will deal with a theoretical notion which has become more and more important in the course of our analyses, which is the notion of *part of*. We shall also use this discussion to apply some ideas from one version of *Situation Semantics* to our framework.

2.4.4 Elaborating the framework: An investigation of the notion "part of" in the theory of activity

In this section, we shall be looking briefly at the theoretical notion *part of*. The relationship *part of* can be said to obtain, in different ways, between certain sub-ACTIONS and their superordinate ACTION(S), as for example between ACTIONS 1.1.-1.4. and ACTION 1 in section 2.4.3., as well as between ACTIONS and their elements, and, in a different way again, between elements of ACTIONS and OPERATIONS filling them. Our aim in this exploration is twofold:

- By a clarification of the notion of *part of* within our framework, we want to contribute towards the clarification of the relationship between ACTIONS and sub-ACTIONS on the one hand, and between ACTIONS, their elements, and OPERATIONS on the other.
- By using a specific approach, that of the standard version of *Situation Semantics* (cf. Barwise & Perry 1983), we want to relate our own notions to a framework in which particular attention has been paid to the notion of *Situation*.

Following the thoughts of Barwise and Perry (1983: 53ff.), we can characterize our superordinate ACTION as a *situation type*:

in s: build, children, house; yes.
This is a weaker formulation than
S: build, children, house; yes,
which would seem to require an exhaustive description.

Situation types of superordinate ACTIONS and of their sub- ACTIONS would seem to meet the criteria for coherence and compatibility (Barwise & Perry 1983: 53ff.):

> A situation-type s is *coherent* if the following three conditions are met:
> (i) s does not assign two values to any constituent sequence, that is, not both,
> in s: $r,x_1,...,x_n$;yes
> in s: $r,x_1,...,x_n$;no.
> (ii) s does not represent two different objects as being the same, that is, in s: same, a,b;yes implies a=b.
> (iii) s does not represent anything as being different from itself, that is, not
> in s: same, a,a;no.
> If (i), (ii), or (iii) fail, s is incoherent. Situation- types s and s' are *compatible* if their union is coherent. The Law of Noncontradiction, a basic "structural constraint", states that actual situations are coherent. (emphasis B&P).

If we add the spatio-temporal dimension to our description of the play session, we get what is called a *state of affairs* (Barwise & Perry 1983: 55): A pair S=(l,s) of a spatio-temporal location and a situation type. The relationship of *part of* is defined, by Barwise and Perry, on states of affairs.

Let us mention at this point that what we are describing here would seem to be a factual, but not necessarily an actual state of affairs.

Now, Barwise and Perry define the relationship of *part of* in the following way (1983: 55):

> "A state of affairs s is part of a state of affairs s' if s and s' have the same location and the type of s is contained in the type of s'."

The expression *is contained* here just means set theoretical inclusion.
A course of events, then, is essentially defined as a set of states of affairs (Barwise & Perry 1983: 56), and some course of events x is defined to be a subset of a course of events y if and only if any state of affairs in e_x is part of some state of affairs in e_y.
We want to investigate, at this point, whether we can use this relationship of *part of* to operationalize our notions of *embedded* ACTION and *element of* ACTION.
Our ACTION *build, children, house* can be represented either as some sort of tree diagram (cf.2.4.3.), or simply in a functional notation. Taking as variables the following, we obtain the functional description in Figure 9.

A	=	ACTION	MO	=	MOTIVATION
OR	=	orient	PL	=	PLANNING
PRO	=	project	EX	=	EXECUTION
SPEC	=	specify	EV	=	EVALUATION
O	=	OPERATION			

and as constants:

u	=	utterance
m	=	movement;

$$\mathrm{A\,1} = \begin{bmatrix} \mathrm{Mo} = \begin{bmatrix} \mathrm{OR\,1} = \mathrm{u} \\ \mathrm{OR\,2} = \mathrm{u} \end{bmatrix} \\ \mathrm{Pl} = \begin{bmatrix} \mathrm{PROJ\,1} = \mathrm{u} \\ \mathrm{PROJ\,2} = \mathrm{u} \\ \mathrm{SPEC\,1} = \mathrm{u} \\ \mathrm{SPEC\,2} = \mathrm{u} \end{bmatrix} \\ \mathrm{EX} = \begin{bmatrix} \mathrm{A\,1.1} = \begin{bmatrix} \mathrm{MO} = \mathrm{O} \\ \mathrm{PL} = \mathrm{O} \\ \mathrm{EX} = \mathrm{O} \\ \mathrm{EV} = \mathrm{O} \end{bmatrix} \\ \mathrm{A\,1.2} = \begin{bmatrix} \mathrm{MO} = \mathrm{O} \\ \mathrm{PL} = \mathrm{O} \\ \mathrm{EX} = \mathrm{O} \\ \mathrm{EV} = \mathrm{O} \end{bmatrix} \\ \mathrm{A\,1.3} = \begin{bmatrix} \mathrm{MO} = \mathrm{O} \\ \mathrm{PL} = \mathrm{O} \\ \mathrm{EX} = \mathrm{O} \\ \mathrm{EV} = \mathrm{O} \end{bmatrix} \\ \mathrm{A\,1.4} = \begin{bmatrix} \mathrm{MO} = \mathrm{O} \\ \mathrm{PL} = \mathrm{O} \\ \mathrm{EX} = \mathrm{O} \\ \mathrm{EV} = \mathrm{O} \end{bmatrix} \end{bmatrix} \\ \mathrm{EV} = \mathrm{u} \end{bmatrix}$$

Figure 9. An analysis of activity in a functional notation (2)

Basically, instead of having the constant u, we could enter the linguistic system at this point re-writing our *Functional Component - Selection Expression - Realization* tables (cf. 2.4.1.-2.4.3.) as attribute-value pairs. Yet, this approach would clearly seem to be premature, because the functional notation, just like an ordinary tree diagram, represents less information than our functional trees which do make a distinction between the relationships of componence, filling, and exponence.

Assuming now that A1 and A1.1.-A1.4 have the status of courses of events, our description of A1 would be as follows:

Course of events A1:

At l : build, children, doors;yes
At l' : build, children, walls;yes
At l'' : build, children, interiors;yes
At l''' : build, children, windows & shutters;yes
AND
A1: At l'''': build, children, house;yes,
where A1 is the superordinate ACTION.
Also: (l o l' o l'' o l''') <t l''''
(l @ l' @ l'' @ l''') <s l''''

where o and @ mean "overlap" and < means "inclusion" (B&P. 1983 : 51). "l", "s", and "t" stand for "location", "spatial", and "temporal" respectively.

Now, we can see that the embedded ACTIONS, or rather, the situationtypes are contained in the superordinate ACTION in the sense defined by Barwise and Perry. The spatiotemporal locations of the embedded ACTIONS are not identical, but only included in the spatiotemporal location of the superordinate ACTION. As identity of l is only required for the *part of* relationship between states of affairs, not for courses of events as a whole, we might recognize a *part of* relationship here. However, there is a remaining difficulty:
It is not immediately obvious where the borderline is between a state of affairs and a course of events, except that the latter is defined as sets of the former (Barwise & Perry 1983: 56). In other words, a course of events with just the elements (l,y,i) with

l=spatio-temporal location,
y=constituent sequence $(r,x_1...x_n)$,
i=0 or 1,

would seem to consist only of a state of affairs. Intuitively, it would seem as if the *r* in the description of a state of affairs could only be instantiated linguistically by stative verbs, and the *r* in the description of some course of events would be instantiated by non-stative verbs. In talking about the relationship of *part of*, it is essential that we know whether we are talking about states of affairs or about courses of events, because the definition of that relationship is not the same in both cases.

What we can see from this section, then, is this: an attempt at formalization can only help us in areas where our theoretical concepts are sufficiently clear. Beyond this point, formalization just helps to bring out the sources of ambiguity, yet if these are overlooked, a deceptive sense of precision is the result. It is, however, certainly worthwhile exploring aspects of situation semantics further as far as they have a bearing on the framework which we have begun to investigate.

2.4.5 The interface between general actions and linguistic actions: a Systemic Linguistics based model of text production

So far, in our modelling of linguistic utterances as goal-directed ACTIONS, we have assumed the clause as the highest rank. In other words, in the case of linguistic ACTIONS the terminal elements for the grammar of goal-directed action were something like *speech acts*, serving as a point of entry for the linguistic grammar. As a generalization about all cases of linguistic actions, this is not the only possible case. Just as actions can be described on levels and ranks, so can linguistic actions. Thus, we are using *levels* and *ranks* here in the same sense as the concept of *granularity of knowledge representation* is used in the area of problem solving in artificial intelligence (Patten 1988: 14ff.).

In this section, then, we shall posit a hierarchy of linguistic units on ranks beyond the clause, their elements, and the relations between them, thus introducing more large scale packaging of linguistic information. We shall then attempt to link these higher rank units with our theory of goal-directd action in a systematic way. In doing so, we intend to develop our ideas up to the point where a formalization like the one in Patten (1988: 77ff.) becomes possible. We shall not attempt such a formalization here, but we shall link the concepts developed here to Patten's formalization of Systemic Grammar at several points (cf. also Patten & Ritchie 1987).

The section will be structured as follows:

First we shall outline the particular aims we have set ourselves for this section. Then, we shall give an advance organizer for the model of production, i.e. we shall relate the individual steps to be followed in the analysis itself to the structure of representations generated by our model. We shall then carry out the analysis itself using a text taken from Hovy (1988). Finally, we shall discuss research goals deriving from the approach advocated in this section and the relationship of this approach to other models. This section can be seen as making contact with related work in Hovy (1988), Patten (1988) and Bateman and Paris (1989). It also forms part of the basis for work in text generation in the project KOMET under development at the *Institut für Integrierte Publikations- und Informationssysteme of the Gesellschaft für Mathematik und Datenverarbeitung* in Darmstadt (cf. Steiner et al. 1990).

Let us now give a preliminary list of factors which a model of text production has to take into account, placing our own suggestions into their place with respect to a computational model of text production. Such a model must incorporate:

(1) A grammar of linguistic form up to the clause/sentence level. There are different variants of SFG available for such a grammar: Either, basically, a semantic grammar only with the realization component handling constituent structure and syntactic function realization, lexical realization, and intonational realization. Ideally, the lexicon in that approach becomes simply most delicate grammar. Still, even in that approach, a separate lexicon is quite feasible with the feature descriptions associated with lexical items unifying with feature descriptions of grammatical constituents under the usual completeness and coherence constraints, as in the work of Fawcett (1987) or Steiner et al. (1988). Alternatively, within SFG, one may choose to work with separate grammars for semantics and syntax of the clause, where then both levels have to be linked by *pre-selection*, as in the generation projects NIGEL, or SLANG, or as in Halliday's own writings. Such a grammar should specify the language to be generated syntactically and semantically, independently of other components of the overall model.

(2) A component for driving the choices in the grammar(s) at all the points where there are choices between two or more correct formal structures. A conceptual and computational tool developed for that purpose is the NIGEL concept of a *chooser* (Matthiessen 1987), which addresses representations of states of affairs and courses of events in a sentence planning language (SPL, cf. Kasper & Whitney 1989) in the process of generating a natural language sentence out of a non-linguistic representation of that same knowledge. Concepts used in SPL are partly concepts from a level of representation called "Upper Model", which represents a level of representation abstracted from linguistic knowledge (cf. Bateman, Kasper, Moore & Whitney 1989).

(3) A component generating the number of sentences and their linear arrangements.

(4) A component for the control of paragraphing, i.e. chunking of coherent clusters of clause-complexes/sentences

(5) A component guiding factors to do with *register*, i.e. formality, simplicity, detail, choice of words (cf. Bateman & Paris 1989)

(6) A component generating a model, a SITUATION, with respect to which referring expressions can be interpreted. In a system of the architecture indicated in (2) above, the SITUATION would be part of the upper model.

(7) In the case of interactive, dialogical texts, we also need a component handling discourse structure.

Like many other theories, Systemic Linguistics has a lot to say about (1), and also partly about (2), especially if we think of something like Systemic accounts of cohesion on the one hand, and of the NIGEL chooser & inquiry framework, which we shall discuss in some more detail in section 2.6.. A fully developed *rhetorical structure theory* (Mann & Thompson 1987 a,b), if it were linked to a component for goal-driven text generation would also go some way towards satisfying (3) (cf. Moore & Paris 1989). The decisive component lacking so far is something like (6). Work such as in the present study can be seen as one attempt at beginning to close this gap. On this general level, earlier work as in Sacerdoti (1975), Appelt (1985) and in Patten (1988) would seem to fall into the same category.

In the following, we shall look at a sample text reproduced below, trying to illustrate in some more detail the interplay of the factors just mentioned. Our goal in this context is to generate the particular structure of the text as fully as possible, trying to indicate where we think there are gaps in our model so far.

> On April 4, concerned Yale students constructed a shantytown on Boesak Plaza as a reminder to those in Woodbridge Hall (and all over campus and the community) that Yale is complicit [sic] with the system of apartheid that creates shantytowns where thousands of blacks are forced to live in squalor and fear. The shantytown, Winnie Mandela City, served as a focal point of education concerning South Africa and Yale's investment there. At 5:30 am on April 14 the Yale Administration had the shantytown torn down and had 76 students and community members who were defending the shanties arrested. After a huge outcry, the Administration allowed the shanties to be rebuilt. We will not be silenced; we will continue to challenge the University on their moral failure. (From: protester literature; the protesters renamed the plaza after the South African churchman Allan Boesak).

Text taken from Hovy 1988.

In order to generate such a text, we first need a component containing relevant *domain-knowledge*, because without this domain knowledge, there is nothing to encode, i.e. there would be no states of affairs and courses of events to encode. Such a component includes knowledge of the type illustrated in Table 36.

Table 36. Domain knowledge

build (x,y)	x=Yale students y=shanty town etc.
temporal location (a,b)	a=build (x,y) b=4.4.86 etc.

In addition to domain-knowledge, we need a component containing conceptual, i.e. general knowledge in the sense of a NIGEL-type upper model. A possible fragment of such a model might look as shown in Table 37.

Table 37. A fragment of an upper model

specialize (house, building) process(build)...

Next, we need a component creating ACTIONS and SITUATIONS out of our domain knowledge, i.e. goals, means, strategies etc. This component, i.e. our point (6) mentioned above, will be our focus here.

We thus have arrived at a formulation of our main goal for the present explorations: We shall explore a model of human goal-directed action containing as an essential part a model for *situations*. This model generates linguistic texts as a special case of products of human goal-directed actions. Viewed in the direction of analysis rather than generation, the model generates representations for texts - representations which have as categories functional categories of the theory of goal-directed action (phases of action) and linguistic functions and structures as special cases of these. Whereas we have explored such a model before in 2.3, we have not investigated text forming structures as special cases of elements of goal-directed actions to any great extent up to now.

Let us investigate some aspects of a model of text production along the lines indicated above. The investigation will take the form of an analysis of a text, which is quite usual for production models in linguistics. Our claim that this analysis is a reconstruction of the production of the text is, of course, a very strong one, but we shall maintain it here for methodological reasons.

Before we start our sample analysis, we shall summarize its structure. This summary should serve as an advance organizer through the analysis. At the end of this advance organizer, we shall give a partial representation of the ACTION to be analysed in the form of a tree diagramm.

(1) Our analysis will deal with the generation of linguistic units on the following ranks: text, paragraph, clause complex, clause. In terms of the theory of ACTION, these linguistic ranks are all generated as ACTIONS, i.e. through recursion of the category/unit of ACTION as a filler of elements of an ACTION.
(2) For each linguistic rank$_n$ in the analysis, we shall set up a SITUATION frame, containing the expounded unit (a constituent on rank$_n$) as a filler in its INSTRUMENT slot, and containing the function of that unit as a whole (the function on rank$_n$ into which the unit on rank$_n$ is mapped) as a filler in its GOAL slot. The unit is a thus a constituent analysed with respect to some set v, where v contains as elements a list of (sets of) possible functions for units on that rank (cf. Patten. 1988: 80. Def.1.2). We have to include the possibility of multiple functions for our units here because we want to follow a multi-functional approach in the sense of Systemic Linguistics.
(3) For each linguistic rank$_n$ in the analysis, we shall give an ACTION analysis, containing the elements (functions of its constituents) of the generated unit in

its PLANNING phase. The functional elements of the generated unit rank are on rank_{n+1} (where increasing *n* stands for downward moves on the rankscale). In cases of rankshift, a function on rank_{n+1} is filled by a unit on some rank with a smaller index.

(4) According to (1)-(3) above, for each unit on a given rank_n, the function of that unit as a whole is derived from the GOAL of the SITUATION in which it is an INSTRUMENT. Its elements, i.e. the functional slots of that unit on rank_{n+1}, are created in the PLANNING of that unit itself. The units filling these slots are created through recursion/indirect self-embedding of the ACTION category. Earlier on, we have stated explicitly

- that elements of ACTIONS are finally filled by OPERATIONS;
- that a linguistic unit on whatever rank may be generated as ACTION or OPERATION, even if OPERATION is much more likely the further down we move on the rank scale;
- that rankshift is possible both in the theory of ACTION and in grammar.

The notions of *rank, unit, function* are used here as in Patten (1988: 79ff. Definitions 1.1.-1.6). We use the term *unit* in the sense in which Patten uses *constituent*, for reasons of compatibility with the remainder of our study here.

Let us now give a brief and simple example of the type of analysis advocated here , using the familiar linguistic structure of a nominal group (NG). Thereby, we are claiming that this NG was generated as an ACTION, which is a somewhat untypical case, but may serve as an illustration (cf. Figure 10).

$$\text{SITUATION}_n = \begin{bmatrix} \text{INSTRUMENT} = \text{NG [rank = group]} \\ \\ \text{GOAL} = \text{Subject/Agent/Theme/Given} \end{bmatrix}$$

$$\text{ACTION}_n = \begin{bmatrix} \text{MOTIVATION} \\ \text{PLANNING} = \text{some subset of NG Functions } \{d, m, e, n, h, q\} \\ \text{EXECUTION} \\ \text{EVALUATION} \end{bmatrix}$$

Figure 10. An action analysis of a nominal group

With respect to the example in Figure 10, though, we have to be careful to make the following distinction: A grammatical function, such as *Subject, Theme, Agent* etc. is the grammaticalized relationship between some unit (constituent) and its elements. It is within the boundaries of that unit alone that constraints hold as far as precedence, absence, filling, conflation etc. of functions is concerned. In grammar beyond the clause, on the other hand, the notion of *function* appears to be relatively weak, essentially restricted to the head-modifier relationship, as in the analysis of hypotaxis and parataxis, with an accompanying rich set of weakly grammaticalized rhetorical relations of some sort. In Halliday's analysis of clause combining (1985a), for example, we find both an account of taxis and an account of the rhetorical/functional elements (clause combining relations) in the clause complex. For the time being in our analysis, we shall use elements of the set of relations on rank_n as predicates which take as their arguments functions on rank_n.

An alternative possibility would be to take *head* and *dependent* as the only functions of constituents, where *h,d* each is an attribute taking as values the set of relations of their rank. Given a straightforward dependency analysis of that kind, the relations would be for:

- NG {d,m,e,n,h,q}, i.e. the set of NG elements;
- Clause {{Subj,Pred,Obj,...}, {Agent,Affected,...}, {Theme,Rheme,...}, {Given,New,...}}, i.e. the sets of clause elements
- Clause complex {set of clause combining-relations, such as elaboration, projection, etc}
- Paragraph {set of paragraph relations}.

In fact, the stipulation of rhetorical relations as ranging over *nucleus-satelite* configurations in rhetorical structure theory (Mann & Thompson 1987 a,b) seems to envisage that type of approach for larger constituents of texts.

The overview in Table 38 outlines the structure of our analysis. As for this outline, it should be observed that SITUATIONS and ACTIONS have a greater number of slots than illustrated in this outline. The full number of slots will be used in the analyses afterwards. It is important to realize that in our outline, we shall not follow the structure of our sample text in every respect (cf. ACTION 1.1 and ACTION 1.1.1.), because we want to bring out the general structure of the approach, rather than only the structure of one specific text.

It is in SITUATION 1.1.1.1. and ACTION 1.1.1.1. in Table 38 that the clause grammar takes over in the usual and by now standard Systemic sense.

Figure 11 again summarizes the approach, with functions of constituents on the rank concerned appearing in curly brackets, the daughters of a given constituent/unit appearing in square brackets, and functional elements making up a relation occuring in round brackets after the relation name.

The tree diagramm in Figure 12 is the representation of the sample text assigned by our analysis of goal-directed action.

Interpreting the diagramm in Figure 12 top down, levels 2–5 in the tree have as exponents texts, paragraphs, clause-complexes, and clauses respectively. The tree is restricted to the rank of ACTION. The interpretation of the dominance relation in this tree is *consists of*. The interpretation of linear precedence of categories on one level in the tree is, tentatively, *is followed by*, except for cases of discontinuity. Necessarily, the set of units filling a given element (say Pl1) on the next lower

Table 38. Overview of analysis

SITUATION 1: GOAL = functions of texts (declare, inform,...,etc)
INSTRUMENT = text

where GOAL and INSTRUMENT are slots in a SITUATION frame, and where (declare, inform,....,) is a list of functions of texts in some SITUATION.

ACTION 1: PLANNING = generating elements of a text
text(background(pinform,pdeclare))

where *(pinform,pdeclare,....,)* is a list of functions of paragraphs in text structure, and (background, motivation,...) etc. is a list of rhetorical relations. Functions linked through rhetorical relations may be in *nucleus-satellite* or in *list* relationships.

SITUATION 1.1. GOAL = pinform
(from PLANNING ACTION 1)
INSTRUMENT = paragraph

ACTION 1.1. PLANNING = generating elements of a paragraph:
paragraph(background(ccinform1, ccinform2),background(ccinform2, ccinform3),consequence(ccinform4, ccinform3))

where *(ccinform$_{1,\ldots n}$)* is a list of functions of clause complexes, and (background, motivation,consequence...) is a list of rhetorical relations as above.

SITUATION 1.1.1 GOAL = ccinform1
(from PLANNING ACTION 1.1)
INSTRUMENT = clause complex

ACTION 1.1.1. PLANNING = generating elements of a clause complex:
clause complex (extension, (information giver,information giver))

where (information giver, information seeker,...) is a list of elements of clause-complex structure, and (extension, elaboration,...) is a list of clause combining relations as in Halliday.1985:192ff

SITUATION 1.1.1.1. GOAL = information-giver
INSTRUMENT = clause

ACTION 1.1.1.1. PLANNING = clause (action(agent,affected))

where (information-giver, information seeker...) is a list of features from Systemic illocutionary force - or mood - networks, and where (action, mental process,...) is a list of predicate types, and (agent, affected,...) etc. is a list of participant roles.

SITUATION 1 Text {function = X/X **E** set of functions of texts}

ACTION 1 Text [background (pinform, pdeclare)]

SITUATION 1.1 Paragraph (function = pinform)

ACTION 1.1

$$\text{Paragraph}\begin{bmatrix}\text{background (ccinform}_1\text{, ccinform}_2\text{)}\\ \text{background (ccinform}_2\text{, ccinform}_3\text{)}\\ \text{consequence (ccinform}_4\text{, ccinform}_5\text{)}\end{bmatrix}$$

SITUATION 1.1.1 Clause Complex$_1$ {function = ccinform$_1$}

ACTION 1.1.1 Clause Complex$_1$ [Extension (information-giver$_1$, information-giver$_2$)]

SITUATION 1.1.1.1 clause$_1$ {function = information-giver}

ACTION 1.1.1.1

$$\text{clause}_1\begin{bmatrix}\text{Action (Agent, Affected)}\\ \text{Theme} = \text{X}\\ \text{Rheme} = \text{Y}\\ \text{Given} = \text{A}\\ \cdot\\ \cdot\\ \cdot\end{bmatrix}$$

Figure 11. Text structure

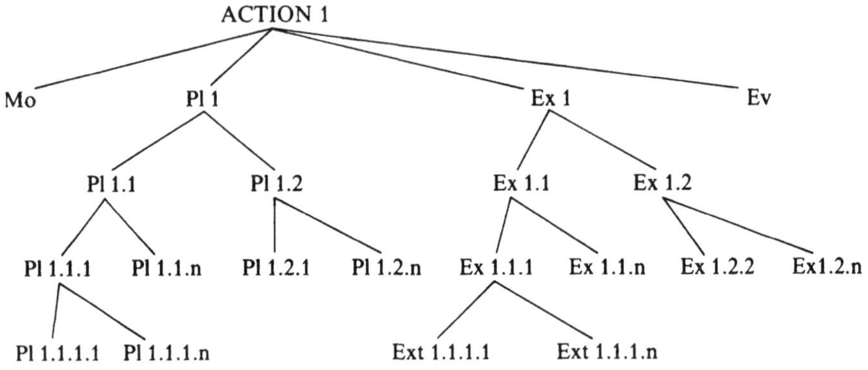

Figure 12. Action structure

rank (OPERATION) is identical to the combined sets of units filling the constituent elements. It is important to remember that the tree in Figure 12 is not a systemic tree in the classical sense. Our tree here stays on one rank on the level of activity. Where the realizing structures of an ACTION are linguistic structures, as in our example here, elements of ACTION from a given level in the hierarchy in the tree are mapped into linguistic units of specific ranks, as outlined in the advance organizer.

We shall now give an analysis of our sample text. To start with, on the level of ACTIVITIES, i.e. the top rank in a grammar of ACTION, we would only find a structure such as in Table 39.

Table 39. Rank: activity

ACTIVITY producing the text:	communication
NEED :	co-ordination of future ACTIVITIES
OBJECTIVE:	co-ordinate struggle for divestment

Next, we generate an ACTION 1, filling our ACTIVITY and serving as a superordinate ACTION for embedded ACTIONS. We shall also try to specify at each step which aspect of linguistic structure is generated by what aspect of the generated ACTION. An analysis of an ACTION will always consists of two parts:

- A Situation specific to that ACTION
- A structural diagram reflecting the constituency, i.e. the logical structure of the ACTION. Observe that "logical structure" is meant here in the sense of the theory of goal-directed action, i.e. we do not refer to here to logical structures of language in terms of grammar. The constituency is abstract in the sense that

it abstracts away from the temporal sequence in which steps of the ACTION are carried out. Discontinuities and scrambling of elements of units have to be accounted for separately (cf. Table 40).

Table 40. Situation 1.

SITUATION 1.	
AGENT	group of students
MATERIALS	fellow citizens
INSTRUMENTS	language in the medium of writing (handout): text
GOAL	inform people of morally bad Yale behaviour & declare continuing resistance: inform & declare
PRODUCT	unspecified (perlocutionary effect of the text)
TIME	some time after April 4 1986
PLACE	somewhere around Yale (presumably)

The situational frame of our SITUATION 1 consists of attributes (slots) and values (fillers). Each attribute/value pair can be called a feature of the SITUATION. The particular list of attributes is independently motivated (cf. Steiner 1985 b). In a more developed approach, the range of possible values for each attribute should come from the domain-knowledge. The formulation of motivated restrictions on the range of values for a given attribute is beyond what we understand presently, if we think of non-ad hoc restrictions. Under the GOAL attribute we introduce functions, i.e. goals of the text as a whole within the SITUATION. While the domain knowledge thus contains knowledge from previous utterances, the situational frame introduces new knowledge for the speech situatioon. New knowledge may come about as a consequence of goals and consequences (PRODUCT) of an ACTION. ACTION 1 takes a form such as Table 41.

The direct realization of ACTION 1, under the interpretation above, would only be the creation of a rhetorical relation between paragraphs 1 and 2 (a rhetorical relation in terms of rhetorical structure theory), with two functional labels for these paragraphes, such as *pinform* plus *pdeclare* continuing resistance. The prefix "p-" here will simply identify labels for paragraph functions, rather than functions of units on lower ranks. We have furthermore generated the sequence between them, plus a potential paragraph boundary which, though, in the present text is not realized typographically. Our claim would be, then, that it is this underlying structure of the text so far which gives it coherence. The OPERATIONS filling this kind of structure would be on the level of creating cohesion in the sense of Halliday and Hasan

Table 41. Action 1.

ACTION 1.			
MOTIVATION	PLANNING	EXECUTION	EVALUATION
1. Reasons for informing people of Yale behaviour & for declaring continuing resistance 2. What are the available means for pursuing GOAL?	Create sub-goals: ACTION 1.1.: pinform people about events & get people to share our perspective ACTION 1.2:pdeclare continuing resistance create rhetorical relation of *background* between 1.1. & 1.2	fill by 1.1 & 1.2	not given

(1977). The expounding unit is the whole text . Whether or not the two paragraphs have topic continuity is not a question which is settled through the model as such. Topic continuity may or may not be a means of achieving the author's GOAL on this level. What makes the text hang together, so far, is a question of the coherence of goals. Also, theoretically we might still be generating one or two sentences only. Otherwise, all that we have done so far, apart from what we have just said, is to set two pointers to ACTIONS filling our ACTION 1. Below, these ACTIONS will be referred to as ACTIONS 1.1. and 1.2. In terms of the text we are generating, ACTION 1.1. is expounded by sentences 1-4, i.e. from *On April...* to ***be rebuilt.*** ACTION 1.2. is expounded by the last sentence *we will not...failure*. In our analysis we shall use *clause complex* and *sentence* interchangeably - the sentence being a unit of written language, and the clause being a unit of spoken language. A clause complex is then any combination of clauses which are linked by some grammatical device in the sense of Halliday (1985a: 192ff).

We are now moving on to the next rank of language, which in terms of the theory of ACTION is reached through embedding, i.e. realized as ACTIONS filling elements of structure of other ACTIONS (cf. Tables 42 and 43). Cases of rankshift, on the other hand, involve recursion of the ACTION category as an OPERATION. Clause complexes are the filling units of elements of paragraph structure. So, just as a text here is taken to realize an ACTION, and having a structure of elements given in a certain relation in the analysis of ACTION 1 under PLANNING i.e. directly deriving from the GOALS of that ACTION, with our two paragraphs filling these elements, so our two paragraphs, in turn, have a structure consisting of elements plus relations listed under PLANNING of ACTION 1.1. and 1.2., each of which elements will be filled by a clause complex (cf. Table 43).

Table 42. Situation 1.1.

SITUATION 1.1.	
AGENT	read in from ACTION 1
MATERIALS	read in from ACTION 1
INSTRUMENTS	paragraph
GOAL	people are informed of morally bad Yale behaviour & take sides with AGENT : pinform (from PLANNING ACTION 1)
PRODUCT	unspecified (perlocutionary effect of the paragraph)
TIME	part of TIME of ACTION 1
PLACE	part of PLACE of ACTION 1

The fact that the two top slots are filled by the same referents as in the case of ACTION 1 is an empirical question, i.e. there is no stipulation in the theory of ACTION that this is necessarily the case - except in the case of the AGENT slot, where, as in the case of causatives, at least the *Causer* must be identical to the AGENT of some superordinate ACTION. Sub-goals are linked to superordinate goals through necessary inferences. TIME and PLACE of subordinate ACTIONS are linked to the corresponding slots in superordinate ACTIONS through the *part-of* relation, which is more fully investigated in earlier sections.

In the analyses of ACTIONS 1.1. and 1.2., the prefix "cc-" identifies "clause complex functions". i.e. the functions which a clause complex has in the structure of a paragraph. As such, they will re-appear as GOALS of SITUATIONS 1.1.1. and 1.2.1. In general, GOALS of one level in our analyses are always directly derived from the PLANNING phases of the corresponding ACTION one level further up. Conversely, the functions of units identified in some PLANNING phase always become GOALS on the next level further down.

The question to what extent the perlocutionary effects are part of the conscious planning of an ACTION is again an empirical one: However, perlocutionary effects, to the extent that they are not consciously planned, are part of the effects of an ACTION, not part of the ACTION itself.

We give an analysis of SITUATION 1.2. and of ACTION 1.2 in Tables 44 and 45.

So far, we have generated, within our two paragraphs, functional labels for clause complexes plus rhetorical relations between the clause complexes.

The next recursion of the ACTION category now leads us to the generation of clause complexes plus clause combining relations within them. That is to say, we generate interpersonal functions of clauses plus clause combinbing relations between them. We shall, at this point, focus on ACTION 1.1.1., i.e. on the generation of the clause complex *On April 4,..., and fear* (Tables 46 and 47).

ACTION 1.1.1., in spite of the superficial fact that the first sentence seems to *consist of* several clauses, only generates one clause complex consisting of one

Table 43. Action 1.1.

ACTION 1.1.			
MOTIVATION	PLANNING	EXECUTION	EVALUATION
1. Reasons for informing people plus MOTIVATION ACTION 1 2. What are the available means for pursuing GOAL	ccinform1 ccinform2 ccinform3 ccinform4 + rhetorical relations between 1-4, i.e. background (1,2) background (2,3) background (3,4) + perlocutionary effects of 1.-4.?	goto ACTIONS 1.1.1. - 1.1.4.	

Table 44. Situation 1.2.

SITUATION 1.2.	
AGENT	read in from ACTION 1
MATERIALS	read in from ACTION 1
INSTRUMENTS	paragraph
GOAL	pdeclare continuing resistance (from PLANNING ACTION 1)
PRODUCT	unspecified
TIME	part of TIME of ACTION 1
PLACE	part of PLACE of ACTION 1

clause. The simple reason is that the three embedded clauses in the first complex are all relative clauses, i.e. there is no direct relationship between them and the topmost clause. The relative clauses will all be generated within the nominal groups of which they fill functional slots, i.e. at a much later stage. As an illustration of how we handle clause complexes which have as constituents more than one clause, we shall later inspect ACTION 1.2.1.

Observe that the relationship between the first two clause complexes is already generated as rhetorical structure as part of ACTION 1.1. Clause complex 1, although fairly complex in terms of embedding, has no complex structure in terms of clause combining.

To give an illustration where a bit more is happening on this rank, let us have a look at ACTION 1.2.1., which is realized in the last sentence of our text, which is a clause complex with the clause combining relation of *exposition* between the constituent clauses (cf. Tables 48 and 49).

Table 45. Action 1.2.

ACTION 1.2.			
MOTIVATION	PLANNING	EXECUTION	EVALUATION
1. Reasons for continuing resistance plus MOTIVATION of ACTION 1 2. Taking stock of available means for ACTION 1.2.	Declaration of intent *to do x* ccdeclare x	goto ACTION 1.2.1.	?

Table 46. Situation 1.1.1.

SITUATION 1.1.1.	
AGENT	read in
MATERIALS	read in
INSTRUMENTS	clause complexes
GOAL	ccinform (from PLANNING ACTION 1.1.)
PRODUCT	not known
TIME	included in time of SIT 1.1
PLACE	included in place of SIT 1.1.

Table 47. Action 1.1.1.

ACTION 1.1.1.			
MOTIVATION	PLANNING	EXECUTION	EVALUATION
		1. information-giver	goto ACTION 1.1.1.1.-n

With the next re-entry of the ACTION category, we shall be generating clauses, with their illocutionary force as their goal and with predicate types and participant roles as their elements (cf. Tables 50-53). Because of the multi-functional nature of language, clauses, of course, have functional elements along several dimensions, along with predicate-argument structures. These other dimensions are, at least, thematic structure, information structure, and logical structure. Observe that we have already covered the mood structure by using the features generating it as the decisive link (GOAL) to the theory of ACTION.

Let us finally identify research goals deriving from the model outlined abobve, and let us also reflect on the relationship of this model to other models.

- Which aspects of text structure, and here we mean formal, linguistic structures, are controlled, i.e generated by ACTIONS and SITUATIONS on the ranks of *text* and

Table 48. Situation 1.2.1.

SITUATION 1.2.1.	
AGENT	read in
MATERIALS	read in
INSTRUMENTS	clause complex
GOAL	ccdeclare (from PLANNING ACTION 1.2)
PRODUCT	unspecified
TIME	part of TIME 1.2.
PLACE	part of PLACE 1.2.

Table 49. Action 1.2.1.

ACTION 1.2.1.			
MOTIVATION	PLANNING	EXECUTION	EVALUATION
	1. exposition (information-giver, information-giver)		

Table 50. Situation 1.1.1.1.

SITUATION 1.1.1.1.	
AGENT	read in
MATERIALS	read in
INSTRUMENTS	clause
GOAL	information-giver
PRODUCT	unspecified
TIME	part of TIME 1.1.1.
PLACE	part of PLACE 1.1.1.

Table 51. Action 1.1.1.1.

ACTION 1.1.1.1.			
MOTIVATION	PLANNING	EXECUTION	EVALUATION
	1. action (agent,effected)		

paragraph? Most of the structure which we are postulating for the ranks of text and paragraph needs to be substantiated and filled in the course of empirical work.

- Can we produce some reasonably stable list of ACTION goals for some domain, a true sub-set of which would be those GOALS being realized in linguistic structures (i.e. those in the GOAL-slots of our SITUATION frames)? A case in question might be extensive lists of possible speech acts for large sub-parts of the German verb system (cf. Ballmer & Brennenstuhl 1981). Such a list of ACTION goals would

Table 52. Situation 1.2.1.1.

SITUATION 1.2.1.1.	
AGENT	read in
MATERIALS	read in
INSTRUMENTS	clause
GOAL	information-giver
PRODUCT	unspecified
TIME	part of TIME 1.2.1.
PLACE	part of PLACE 1.2.1.

Table 53. Action 1.2.1.1.

ACTION 1.2.1.1.			
MOTIVATION	PLANNING	EXECUTION	EVALUATION
	1. NOT (action(agent,affected))		

be the decisive external driving force for text generation. "External" here means "outside the linguistic system". We need to formulate more precisely how the GOALS interact with the rest of the slots in a SITUATION. In the context of automatic generation in particular, it needs to be kept in mind that without such external driving forces, we only have generators which generate random and uninterpreted text. A solution which is frequently proposed in current work is that "somehow the generator is told from the outside what to encode, and then its job is merely the encoding itself". What appears basically wrong in such an approach is that there simply is no unmotivated list of facts anywhere in the world merely waiting to be encoded - the force which arranges such facts into particular constellations and drives their encoding in particular shapes is human goal-directed action. To attribute ACTIONS structures to the observable "behaviour" of some interactant is what should constitute a very major part of what is currently called "user modelling". We need models of how to generate goals in some SITUATION (cf. Moore & Paris 1989).

- Texts need for their interpretation a model of the world with respect to which reference is established. To what extent do we have to refine the present model of a SITUATION to provide such a model?

- The reasonable pursuing of any goal, and certainly of a linguistic goal, requires the appropriate setting of a number of linguistic parameters other than those controlled directly by the goal itself. These parameters have essentially been known at least since the time of traditional rhetoric (cf. Aristoteles *Rhetorica*, Quintillian's Rhetoric etc.), and some of them have received more modern, and partly more explicit formulations in Systemic register theory and in work in text generation such as Hovy (1988). The setting of these additional parameters will normally be instrumental, to the extent that it is done consciously, or otherwise will take the form of OPERATIONS. However, a more precise formulation of the interaction between those parameters which can be related directly to the GOALS of some speaker, and those which are only secondary needs to be made much more precise. To give a simple example: In ordinary goal-directed ACTIONS, one does not talk to someone primarily *in order to* appear sociable. Yet, in those not infrequent cases of "phatic communion" (Malinowski 1935) between people, this may actually become the primary goal, thus making other goals, such as the encoding of content, derivative. What we are saying here is that whereas all the parameters having to do with *register* will always play a role in the generation of any text, their precise relative weight in the generation of each particular text-type (where "type" needs to be defined in terms of GOALS) is the important issue for research.

- The categories of our SITUATIONS, such as *Agent, Instrument etc.* are at least partly also categories of our clause grammars, where they appear as participant roles on arguments or circumstantial roles on any predicate. It needs to be made clear in detail what the precise relationships are here. We argued in 2.3 that there can be no isomorphism between the two levels of representation, and that therefore precise realization rules have to be formulated.

- We need to compare systematically our use of rhetorical relations with the standard variant of rhetorical structure theory. As far as the interface between linguistic structures and non-linguistic strategies of text planning, generation, and analysis is concerned, rhetorical structure theory draws a boundary between non-grammaticalized realizations of rhetorical strategies and those which are grammaticalized. While in principle some rhetorical structure and/or some rhetorical relations may be grammaticalized in a grammatical unit at any rank (within the internal structure of the nominal group or between prepositional phrases and verbal groups, etc.), the highest rank where we find grammaticalization, at least in English, would be that of the clause complex. Clause combining relations are, in English, grammaticalizations of rhetorical strategies on the highest rank. If we accept this, then the inevitable question is how we as investigators, and how the interpreter of any text identifies the higher rank rhetorical relations and rhetorical structures. One of the usual answers is that those strategies of textgeneration and analysis which are not (yet or any more) grammaticalized are semi-fixed in other socially normed processes of generation and analysis - which is very probably true and also obvious, if we think of the conscious expression of these norm-giving practices in education. This answer may be largely true, but it certainly relegates an investigation of such processes to areas somewhat outside of what is currently perceived to be linguistics. The approach followed here postulates ranks above that of the clause complex, namely those of *text* and *paragraph*, both of which are related to INSTRUMENT - slots in our SITUATION frame, and both of which have structural elements which are related to the PLANNING phases of ACTIONS just in the same way as units and their elements in other parts of the grammar are related to these categories. Language, on a very general level, is thus shown to be nothing but the cristalized, i.e. grammaticalized form of human action. To what extent such grammaticalized ranks exist is an empirical and, furthermore, culture- and language-specific question.

- We need a more elaborate investigation of the category of "plot" in the context of the current approach. The category of "propositional content" and, operating on it, truth conditions, share a prominent status in the more philosophically oriented linguistic theories. And, certainly, it appears to be a necessary and central concept for any account of the control of such text phenomena as lexical choice and phenomena in the Systemic *logical compenent* (generating conjunctions, prepositions, negations etc.). But within the method indicated in this section, a the generation of a *plot* is the product of moving down a rank scale of ACTIONS and linguistic ACTIONS in particular, where on each rank the particular function of some unit controles the *what* and *how* of what is encoded. Quite clearly, SITUATIONS are generated, and with them propositions, for the entire SITUATION as well as for individual slots. But whether or not, say, an [action, agent-oriented] verb in terms of grammatical transitivity is chosen, is not so much the product of some unguided mapping from SITUATIONS to propositions, but, as shown in detail in the analysis, the product of the goal/function of a unit or element on a given rank. Processes and participant roles, for example, are the clause level expressions of PLANNING phases and of the goal in the connected situation. And this is why a simple fact like *human(hugo)* may be expressed, variously, as *hugo is a man, hugo reminds of a man, hugo seems to be a man, hugo makes a (nice) man* etc. This appears like a connection between human action and language which any theory that calls itself *functional* in our sense has to account for. So, plots and propositional contents do have a place in the present perspective, and even a prominent one, yet they are methodologically treated as generated by functions of language, that is, by goals of speakers, and are thus intimately linked to the other functions of language. Which of these functions is primary appears to be, in the present context, an unnecessary question, because there is, so far, no real interpretation attached to it.

- Which aspects of linguistic structure are accounted for by such an approach as the one advocated here? First, there are structures on the highest ranks of linguistic structure, such as paragraphing and sequence of clause complexes within a paragraph. Most of the substantive knowledge to be included in these components still needs a coherent formulation, but researchers inside and outside Systemic Linguistics have contributed already a lot of detail there. Next, and very importantly, lexical insertion: A model of text generation needs to "know" not only what class of verbs have which number and types of participant roles , but also which particular verb should govern which particular sentence in which part of a text. We thus need *knowledge*, which is, in most frameworks using a knowledge-based approach, mapped into *linguistic knowledge*. In our particular approach here, there is no sharp mapped into *linguistic knowledge*. In our particular approach here, there is no sharp dividing line: all knowledge is in the form of potential goal-directed actions, and a sub-part of that knowledge is always realized as linguistic knowledge.

This is as far as we shall go in the present context. The main function of this section within the overall study has been to outline an overall model of text production which interprets text generation as a special case of goal-directed action, moving up to higher ranks than before, or, expressed differently, decreasing the degree of granularity at which linguistic strcutures are inspected. We shall now go back to the question of research hypotheses concerning semantic complexity which can be derived from the theory of goal-directed action outlined in the present study.

2.5 Predictions of the theory of activity for some aspects of semantic complexity in child language: a preliminary discussion

In this section, we shall consider predictions of the theory of ACTIVITY as outlined so far for some aspects of semantic complexity in child language. These predictions will be formulated in their final quantifiable version in sections 3.3.-3.10, where they will also be tested. Let us first discuss some classes of predictions which can be derived from a theory such as the one we have been discussing:

- In the first place, one might want to investigate the structure of ACTIVITIES as such. With respect to our data, the independent variables could be age, sex, social class, or situation type. One could then derive measures of complexity, such as *unit : structure complexity, element : filler complexity, embedding complexity etc.*, which could serve as dependent variables.
- In the second place, one could interpret our theory of ACTIVITY as a kind of story grammar, and then investigate the structure of stories in terms of representations generated by our ACTION-grammar for stories. We have indicated such an approach in 2.4.1., yet we shall not pursue it any further in our present context. An approach along similar lines, yet using a different theory of *story structure* can be seen, for example, in Klann-Delius et al. (1985: 343ff).
- In the third place, one could investigate semantic complexity of the language in a given corpus in terms of a theory of linguistic semantics, taking as independent variables linguistic vs. non-linguistic ACTIONS. In this case, the theory of ACTIVITY would generate the independent variables, but complexity would not be measured in terms of the theory itself.

We shall look at predictions from the theory of ACTIVITY in a way similar to the third perspective just indicated: In our transcripts from the child language development project of the Polytechnic of Wales (cf. Appendices 1 and 2), we have linguistic data taken from, mostly, non-linguistic ACTIONS, at least as far as the play sessions are concerned. Within these data, we shall use *element of* ACTION as independent variable. We shall investigate certain types of semantic complexity in PLANNING phases vs. EXECUTION phases, using the semantic theory of Systemic Linguistics as a tool for analysis. This will, from now on, gradually lead us back to a purely linguistic focus. The primary goal of the current investigation, it should be remembered, is the further development of some aspects of Systemic Linguistics (cf. section 1). We have pursued this primary goal up to now in so far as we have been elaborating a concept for the level of *context of situation* within Systemic Linguistics, which is new within the theory as such. In chapter 3, we shall pursue our primary goal further in that we shall be applying existing analytical tools from Systemic Linguistics in an empirical investigation which is inspired by our theory of ACTIVITY. In this process, it is necessary to evaluate critically these existing tools and, where necessary, modify them. In the course of the very same process, we shall be working towards our secondary goal, which is an investigation of certain phenomena in child language development, and again, it is our theory of ACTIVITY, which points out these phenomena as areas for research.

The representations assigned by the theory of ACTIVITY to the ACTIONS (partly) instantiated by our data will give us PLANNING phases and EXECUTION phases as independent variables. Our dependent variables will be aspects of *context dependency, transitivity, thematic structure, circumstances, time, logical relationships, and Aktionsarten.* Generally speaking, the theory of ACTIVITY would for each of these dependent variables predict that the semantic complexity in PLANNING vs. EXECUTION phases is either different in an overall sense, or, at least, different in certain respects which will be made more specific in each of the sections where we shall investigate semantic complexity.

Why would one formulate hypotheses such as these against the background of our theory of ACTIVITY?

In the play session which we shall be investigating, we have essentially non-linguistic ACTIONS. That is to say, in the EXECUTION phases, language will, as a rule, come in as OPERATIONS which are not filling the main element as such, but which merely function in an instrumental way within the EXECUTION. They are, by definition, not consciously planned. In the PLANNING phases, on the other hand, language is the dominant filler of the element, because in interactive, collective PLANNING, language is necessarily the dominant filler. This also implies that, in those cases where PLANNING itself has any embedded ACTIONS, which will be the case in several places, we can even expect language which is consciously planned. In PLANNING, language has to encode *possible worlds*, possible states of affairs and courses of events, without relying on the immediate situation predominantly. In the EXECUTION of a non-linguistic ACTION, on the other hand, language will primarily function as a means for coordinating ongoing OPERATIONS, and only within this function, and because language always encodes some picture of a situation, will language serve as a reflection of reality. Given an overall functional perspective on language, one would clearly expect these radically different functions to be reflected somewhere in the semantic structure of the language used.

Before going into the investigation of aspects of semantic complexity in English child language, we shall discuss a certain class of possible alternatives to the way of analyzing human goal-directed action suggested in the present study.

2.6 Some frameworks for knowledge representation in artificial intelligence and their implications for the present study

2.6.1 The focus of this section

This section will be rather detailed for a section discussing alternatives to the main approach put forward in this study. However, this appears to be necessary in view of the fact that *artificial intelligence* techniques for representing knowledge of the *context of situation* are currently widely discussed inside and outside of Systemic Linguistics. Also, we should like to enable people from outside Systemic Linguistics to relate our own proposals to some of these techniques, especially because in 3.2. below, we shall interpret the representations resulting from an application of the theory of ACTIVITY to our data as a kind of knowledge representation. Finally, we should like to point out why we have chosen a theory from the psychology of action as a background for representing knowledge about certain kinds of SITUATION, rather than one of the currently popular theories in artificial intelligence. It will be seen, though, that the choice does not have to be strictly one or the other: Techniques of knowledge representation in artificial intelligence do have a lot to offer from the point of view of the present study, and we want to bring out as clearly as possible what it is that one might want to import from such techniques given our present framework. On the other hand, it should also become apparent that quite a few of the issues which nowadays appear to be (re-)discovered in the field of artificial intelligence have been under discussion for some time in fields like linguistics and psychology.

Within the scope of the present study, it is neither possible nor desirable to give anything like a comprehensive account of techniques of knowledge representation in artificial intelligence. We shall, however, try to discuss those aspects which have a bearing on questions of content and form of rules and representations introduced in our sections on the theory of ACTIVITY.

As for the function of this section within the overall structure of the present study, the following point should be observed:

Sections 2.6.2. to 2.6.6. present a general discussion of the topic. In these sections, we shall not primarily aim at discussing the most recent approaches, nor only such approaches which should be used directly in an implementation of our ideas. The approaches discussed are not necessarily the most current ones in the field, they rather have the status of representative approaches. It is our conviction, though, that they still present relevant developments in the field, most clearly showing the basic ideas. To counterbalance these sections, we shall conclude with a section 2.6.7. which directly builds on our previous section 2.4.5. and which does outline how our own ideas could be implemented into a text generation system. In this section, then, we shall consider only such approaches which are directly relevant to an implementation of our own ideas, and which have been explored in that connection. They are therefore also more recent than approaches discussed in the more general sections. The line of argumentation which we shall follow there is as follows:

In the direction of analysis, representations of ACTIONS and SITUATIONS will be built in two respects: If the text is of some genre encoding events that admit of types of representations we envisage, broadly "story"-type genres, or problem solving *plots*, a listener/reader will assign such representations to the plot. These representations are necessarily underdetermied by the purely linguistic structure and thus require both a systematic link to linguistic semantics and preference criteria of their own. For other types of *plot*, i.e. the message encoded in some text, other types of representation are needed. Whichever type of text we are faced with, though, a listener/reader of the text will attribute an ACTION and a SITUATION representation to the situation in which the text was produced, s/he will attribute a goal-structure to the model of the author. Text production, in the current perspective, parallels analysis in these respects. So far, then, we have a modelling of certain types of *content* and of hearers/readers.

We shall now first go into the more general parts of our discussion, finally coming back to a discussion of the more specific issues pertaining to our own approach.

2.6.2 The place of linguistics in artificial intelligence

In order to arrive at a realistic picture of what the place of linguistics is relative to artificial intelligence, we shall first have a brief look at the field of artificial intelligence as a whole, asking where in this field a linguistic input of some sort seems to be required. Our main sources here are Wahlster (1984 a,b, 1984/85), as well as Winograd (1983).

A list of the main fields of work within artificial intelligence would appear to have to contain at least the following entries:

- techniques of knowledge representation
- natural language systems
- deduction systems
- heuristic search procedures
- robot technology
- processing of visual information

An input from linguistics seems to be required most obviously in the cases of natural language systems and of techniques of knowledge representation. Natural language systems, in turn, seem to fall into the following categories at least:

- machine translation
- integrated question answering and dialogue systems
- data base retrieval and data formating
- text analysis and text comprehension
- text generation
- theory motivated systems
- language learning
- comprehension of spoken language
- natural language programming
- automatic abstracting
- natural language descriptions of visual information

Such a list, at the current rate of development of the field, is, of course, neither comprehensive nor very stable. Even from such a list, it should be obvious that, within the sub-field of natural language systems, linguistics has to make a substantial contribution. So far, at least the more ambitious projects have to a greater or lesser extent incorporated ideas from syntactic and semantic theories developed within linguistics (cf. surveys of the field in Danlos 1987; Nirenburg 1987; Grishman 1986; Kempen 1987). Systemic Functional Grammar in particular has gained influence, as we have tried to indicate at various places in this study. Recently, ideas from textlinguistics, discourse analysis, and pragmatics have begun to make an impact on natural language systems. Quite similar to the way in which linguistics in general has been moving more and more towards an integration of various models of *context* and *situation* into its field, natural language systems are increasingly projected and implemented in interaction with knowledge bases in the broadest sense, covering a wide field from the storage of factual information about "the world" to the constitution of "possible worlds" and partner models in discourse. There is, of course, still the linguistic knowledge in a narrower sense, covering syntax, semantics and phonology. In the following sections, we shall be looking at some of the most influential techniques for representing world knowledge, because these techniques have reflected back on linguistic theories to some extent.

2.6.3 The place of knowledge representation in artificial intelligence

Depending on the particular area one is concentrating on, knowledge bases will play a more or less important role, and they will consist of very different types of objects and processes in each particular case. It is possible, however, to generalize about the components of knowledge bases and/or about the processes that are connected to or form part of a knowledge base:

- any knowledge base needs some technique for the representation of knowledge;
- any knowledge base needs techniques for the transformation of input-data into an internal representation;
- a part of any knowledge base will also be search processes and inferencing mechanisms operating on the representations.

Seen in the present perspective, the area of knowledge representation and of accessing that knowledge is in some way fundamental, because our framework for representing structured information about ACTIONS and SITUATIONS might fulfil a similar role within Systemic Linguistics, at least for certain types of text.

A question related to the concept of a knowledge base is that of whether it is possible or useful to make a strict distinction between linguistic and non-linguistic knowledge. To some, there may appear to exist a strict borderline between these types of knowledge. As we shall see, however, this borderline is in many places breaking down, especially in those cases in which one has to use aspects of linguistic knowledge to define concepts relating to non-linguistic knowledge, and vice versa. In the present section, where we are concentrating on techniques in artificial intelligence, rather than linguistic techniques, we shall investigate some techniques for representing so-called *non-linguistic knowledge* in order to find out to what extent they can make a contribution towards linguistic models of *context of situation.*

2.6.4 Discussion of an example

In order to bring out clearly what an interface between linguistic and non-linguistic knowledge in a modern sense looks like, we shall discuss a specific example, the German HAM-ANS system. In doing so, we shall rely on Engelberg & Knöpfler (1982), Hoeppner & Morik (1983), Hoeppner (1982), Busemann et al (ms).

We shall only briefly discuss the overall process of analysis before connection with the knowledge base is made: the system HAM-ANS has three types of application:

- a booking system for hotel rooms
- a system for the analysis of a series of visual representations of events at a traffic junction
- a databank system.

Communication has to take the form of written rather than spoken language. To start our short investigation, we shall first have a look at a sample dialogue from the hotel room booking environment (taken from Hoeppner & Morik 1983: 11):

1 ? (040 4123 3315)
2 hotel zum fetten ochsen, guten abend!
3 ? Hallo hier ist Karlchen Müller, Fuchshausen
4 was kann ich für sie tun?
5 ? Sagen sie, ich möchte ein Doppelzimmer für zwei Tage
6 gewiss ich will mal sehen ...
7 ein doppelzimmer bis zum 25.4. hätten sie gern?
8 ? Nein, das habe ich anders gemeint.
9 entschuldigung, da habe ich sie wohl mißverstanden
10 ? Ich möchte ein Doppelzimmer für drei Nächte mit Bad
11 ein doppelzimmer mit bad bis zum 26.4. hätten sie gern?
12 ? Ja genau
13 ja, da ist noch etwas frei. haben sie noch irgendeinen besonderen wunsch?
14 ? Gibt es im Zimmer einen Sessel oder einen großen Stuhl?
15 ein großer stuhl steht nicht zur verfügung, aber ein sessel.
16 ? Wieviele von den Sitzgelegenheiten sind bequem?
17 eine von den vier ist relativ bequem.
18 ? Der Sessel?
19 ja, relativ bequem.
20 ? Ausgesprochen bequem?
21 nein, relativ bequem.
22 ? Ist dieser Sessel vielleicht weiß?
23 nein, der sessel ist gelb.
24 darf ich ein doppelzimmer dann auf den namen karlchen müller, fuchshausen buchen?
25 ? Augenblick, ich habe noch eine Frage
26 ja bitte?
27 ? Wo?
28 bitte wie meinen sie das?
29 ? Wo steht denn dieser Sessel?
30 der sessel ist vor dem fenster.
31 ? Und neben was?
32 der sessel ist neben einem niedrigen couchtisch
33 darf ich ein doppelzimmer dann auf den namen karlchen müller, fuchshausen buchen?
34 ? Nein, ich möchte noch was anderes wissen.
35 ja bitte?
36 ? Was befindet sich eigentlich auf diesem Couchtisch, der neben dem Sessel steht?
37 kein ding ist auf dem couchtisch, der neben dem sessel ist.
38 ? Das Zimmer ist doch dunkel?
39 nein.
40 ? Also hell?
41 ja, vermutlich hell.
42 ? Tatsächlich?
43 ein fenster von ihm ist groß
44 darf ich ein doppelzimmer dann auf den namen karlchen müller, fuchshausen buchen?
45 ? Ja, nun habe ich keine weiteren Fragen.

46 ich habe also ein doppelzimmer vom 23.4. bis 26.4. auf den namen karlchen müller, fuchshausen gebucht.
47 vielen dank und auf wiederhören
48 ? Auf Wiederhören

ENDE

In this dialogue, contributions by the system are distinguished by lower case spelling throughout.

The opening phase of the dialogue is not controlled by a linguistic grammar on the side of the system: the first steps are carried through as standardized formulas (greeting and introduction of the hotel, invitation of the client to formulate requests, paraphrasing of the client's requests, confirmation of vacancies). This stage covers lines 1-13 of our sample dialogue. It is the central part of the dialogue, where the system and the client have a kind of discussion about the client's particular requirements, that the system uses its grammar (lines 14-44). In lines 24, 33, and 45 the system tries to enter its final actual booking exchange, which is again carried out with the help of standardized formulas.

We shall now concentrate on the processes of syntactic and semantic analysis, without going into too much detail. The first part of the analysis consists of three major sub-tasks: Lexical analysis, syntactic analysis, and the identification of ellipses. During lexical analysis, most bound morphemes are identified and interpreted, syntagmatic lexical units are identified and spelling mistakes are automatically corrected. The syntactic analysis carries through the disambiguation of morphological structures, a multi-strategy parsing with *augmented transition networks* of the sentences into configurations of semantic cases and processes, or, in the case of relational (*be-type*) predicates into something like a semantic equation, and the generation of a semantic representation. For elements which have been identified as being ellipted, their full semantic representation is generated. An intermediary product in this analysis is a so-called *surf-representation*, like the following for part of line 14 of our sample dialogue (cf. Hoeppner & Morik 1983: 1ff):

```
[14-b]    (af-d:IS
            (t-o:OR
              (t-s:(q-qt:E-) (lambda:x1(af-a:ISA x1 SESSEL)))
                (t-s:(q-qt:E-)
                  (d-o:AND
                    (lambda:x3(af-a:ISA x3STUHL))
                      (lambda:x2(af-a:REF x2GROSS)))))
       T)
```

The representation above does not seem to contain the constituent *Im Zimmer*, yet this is not essential for our illustration. *Surf-representations* are then transformed into *deep-representations* which, in turn, are the input to the interpretation component, i.e. the knowledge base carrying the world knowledge. The *deep-*

representation appears to differ from its corresponding *surf-representation* among other things in that it contains explicit markings for the scope of quantifiers, which is to be expected in any kind of logical form.

It should perhaps be added at this point that in the example we are discussing here, there is no analysis of the syntactic structure into a configuration of semantic cases and processes/events, due to the fact that our predicate here is of the *be-type*. Whether or not such different strategies of semantic analysis for relational vs. other types of predicates are useful, is a question which remains open. There are certainly valid reasons for adopting the same strategy for both types of predicates, yet this issue is not of overriding importance here.

Let us now look somewhat more closely at how HAM-ANS accesses its knowledge base from its *deep-representations*. In the process of interpretation, i.e. translation, of *deep-representations* into reactions of the system, HAM-ANS accesses three sources of knowledge:

The conceptual network, the referential semantic network, and the visual data. Figure 13 contains an excerpt of the HAM-ANS networks (Hoeppner & Morik 1983: 20).

In conceptual networks, nodes represent concepts and arcs represent relations between these. HAM-ANS uses the following set of relations: hyponymy (*U*), part-of (*T*), quality (*E*), set of values of a quality (*V*), inherent property (*D*), class membership (*ISA*), property of an object (*REF*), referential part-of relation (*HAP*). Of these, the relations *ISA* and *HAP* are characteristic of the referential semantic network, i.e. they are meant to characterize the instantiation rather than the concept. The objects which are present in the visual data are given an index and are connected through the *ISA* relation to the conceptual semantic network. The use of numerical values for "strength" of a certain property will not be discussed here.

The process of interpretation of a *deep-formula* takes the following form:

The *deep-formula* contains lexical items and semantic cases, where they are applicable. These are now treated as variables for which the entities from the referential network are tested as possible values. For every fully instantiated formula, the test procedures of the knowledge base compute truth values. In order for these procedures to function, it is essential that values from the referential semantic network are connected to the input from the visual data on the one hand, so that many properties of entities can be tested through the *REF* relation, and through the arcs in the conceptual network to concepts on the other hand. Between these concepts obtain the semantic relations discussed above. By computing the implications of these relations for any concept with which an entity from the referential semantic network is connected, the system can access, or rather *generate*, much more knowledge than is given through the input from the visual data. Essential in this context are properties like the restricted or unrestricted inheritance of qualities through certain relations and the logical characteristics of the relation, such as transitivity,

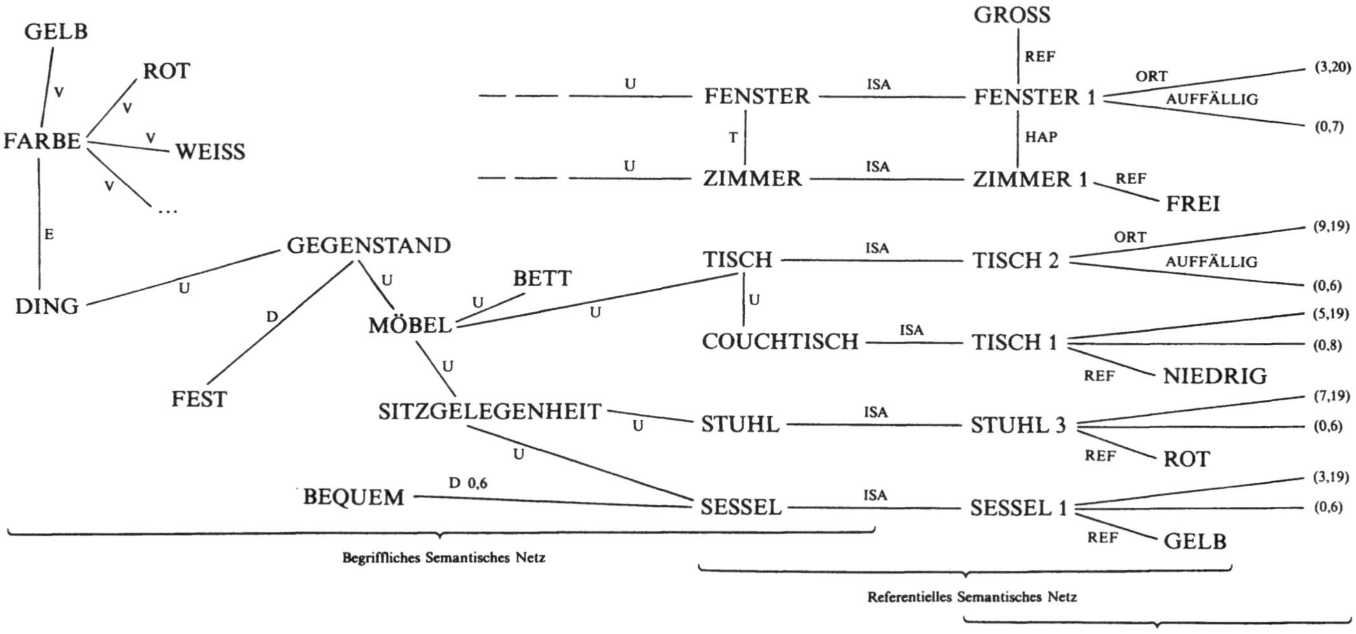

U: Ober-Unterbegriffsrelation
T: Teil-von-Relation
E: Eigenschaftsbezeichnung
V: Werteskala einer Eigenschaft
D: Inhärente Eigenschaft

ISA: Klassenzugehörigkeit
REF: Merkmal eines Objektes
HAP: Referentielle Teil-von-Relation

ORT: Koordination für Objekte
AUFFÄLLIG: Anfangsauffälligkeit

Figure 13. Conceptual and referential knowledge in HAM-ANS
I am grateful to the authors for giving permission to reproduce the material in Figure 13.

reflexivity, reciprocity, etc.. Inferencing in this way may take quite complex forms and may proceed through various types of semantic or conceptual relations.

This is as far as we shall take our presentation of a specific example of the interaction of syntactico-semantic analysis with the knowledge base in the environment of an artificial intelligence - system for modelling man-machine dialogue. Quite obviously, we have left out of account many of the features of HAM-ANS which are essential for the system as such. However, in our discussion we had a very specific and limited purpose: The illustration of the interface between linguistic representations and processes in a knowledge base for capturing world knowledge. We want this to serve as a background for our discussion of conceptions of knowledge representation which follows in the next section. Also, there is a general parallel with what we discussed in connection with the interaction between representations of Systemic grammar and their interaction with representations generated by our analysis of ACTIVITY: This interaction, within the present approach, realizes the interface between *language* and *context*. It is precisely at the points where OPERATIONS are realized by semantic features (cf. the analyses in 2.4.1-2.4.3.) that we encounter this interface.

2.6.5 Frameworks for knowledge representation

2.6.5.1 Adjusting our focus. For our discussion of the field of knowledge representation in the present section, we are deeply indebted to the very useful survey given in Engelberg and Knöpfler (1982: 13ff.) Let us begin by examining in some more detail what we mean by the term "knowledge":
For some time, roughly 1960-1975, there was a wide-spread assumption among practitioners in the field that *knowledge* could be reasonably well divided into linguistic knowledge on the one hand, and non-linguistic knowledge, or knowledge of the world, on the other. Linguistic knowledge, in this perspective, was conceived of as (the largely unconscious) knowledge of concepts and rules from the phonological, the morphological, and syntactic components. Furthermore, there was the assumption of some kind of *lexicon* as well as of concepts and rules of some semantic component. To these types of knowledge would have to be added the knowledge of rules for mapping representations from each of these components onto one or several of the others. Non-linguistic encyclopaedic knowledge would, according to this view, be distinct in content and form from linguistic knowledge. Above all, linguistic knowledge was assumed to be innate to a considerable extent. Linguistic representations would be generated on the basis of linguistic knowledge thus conceived. The process of interpretation would then give access to and operate on non-linguistic knowledge.

The point of view just described was really never more than a majority view, which implies that there were diverging opinions even then, yet it was part of the dominating paradigm in linguistics and also cognitive psychology, and thus had considerable influence in artificial intelligence as well. However, the view that linguistic and non-linguistic types of knowledge can be neatly separated has increasingly come under attack in recent years, and it is nowadays widely recognized in all of the disciplines concerned that linguistic and non-linguistic knowledge shade into each other at least in the borderline areas (cf. Rumelhart, Winton & McClelland 1986). It is no longer seriously doubted in many schools of linguistics, for example, that the consideration of various types of context is part of linguistics, and it is within this area that the borderlines between the two types of knowledge become perhaps hardest to draw. The same applies to many modern natural language systems in artificial intelligence and computational linguistics. In the analysis of an utterance, for example, there are stages of the overall process which appear to be relatively clearly *linguistic*, like phonological, morphological, and syntactic analysis. This is illustrated by our *surf-representations* in the preceding section. We begin to appraoch the borderline area, though, as soon as we enter the field of semantics: Can, for example, *features* of lexical items or semantic *cases* be arrived at without taking into account information from the *situation*, or from referential networks, or instantiations of frames, or scripts? Or, vice versa, to what extent are referential networks, frames, scripts etc. structured independently of linguistic categorizations? Questions such as these imply that the differentiation between linguistic and non-linguistic knowledge is losing much of its significance and may even become something of a hindrance for theoretical and practical progress.

Let us now turn to some of the questions associated with the representation of knowledge as such: There is a first fundamental distinction between analoguous and symbolic representations of knowledge. An analoguous representation preserves certain types of spatial isomorphism with the domain which the knowledge is about. In particular, the *domain* may be nothing but another representation of the same knowledge, but we shall not enter into epistemological questions associated with this assumption. A picture, or a drawing of some scene, for example, is analoguous in that sense, but also more abstract representations or encodings, as long as they preserve certain spatial relationships directly. Analoguous representations seem inadequate for many types of knowledge, especially for knowledge which itself consists partly of conceptual and/or propositional relationships or representations. Therefore, natural language systems often prefer symbolic representations for their knowledge bases.

Within the symbolic type of representation, we in turn find two sub-types: Linear vs. non-linear representations. The linear type of representation of knowledge is most closely associated with representations in propositional form (cf. Kintsch 1977). In this approach, knowledge is represented and stored as sets of propositions defining concepts and relations. This type of representation has its adherents in linguistics as well as in other disciplines (van Dijk 1979; Sperber & Wilson 1986). We shall not discuss this way of representing knowledge extensively here. One important objection to it is within artificial intelligence, that operations over these representations (inferencing etc.) tend to be slow. From a linguistic point of view, it has been argued that a propositional representation of world knowledge does not add anything substantial to already existing, even if unsystematic, knowledge already present in more narrowly linguistic representations (Brown & Yule 1983: 106ff.). Such arguments should at the moment not be taken as final, and to many of those active in the field, there is much that seems to recommend propositional types of knowledge representation, such as the status of predicate calculus as an inferencing system, yet we shall focus here on non-linear types of representation, because they are much closer to the framework which we have been discussing in sections 2.3. and 2.4. Let us summarize the relationships between types of knowledge representation as in Figure 14.

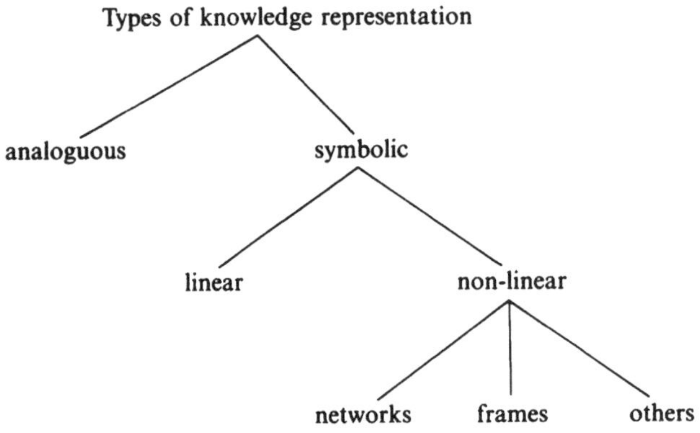

Figure 14. Types of knowledge representation

We shall concentrate on knowledge representations in the form of networks and frames, because they seem to represent a major line of development and they can easily related to what we have been discussing in previous sections. A further development of the *network-* and *frame* approaches are knowledge representation languages such as KL-ONE (cf. Brachman & Schmolze 1985) and its derived languages, such as LOOM (cf. MacGregor & Bates 1987). We shall come back to LOOM in particular in 2.6.7. as one way of implementing semantic levels of information such as the *upper model*.

2.6.5.2 Networks. A network is a graph with nodes and links connecting them (Engelberg & Knöpfler 1982: 19ff.; Sowa 1983; Patten & Ritchie 1987 for Systemic networks). In the case of conceptual networks, the nodes represent concepts and the links between them certain relationships. On this general level, the same applies to referential networks, only that in their case we are dealing not with *types*, but with *tokens*, i.e. not with concepts and classes, but with instantiations and elements. The by now classical approach to networks in this sense can be found in Quillian's *semantic memory* (Quillian 1968). He assumes the following types of relationships between concepts:

sub-class
super-class
modification by adjective/adverb
disjunction
conjunction
two further unspecific categories.

From a linguistic point of view, there are obvious links to the idea of the "Wortfeld" and to *strucural semantics* as represented in the work of Lyons (1977 Vol.1: 270ff.). The linguistic framework of Lyons is comparatively rich, as far as number and types of "sense relations" are concerned. For several of these, however, the tests for identification seem to be somewhat intuitive and therefore not easily applicable. Another candidate from within linguistics for a related approach would be the system network representation of lexical items in the tradition of Systemic Linguistics (Fawcett 1980: 151ff.; Berry 1977: 62ff.). In some respects, Quillian's approach may be considered outdated by now. Progress in essentially the same direction can be seen in work such as in the HAM-ANS project, which we have discussed. Their networks represent further developments in at least the following ways:
To arcs/links between concepts in their conceptual networks are attached numerical values indicating in what percentage of cases the postulated relationship obtains for a specific domain, which is important if at some stage one wants to incorporate a notion like "strength of activation" (cf. Rumelhart, Winton & McClelland 1986: 48ff.). Secondly, they draw a distinction between conceptual and referential networks, although both are intimately related to each other.

Working with probabilities in the way just mentioned does not seem to be a very principled way of dealing with relationships between concepts, as long as there is no theory which entails an account of what these probabilities express. Such theories, however, have been envisaged (as for example in Rumelhart, McClelland & the PDP Research Group 1986), and from a more pragmatic point of view, probabilities seem to be essential to improve the performance of systems such as the ones we have been discussing. Also, we are reminded of the use made of probabilities in connection with the linguistic concept of "collocation" as embodied, for example, in the *cloc*-package developed at the University of Birmingham following ideas of John Sinclair and other Systemic linguists (cf. Reed 1984), a software tool which computes collocations of lexical items for a given text. The transition between conceptual and referential networks seems to correspond roughly to the traditional borderline between linguistic and non-linguistic knowledge, and precise formulations in this area may help us to obtain new insights into the nature of that distinction, to the extent that it is adequate.

Let us consider network approaches to the representation of knowledge in some more detail: If the knowledge base is connected to some linguistic analysis of natural language input, then the syntactic structure of sentences and clauses is analyzed into a semantic structure where the semantic structure is a configuration of predicate types, semantic cases and circumstantials of various types, with additional representations for *modality, time, and mood.* The semantic structures which we shall be discussing in chapter 3 of this study are instances of such structures. From a linguistic point of view, it is important to observe a theoretical distinction between valency bound elements and non-valency bound elements, because verbs can only assign cases to elements which are bound by them. The semantic representation of non valency bound elements like circumstantials has to be computed through an analysis of their internal structure, which is perhaps easiest to see in the case of prepositional groups. It should also be said here that the concept of syntactic and semantic valency is, at least in artificial intelligence, usually applied to verbs only, whereas in principle, it also applies to the other major word classes, although the application is more difficult in several respects (cf. Steiner & Winter 1987). At least two linguistic approaches seem to have had a considerable influence: "Case Grammar", as developed by Fillmore and others (Fillmore 1968, 1977), and Systemic Functional Grammar (Halliday 1967-68, 1985a; Fawcett 1980). Computational work related to *case grammar* includes Simmons (1973) and Somers (1983, 1986), and work related to Systemic Functional Grammar includes Winograd (1972, 1983), Mann and Matthiessen (1985), and Heid, Roesner and Weck (1987). There are several well known difficulties connected with this type of approach, in particular difficulties related to the questions of number and type of semantic cases and predicate types. Unless the range of semantic structures to be covered is not artificially restricted, it is not easy to formulate an approach which relies on well defined categories and rules. Criteria for the identification of semantic cases on the basis of encyclopaedic knowledge are notoriously vague and lead to a serious lack of inter-coder consistency in dictionary coding. Case systems which rely heavily on the formulation of constraints for the syntactic realization of semantic cases, as in variants of Lexical Functional Grammar (cf. Bresnan 1982) or of Systemic Functional Grammar (Steiner et al. 1988), fare better as far as consistency is concerned. Here, though, there is the interesting problem of how, precisely, the set of semantic cases interacts with the concepts and relations in the knowledge base for nonlinguistic knowledge. In spite of these well known difficulties, natural language systems very often incorporate some account of semantic cases, because they are very useful, and possibly essential, for the handling of some classes of linguistic phenomena, such as [affected-centred] vs. [agent-centred] verbs, the representation of semantic ambiguity, the guiding of automatic lexical transfer in machine translation (cf. Eckert & Heid 1988), and others.

So far, the nodes in networks which we have considered are words identical to or at least close to words from natural language. Yet, one may choose to work with the assumption that words from natural language are not the "atomic" units of a semantic representation. Well known approaches in linguistics relying on the assumption that it is useful to decompose the meaning of words into further more basic and universal units included those of the feature analysis of words and "Generative Semantics", which focused on the lexical decomposition of verbs. In Systemic Functional Grammar, the semantic model is expressed in *system networks* (cf. section 3), consisting of features connected by *and/or* connections. The semantic features in these networks become increasingly specific as one moves through them from left to right. Each of the classes, however specific, has to be kept distinct from the set of lexical items which instantiate the class, which implies that the most general classes have the largest number of lexical items realizing them, or being the members of that class.

An influential approach to lexical decompositon was brought into artificial intelligence by Schank and Abelson. Schank (1975) decomposes verbs and abstract nouns into:

a. conceptual categories (*act,pp,pa,loc,t*)
b. primitive actions (*ptrans, propel, move, expel, ingest, grasp, atrans, mtrans*)
c. conceptual roles (*object, recipient, direction, instrumentalis, result, reason, enabling, causation*)

These categories serve to decompose the meaning of words, to describe the proposition-like relationships between these words, and even to relate the expressions representing entire stories. We shall briefly consider two examples of *conceptual dependency descriptions* of this type, one for isolated sentences and the other for a whole sequence of events (cf. Figures 15 and 16). The set of terms used in these representations is slightly larger than the one we listed under a-c above, because our list derives from Schank 1975, whereas our examples, which represent a further development, are taken from Schank and Abelson (1977: 15,29).

Conceptual dependency representations, it is claimed, represent the conceptual structures which underlie central aspects of human information processing. Categories, actions, and roles of the framework have certain semantic, or rather conceptual, properties, as well as relations between them. From the perspective of computation, it is very important that when these elements are combined to form the representation of words and sentences, such properties are inherited in certain specified ways by the larger units which they represent in their combination. This is, on a general level, an approach to *property inheritance* which we shall come back to in our dicussion of *frames* and which we have already encountered in

The symbol ⬆ denotes causality. Some example sentences and their representations are:

John killed Mary.
John **DO**
⬆
Mary **HEALTH** (-10)

John kicked Mary.
John **PROPEL** foot **to** Mary
⬆
foot (John) **BE PHYSICAL CONTACT** (Mary)

John told Mary that Bill was happy.
John **MTRANS** (Bill **BE MENT.ST** (5)) **to** Mary

John read a book.
John **MTRANS** (information) **to** **LTM** (John) **from** book
inst (John **ATTEND** eyes **to** book)

Figure 15. Conceptual dependency representations of sentences (Schank and Abelson 1977: 15)

our dicussion of conceptual and referential networks in the connection with the HAM-ANS approach. Within linguistics, the same general processes are at work in the area of feature percolation, especially in unification-based grammars. Feature percolation, of course, has to be constrained in linguistics, among other things, by the notions of *construction* and *head of construction*, as well as through logical relationships like class-subclass, implication, reflexivity, transitivity, and others.

There are several areas within this field which would merit further consideration, two of which would be the inclusion of quantifiers into networks and the partitioning of networks (cf. Engelberg/Knöpfler 1982: 40ff.). These, however, are outside the scope of the present discussion.

An approach such as the one just discussed is insightful and problematic at the same time: On the one hand, there are, apart from causation, many other relationships between parts of texts, and it is by no means obvious which these types are and how to constrain their assignment to parts of representations in an insightful way. On the other hand, given a certain text, it is not obvious how we can arrive at a *conceptual dependency representation* of the text in such a way as to achieve consistency among different interpreters of a text. Consistency here should

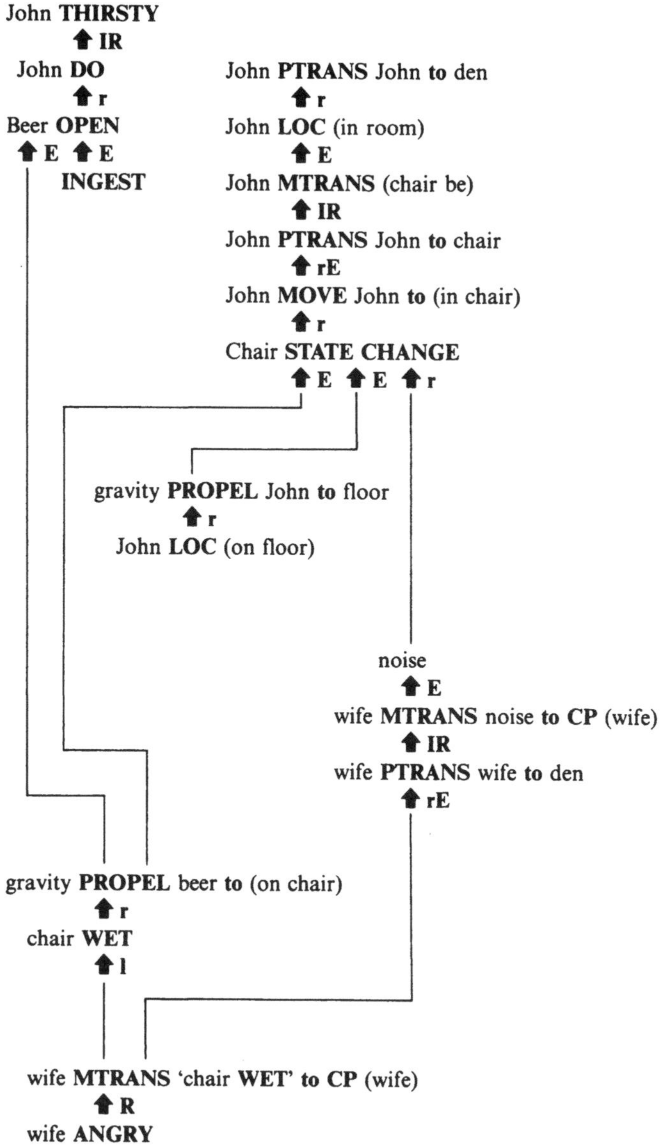

Figure 16. Conceptual dependency representation of a story

I am grateful to Erlbaum publishers for permission to reproduce the material in Figures 15 and 16 (Schank and Abelson 1977: 29).

not be taken to mean "one and only one representation" - indeed, it is a truism that there is more than one interpretation of a text. Consistency simply means "not an arbitrary number of representations" as well as a principled motivation for each single representation.

Our discussion of problems in this context should not be taken to imply a rejection of an approach such as the *conceptual dependency* approach. Rather, we want this discussion to be taken as representative for discussions which are necessary in connection with the whole family of approaches relying on network representations of the types of knowledge which we have been discussing.

Let us briefly go into some issues connected with the implementation of network approaches, in so far as they have a relationship to linguistic analysis:
What is the *semantics* of the relations that are associated with the arcs/ links/ branches in networks; in other words, what kind of processes do they symbolize in terms of an algorithm? It is around this question that some crucial aspects of the *proceduralist vs. declarativist* controversy are built. The proceduralist side holds that the *meaning* of any such relation is nothing but the procedures that the various higher and lower levels of programming prescribe to be carried out by the system (cf. Johnson Laird 1977). As procedures or relations formulated on one level of programming are recoded and ultimately carried out on lower levels, the meaning of the terms and rules of the higher level is realized, where the term *realized* is pretty close to the technical sense of Systemic Functional Grammar. A declarativist, on the other hand, sees the meaning of concepts and relations defined in the declarative propositional storage of knowledge on one level (for a discussion of these issues cf. Bobrow & Collins 1975). When it comes to considering these questions in terms of actual implementation, however, it is not at all obvious that the two positions are all that far apart.

Another set of questions relates to the actual storage of networks in terms of the architecture of the computational system: Networks, obviously, are not stored as they appear on the printed page, but rather in linear sequences of information units with *addresses* (concepts) and pointers which are added to them (relations). In this way, the information contained in a network gets linearized, which is not the same as the propositional approach to knowledge representation which we mentioned earlier. For search procedures in our networks, then, the question is one of strategies: depth-first vs. breadth first, or some combination of these strategies (cf. Engelberg & Knöpfler 1982: 53). Networks, it is claimed, allow for shorter search procedures in terms of computing time than the propositional storage of knowledge in the form of expressions from the predicate calculus, because the structure of networks limits the number of paths to be checked in the case of questions addressed to the knowledge base. Still, for many search procedures, the actual computing would take considerable time unless the procedures are not constrained by some kinds of heuristics, which can take on various forms. In the most simple case, the search procedure may simply be interrupted after a certain time. In other cases, hierarchies of goals and sub-goals may be used to avoid having to search entire networks and possibly families of networks with all the relations between concepts involved.

Further problems relate to questions associated with polysemeous names for concepts and instantiations: Inferencing, in such cases, will produce a large number of undesired results if ambiguity resulting from the polysemy of terms cannot be resolved. At present, there is no universally accepted approach to solve this problem. Technically, this appears to be the same type of problem as the one of deterministic vs. non-deterministic parsing in linguistic syntax or semantics.

Network representations of knowledge have, as we have seen, affinities at various points with linguistic approaches like structural semantics, system networks in Systemic Functional Grammar, lexical decomposition and others. It is partly such affinities which constitute a field of common questions between linguistics and artificial intelligence. One should not forget, however, that the terminology may suggest more commonality of meaning than there is in reality between the two disciplines: Linguistic networks are, in most cases, not the same as the networks which we have discussed in this section, nor is there an absolute identity in the respective meanings of terms used. Respecting this fact should prevent us from jumping to conclusions regarding the precise meaning of the terms used in each of the disciplines involved.

2.6.5.3 Frames. The second type of tool for the non-linear representation of knowledge that we shall discuss here is that of a "frame" (cf. Minsky 1975; Metzing ed. 1980). As a first approximative definition of *frame*, we shall use the following (cf. Engelberg & Knöpfler 1982: 60ff):

A frame is a structured and limited bundle of information units representing knowledge about a stereotype situation or object occurring in everyday life.

As we can see from this definition, there are several related concepts: The notion of a *script*, as developed by Schank and Abelson (cf. the preceding section), which is, in one perspective, a special case of a frame;
the notion of a *schema* as developed within cognitive psychology (Kintsch 1977); and the notion of a *prototype*, in so far as it is used to describe prototypical situations (cf. Rosch & Mervis 1975).

In looking at the concept of a *frame*, we shall start with the exploration of some basic ideas, then go on to consider some applications, after which we shall examine some limitations of the concept of *frame*. Our prime reason for going into these issues is, as before, that the idea of a frame, just like similar ideas, can be considered to be a rival candidate to the concepts of ACTION and SITUATION which we have explored in sections 2.3. and 2.4. earlier on, and that, even if we have opted for the particular approach outlined in these sections, alternative approaches have to be considered. Furthermore, and again, as before, in our discussions of limitations of the concepts of *frames, networks,* etc., we want to make explicit our reasons for choosing our particular framework.

Frames can be viewed as stereotype objects or stereotype events. Figure 17 and Table 54 contain two representative examples.

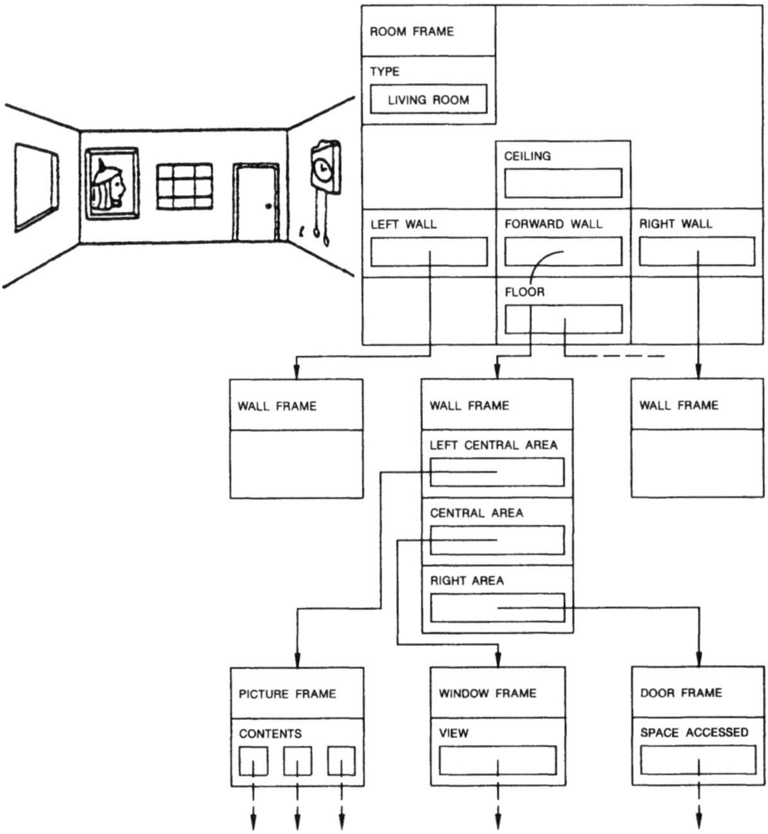

Figure 17. Room frame
Figure 17 is taken from Wahlster 1984a. I am grateful to the author for his permission.

The first distinction which we want to point out here is that between "slots" and "fillers". In the *room* - frame (Figure 17), we can see the slots *left wall, forward wall, right wall, ceiling, floor,* of the *room*-frame. These slots are filled

Table 54. Minsky's *Children's Birthday Party* Frame

Dress	Sunday best
Present	Must please host
	Must be bought and gift-wrapped
Games	Hide and seek. Pin tale on donkey
Decor	Balloons. Favors. Crepe-Paper
Party-Meal	Cake. Ice-Cream. Soda. Hot Dogs.
Cake	Candles. Blow-Out. Wish. Sing Birthday Song.
Ice-Cream	Standard three-Flavor

Table 54 appears as in Engelberg & Knöpfler (1982)

by elements like contents, view, space accessed, but also by other frames, like *wall*-frame, *picture*-frame, etc. All of these elements can be called *fillers*.

In Minsky's frame of an American children's birthday party (Table 54), we find the slots *dress, present, games, decor, party-meal, cake, ice-cream,* and as fillers the corresponding elements on the right. The slots in a frame are interpreted as permanent elements of the long term memory, whereas the fillers are instantiations or values of these slots. Slots and fillers are represented as variables and their values respectively. As we can see in our examples, slots can be filled directly by individual constant values representing the elements of any given situation, or else by frames in turn. This possibility of the instantiation of a slot of a frame by another frame makes the concept of frame a recursive one. In this view, there are rather diverse relationships involved:
We find something like a *class–sub-class* relationship in, say, *wall* = *left wall, forward wall, right wall,* where only specifity on the same level of abstraction seems to be increased. In other cases, we find filling of the slots of one frame by another frame regardless of abstraction and specifity, as in *left central area* = *picture frame*, and, finally, we encounter instantiation of the *type-token* kind, as in the assignment of one specific situational referent to some slot. These different types of relationship are well known from linguistics (cf. the notions of *delicacy, rank, exponence* in Sytemic Functional Grammar, as discussed in 2.3.). Certain default-values are usually assigned to slots in a frame which represent standard assumptions about fillers for these slots in the absence of contradictory information in the description of a situation.

It is part of the essence of the frame-concept that objects as instantiations can be fillers of slots in different frames at the same time, a property which is sometimes referred to as "terminal sharing". If we take our *room*-frame as an example, we can see that back yard, which may be a filler of our slot *space accessed* in the *door*-frame, can also be a filler of a slot *hiding place* in some frame *play hide and seek* of children playing in the neighbourhood. This models what is known as the "multiple view" of one and the same scene by different observers. Individual frames in a knowledge base can be connected through the relationship of instantiation and/or through the class: sub-class relationship. Combinations of frames in these ways are sometimes called "scenario".

While so far our focus has been on frames as stereotype objects, we shall now discuss an example of a frame as a stereotype event, Charniak's well known *painting* frame (Figure 18, cf. Metzing. ed. 1980: 62ff).

Figure 18 contains a simplified version of a frame for the complex event *painting*. The slot *vars* has as fillers preconditions of the overall event, *goal* specifies the goals of the agent of *painting*, and *event* has as ultimate fillers the ACTIONS and OPERATIONS of the agent (in the sense of our model in section 2.3.), without making any theoretical and representational distinction between ranks, though. The slot EVENT is filled, not by constant values, but by variables in turn, with the variable *painting* occurring eight times, in four cases even as second level embedding (*painting* 4-7). *Event*, in this representation, consists of four primary elements (*painting* 1,2,3,8), with *painting* 3 in turn consisting of *painting* 4-7, with *painting* 4 undergoing an (unbounded?) loop. The *leads to* and *comes from painting* statements specify preconditions/causes/reasons and consequences of the individual processes. Obviously, then, relationships between events which are connected by pointers can be, at least, causal and/or temporal. The command *loop* provides for recursion of categories like *painting*.

In the *painting* frame, we encounter a problem connected with the question of *terminal sharing* again: How do we decide, in a non-arbitrary way, which slots to assign to which frames? The slot *painting 1*, for example, which represents the cleaning of objects, has fillers which may occur in many different frames, at least as long as the representation remains on a certain rank. So, the question is whether one could not define a variable like *object not dirty*, which is read into any slot of the type *painting 1*, rather than working with a specific attribute-value pair *painting 1 : object not dirty* in the *painting* frame. In the approach above, such an attribute-value pair would have to be part of all the possible frames in which the cleaning of objects figures as a constituent.

Similarly, if we want to specify for a given instantiation, say, the filler for *instrument* under *vars*, then do we add the particular set of instruments to the slot in our *painting* frame only, or do we read them into the *painting* frame from a possible slot in some frame *storage room for tools*, which may also be part of our knowledge base?

It is problems such as the ones just discussed which need to be solved if the frame concept is implemented in any larger knowledge base. Sometimes these problems are regarded as constituting a fairly serious disadvantage of the entire frame approach (cf. McClelland, Rumelhart & Hinton 1986: 9). We shall come back to some aspects of frames as representations of stereotype events in section 2.6.6.

Let us now consider some applications of frames in the analysis of natural language in order to see what their role might be relative to a linguistic model. In

```
PAINTING (COMPLEX EVENT)
   VARS: (AGENT must be animate)
            (OBJECT must be a solid)
            (PAINT must be a liquid, usually is paint)
            (INSTRUMENT must be a solid, usually is either a roller or a
                                        paint brush, and should be absorbant)
            ...
   GOAL: PAINTING-GOAL (OBJECT has a coat of PAINT on it)
            COMES-FROM: (PAINTING6 via rules which say that
                                        paint on INSTRUMENT will stick to
                                        OBJECT, partially fulfilling the goal)
   EVENT: PAINTING1 (OBJECT not dirty)
                  COMES-FROM: (WASH-GOAL)
                  LEADS-TO: (NOT DIRTY-OBJECT1)
               PAINTING2 (everything nearby covered with newspaper)
               PAINTING3
                  (LOOP PAINTING4 (get PAINT on INSTRUMENT)
                     COMES-FROM: (rules which explain how immersing
                                        INSTRUMENT in PAINT will give desired
                                        result)
                     PAINTING5 (GREATER DRIP-THRESHOLD than the amount
                                        of PAINT on INSTRUMENT)
                     COMES-FROM: (rules showing how the regulation
                                        of pressure regulates the amount
                                        of PAINT)
                     PAINTING6 (INSTRUMENT is in contact with
                                        OBJECT)
                  PAINTING7 (GREATER amount of PAINT on
                                        INSTRUMENT than the
                                        STREAK-THRESHOLD)
                  COMES-FROM: either (regulating pressure)
                                        or (adding more paint via
                                        PAINTING4)
               PAINTING8 (PAINT removed from INSTRUMENT)
                  LEADS-TO: (rules expressing how if it were not removed
                                  INSTRUMENT would stiffen)
```

Figure 18. Charniak's painting frame (cf. Metzing, ed. 1980: 62ff.).
I am grateful to Dieter Metzing for the permission to reprint.

doing so, we are trying to link up with a similar discussion which we undertook in connection with our framework in section 2.4.2. The focus will be on the function of frames of getting access to information which is implicitly present in linguistic material without being structurally encoded. Technically, we are considering a particular kind of inferencing (for some of the following cf. Engelberg & Knöpfler 1982: 72ff).

Let us take the problem of *reference* first: One standard approach in linguistics, that of Systemic Functional Grammar, holds that reference of pro-forms can be *endophoric (anaphoric or cataphoric)*, or *exophoric* (cf. Halliday & Hasan 1976: 31ff). In the case of exephoric reference, is the expression *exophoric* to be interpreted as "present in the physical context of the utterance"? This view would seem to be too simplified, because any representation of the physical context is dependent on, firstly, the perspective of the observer, and, secondly, on the delicacy and the rank and level of description. To give an example: Depending on one's perspective, a given individual may be referred to as "hero, villain, boy, man,...", where the extensional, not, however, the intensional meaning of each of these terms is the same. Also, given a physicalist perspective, do we encode a man as *man*, or by enumerating his body parts, or even by enumerating the neurons making up his body? All this implies that we need some kind of organizing principle which will guide us in generating representations of some context of situation.

Now, let us take a case of text processing, where exophoric reference plays a role:

(14) *John went into a restaurant. The waiter brought him the menu.*

How do we explain linguistically the use of the two definite articles? Or, from the point of view of information retrieval, how do we know which are the referents of the two nominal groups containing *the*? Observe that we are assuming that neither the *waiter*, nor the *menu* have been mentioned in the previous text, yet are now linguistically marked as "identifiable", which implies referential identifiability in the situation of the utterance. A linguistic explanation would rely on the notions of "given" and "new" information: The waiter and the menu would be said to be *given* in the sense that the author of the text assumes the referents of these *nominal groups* to be present in the reader/hearer's memory. These referents, though, are not explicitly mentioned in the preceding text, if there is any, nor are they present in the physical situation of the utterance. Using the frame approach, we might say that a certain frame is "evoked" by the "header" : *restaurant* in the processor of this text. This would imply the evokation of slots like waiter, menu, table, meal, bill etc. automatically, and these slots, or rather the concepts and propositions filling them, may function as referents for exophoric reference in the text. In this way, frames can be used to model what is generally called "non-explicit information in a text", or rather, one aspect of non-explicit information. It should perhaps also be said that the same function in similar ways could be performed by *scripts*, or *schemata* or other types of mental models.

Another way in which the notion of a frame can be said to provide a method of dealing with non-explicit information is illustrated in the following example (Engelberg & Knöpfler 1982: 74):

(15) *John bought a ticket for the concert, but he did not go to hear it.*

The question here is how we can account for the conjunction *but*. If we analyze the two clauses into a logical form, there is no contradiction between them which would explain the adversative conjunction. From a purely logical point of view, there is no particular relationship between the two clauses, certainly not one of contradiciton. We need some way of projecting the states of affairs encoded in the two clauses against some "possible world", mental model, schema, script, or frame, if we want to account for the use of the adversative conjunction. The conjunction here encodes rhetorical structure (cf. Mann & Thompson 1987a,b), or intentions (cf. Grosz & Sidner 1986), rather than merely the connection between two states of affairs in some world. Another way of saying this is that the contradiction involved holds between certain inferences which the reader/hearer of the text draws from the first clause, and the proposition underlying the second clause. More precisely, it is the inferences which the speaker/writer of the text expects the reader/hearer to draw. Now, using an underlying frame representation of a standard situation of *going to a concert*, which would have a slot for, say, *necessary means for admission*, or something functionally equivalent, would help us to represent the inferencing which has to go on in decoding the text.

Another issue in the interpretation of texts is that of disambiguation, as illustrated in the following texts:

(16) *Herbert knew that it was time for him to pay his debts.*
So he went to the bank carrying all his money with him.

(17) *Herbert knew that it was time for him to take a break.*
So he went down to the bank (of the river) to sit down for a while.

In a purely linguistic analysis with non-deterministic parsing, the ambiguity arising from the polysemy of the word *bank* would have to be carried along in the analysis for a considerable time, i.e. there would be at least two lexically motivated representations, due to lexical ambiguity of the word *bank* alone, all the time. In practice, there are many more such lexically motivated representations. In fact, the question is whether the ambiguity could be resolved at all, unless one is willing to rely on extremely specific and ad-hoc semantic features and co-occurrence restrictions. Provided, though, that some data base was accessible which contained the two frames of *paying debts* and *leisure*, the ambiguity would not even arise, at least on the level of semantic interpretation, because only one reading would be accessible in any one of the possible frames to be entered. The important question is, of course, at what stage and dependent on what clue would the system enter one frame, rather than the other. This is easy to control in toy-environments, but far from trivial in large scale data-bases.

The traditional linguistic way of non-deterministic parsing certainly does not represent a plausible hypothesis about human information processing, yet even in a strictly engineering perspective, it has serious disadvantages, at least as far as computing times are concerned. As mentioned before, the opposite extreme of building into a system ad-hoc restrictions is also dangerous and theoretically unsatisfactory.

Yet another linguistic phenomenon where a frame can be helpful is one type of co-reference, as illustrated in the following text:

(18) *Jane walked Mary to the airport. She really was sad to see her go.*

The pronouns in the second clause realize one type of anaphoric reference, under which either *Jane* or *Mary* are available as antecedents for *she* and *her* (cf. our discussion at the end of 2.4.2. for a parallel case in the *Heinz*-story). Without the application of a concept of a frame, or one equivalent to it, it is difficult to see how one can avoid the representation of an ambiguity of reference which does not really exist in terms of information processing.

We shall not go further into applications of the frame-concept to linguistic analysis at this stage. What we have discussed should be sufficient to illustrate that some concept like *frame* is essential if we want to develop plausible and psychologically meaningful hypotheses about human information processing. It should also be clear that the frame concept does not provide a full solution to all our problems. In fact, practically all of the theoretical desiderata which we have discussed with respect to the framework developed in 2.3. exist in relation to the frame concept as well. To the extent that these desiderata can be seen as ways of future development, rather than as inherent weaknesses, the fundamental attraction of the frame concept, and related ideas, is not weakened.

Let us finally discuss a few questions connected with the representation of frames. This discussion is not intended as an in-depth investigation of questions of representation. Rather, it serves two functions in our context: In the first place, some of the questions which we have discussed in this section have to be related to matters of representation to give us a realistic understanding of the meaning of these issues. For example, when we are talking about conceptual or sense relationships between concepts in a knowledge base, the discussion is rather empty, against an artificial intelligence background, if there are no ideas involved about how such relationships can be represented.

In the second place, the questions of representation, which we shall raise very briefly, have a direct bearing on crucial aspects of the representation of such a framework as we have indicated in 2.3. above.

From the point of view of implementation, a frame is a property list or association list, which has the following general form (cf. Engelberg & Knöpfler 1982: 77):

atm	:	(ind1 prop1 ind2 prop2...)
atm	=	atom
ind	=	indicator
prop	=	property

A property is a value of the variable *ind*. If, then, under *atm* the name of the frame is given, *ind* will represent a slot and *prop* the value which the slot takes in the case of instantiation of the frame. Among frame languages are the frame representation language *FRL*, the knowledge representation language *KRL*, and *OBJTALK*. Certain relations between frames have to be defined to make the frame concept economical: A relation "a kind of" (*ako*) can be introduced which defines the relation of one frame to its superordinate frame. The relation "instance" defines the relationship between a frame and its subordinate frames. The terminology here will seem somewhat unfortunate to many linguists, because *the instance of* relationship is commonly applied to the *type-token* distinction, whereas *a kind of* will frequently be used for one direction of the *class-subclass* relationship. *Ako* and *instance* are slots in a frame. Using these relations, we can define property inheritance as the transference of properties from a superpordinate frame to a subordinate frame and its instantiations. The obvious linguistic counterpart would be *hyponymy*. From this perspective, it also follows that a frame can be a subordinate frame (*ako*) of different superordinate frames (a toy car *ako* toy and *ako* car), which, in turn, may enter into all the permitted relationships among themselves. The principle of property inheritance implies that the problem of multiple storage of values of slots is partly solved for those frames which are in an *ako* or an *instance* relationship. It also implies that these relationships have to be handled very carefully in more extensive data-bases if excessive wrong inferencing is to be avoided. A toy car may be *ako* toy and *ako* car, but, say, a birthday party is not *ako* birthday. The linguistic knowledge about classes of compounds should be taken into account here from the very start.

There are certain additional procedures attached to frames to make the data base in which they form part of the structure more economical: In *FRL* or *KRL*, for example, an *if-added*-procedure can be attached to slots in frames, which accomplishes the following: If some value is assigned to a slot in instantiation, that same value will be given to certain other slots in different frames. This will, obviously, be necessary in frames which are connected through property inheritance, but not only in the case of such frames. *If-added* procedures operate on incoming data. A parallel procedure *if-removed* operates on outgoing data, obviously in the opposite direction: Values removed from the slot in one frame will also be removed from certain other frames.

Even from the few points we have mentioned in connection with the representation of frames, it can be seen that, as soon as we approach a process even remotely resembling the complex processes going on in natural language production and comprehension, the question of parallel processing has to be raised (cf., among many others, Bateman 1987: 30ff), because many of these processes, such as the multifunctional determination of sequence and form of linguistic structures (cf. Kay. 1985: 252), may have to be conceived of as parallel processes.

Perhaps the most interesting set of questions connected with frames and their representation from the point of view of current (text-) linguistics is that of inferencing. The term "inferences" is used in various senses:

In the most narrow definition, *inferencing* refers to all the valid propositions which we can derive through the relationship of *implication* from a given proposition in the form permitted by the predicate calculus. This type of inferencing has the advantage of being well defined. It has the disadvantage, from the perspective of text comprehension, that it will not cover the more interesting type of inferencing in natural language processing, while covering a huge amount of inferencing which is probably of only marginal interest in natural language understanding, such as the inference from any positive statement of the negation of its negative counterpart.

In a wider sense, *inferencing* includes pragmatic presuppositions and conventional or conversational implicatures (cf. Grice 1975; Gazdar 1979; Sperber and Wilson 1986).

In yet a wider sense, *inferencing* is used to refer to any type of conclusion that can be drawn with some justification from a sentence, a set of facts, or, indeed, any lawful connection between structures representing knowledge in some data base.

It is the third kind of meaning under which the term *inferencing* has been used in our present discussion, except where explicitly stated otherwise. Although this use of the term is comparatively vague, it seems to be the most appropriate use in connection with natural language processing, certainly as long as the subject of processing is to be taken as human, or some system modelling human information processing. In artificial intelligence systems of that type, we frequently find the distinction between "read time inferences" and between "question time inferences": Read time inferences are inferences which are made at the time of actual input of information and then entered into the database along with the explicitly encoded information. One of the major difficulties in this connection is that of deciding, in a non ad-hoc way, which aspects of information are relevant and which should be dropped. Question time inferences are made only if and when a question is asked requiring the specific information to be inferred. A major problem associated with this type of inferencing is that of search and response time: If the relevant information is deeply embedded in the structure of the data base, the inferencing processes may take a considerable time.

Sometimes, a distinction is also made between "forward inferencing" and "backward inferencing". In the case of forward inferencing, assumptions are deducted from the valid facts in a data base. In the case of backward inferencing, underlying assumptions are deducted from a question posed to the system, and these assumptions are checked against information in the knowledge base.

Probably still at the centre of techniques of inferencing are techniques of theorem-proving. With these techniques, as with the others mentioned, one of the key problems is that of the combinatory explosion of inferences to be made, if at any given point in the process all the inferences which are permitted by the system are actually drawn. Therefore, certain heuristics have to be used to restrict these processes. These techniques may be as crude as setting upper boundaries for computing time and space. Whereas such techniques certainly play a role in human information processing, they do not give us great insight into the more interesting processes.

Another technique for guiding and restricting inferencing relies on expert knowledge of some kind, i.e. in-depth knowledge in a restricted domain. This kind of knowledge can be used to generate certain degrees of likelihood of the validity of a given inference in view of the possible and likely states of affairs for the domain concerned.

We shall not go any further in our discussion of representational aspects and procedural aspects of implementing and operating a frame guided knowledge base. What we have said should enable us to form a somewhat more realistic assessment of the status of the concept of frames: It does open the potential of modelling certain aspects of natural language processing, but this statement has to be understood rather literally. The potential is opened, though in no way exhausted, because current techniques of representation and operation of such a system need to be developed further. Also, as we shall see in the following section, if the conceptual and theoretical status of the concept of *frame* is considered in connection with ideas which were developed earlier in linguistics, the question arises of how much of it is genuinely new, and how much of it is just a reformulation of already existing ideas.

2.6.6 Implications of concepts from artificial intelligence for linguistic semantics

In this section, we shall briefly raise the question of what the implications are for linguistics from what we have said about conceptions of knowledge representation in artificial intelligence. Is there, for example, or should there be, a one-way flow of ideas from linguistics to artificial intelligence, or is it rather the other way round, i.e. should linguistic models for the *context of situation* be derived from models developed in artificial intelligence? There is, of course, the possibility of a mutually beneficial influence between these disciplines, apart from the two extreme alternatives mentioned. The question is not merely a rhetorical one, as many people who are active in one of the fields concerned will admit. It should be noted at the outset that we are not discussing here the case of syntactic theories, such as Lexical Functional Grammar (Bresnan.ed. 1982), Generalized Phrase Structure Grammar (Gazdar et al. 1985), Functional Unification Grammar (Kay 1985), Government & Binding (Chomsky 1981), Head-Driven Phrase Structure Grammar (Pollard & Sag 1987) and others, and their interaction with our field. This would certainly be a highly complex topic of its own, yet is not directly relevant to the points we want to make in our present context, as these theories do not place a major focus on the types of knowledge representation which we have been discussing (but cf. the use of general concepts like "classification" or "unification" in both syntax and semantics in the past, as in Mellish 1988).

It would appear that in the area of knowledge representation in artificial intelligence, the main influences are linguistics, philosophy, and cognitive psychology (cf. also Engelkamp, Lorenz & Sandig 1987). As far as ideas from linguistics are concerned, they usually underwent some simplification in the process of being imported into artificial intelligence. This would seem to apply to semantic networks, such as we have discussed, in particular, which usually contain only a subset of the sense relations formulated in, say, structural semantics. One may suspect that the reason behind these simplifications is partly a simple matter of cost and time, but partly also a matter of insufficiently clear definitions of linguistic sense relations. The same could probably be said about the importation of semantic case roles for the analysis of clauses into many systems. So far, then, one could advocate a more comprehensive input from linguistics into artificial intelligence, provided that linguists are able and willing to define their concepts, like sense relations, semantic cases, semantic features etc., in a way which is sufficiently explicit to serve as a useful input. Once this obligation is recognized within linguistics, it can be regarded as a very useful spin-off effect for linguistics from the collaboration. More practically, working in an artificial intelligence environment context may force a linguist in several respects to clarify his/her thoughts to the point where at least operationalizations can be achieved. Operationalizations, though, should not be confused with ad-hoc devices, which will make anything "run" on a machine for a restricted system.

Now, while for some time in the earlier history of artificial intelligence, one may, with some justification, speak of a mainly one-way flow of ideas from linguistics into artificial intelligence, in so far as there was any influence, the case of frames seems to have reversed that tendency to some extent: In the case of notions like *frame, script, schema, scenario*, the flow of ideas seems to have been from cognitive psychology into artificial intelligence, and either from there, or from cognitive psychology directly, into linguistics. Very frequently, linguists have looked into one of these disciplines rather than into the history of their own discipline. Yet, for a considerable time, there have existed traditions in linguistics trying to incorporate models of context and/or situation and /or activity, such as the traditions associated with J.R. Firth and, following him, Systemic Functional Grammar, as well as

Tagmemics and schools of thought around Dell Hymes (cf. Brown & Yule 1983; Steiner 1985 b for further references and illustrations). All of these models have had their weaknesses, yet these seem to be of a kind like some of the weaknesses of current frame-conceptions, of which we shall briefly mention a few:

One difficulty associated with the idea of a *frame*, which we have alluded to before, should come to mind immediately: How can we reach decisions in a non-arbitrary way about the boundaries and about the specifity of frames? A more detailed formulation of this question would be the following:
Which, precisely, are the slots that must be included in a given frame, and how specific should these slots be? Should we work with rather general slots like, say, ACTION, PLAN, GOAL, MATERIAL OBJECT etc., as we did in sections 2.3 and 2.4., or should we assume more specific slots like, say, *armchair, wheelchair, dinner table*, in the case of some frame *living room*? In existing systems operating with frames, these decisions are usually reached rather pragmatically, yet for the integration of frames into a more extensive knowledge base, general principles are obviously needed.

Another problematic area emerges if we consider the possibility of using frames to model prototypes (cf. Rosch & Mervis 1975). The question is gaining importance as certain linguistic approaches give a central place to the notion of a "prototype" (cf. Langacker 1983; Lakoff & Johnson 1980; Hudson 1984). Approaches incorporating the notions of *prototype* or *stereotype* are particularly attractive if we want to come to grips with the problem of "fuzzy edges" in semantics, a problem which has long been known to plague any semantic approach relying heavily on categorial features of a "yes/no"-type. However, it is not immediately obvious how one should incorporate the idea of a prototypical rather than a "categorial" semantics into the concept of frame. It is true that there is the notion of "default values", which are assigned to slots in the absence of contradicting information, and at least a stereotype could presumably be conceived of as a frame with instantiated default values for its slots. The idea of a prototype, though, seems to present more difficulties: How, for example, should we incorporate the notions of more central and less central features in the definition and identification of any object or situation? What would be a more prototypical token for a given type than some other token within the constraints of a frame approach?

With these remarks, we do not intend to imply that there is no solution within a frame approach for such problems. What we do want to express is that the solution is not automatically given, and, indeed, not obvious.

Let us briefly compare some aspects of the approach used in sections 2.3. and 2.4. with the *painting* frame, because both represent information about human actions (cf. for a reproduction of the *painting* frame section 2.6.5.3., Figure 18):

The framework of ACTIVITY outlined in 2.3. and 2.4. is similar to a generic frame for human goal-directed actions. There are a number of minor differences between such an *action* frame and the *painting* frame: The *painting* frame operates with only one rank of structures, units of which can, however, be generated and assigned recursively. There is no theoretical distinction between a unit and elements of a unit, on the one hand, and other units of a different rank filling this unit, on the other. The theory of activity incorporates recursion of elements on one rank, as well as embedding on different ranks, as outlined above. Both of the approaches have the notion of "re-entry" built into them, the theory of activity through certain types of recursion, the frame approach, as in the *painting* frame through the device of embedded property lists. *Painting* 4-7, for example, are property lists embedded in the property list representing *painting* 3. The slots in our tables representing the SITUATION are very close, indeed, to the slots of the *painting* frame, and instantiation functions in much the same way in both approaches.

We do not intend to imply any major claims of superiority for a more linguistics oriented approach. What we do want to draw attention to is that while the importation of ideas like the frame idea into linguistics is not necessarily unmotivated, the essence of such an idea does not constitute a major new development relative to what has been discussed in the linguistic community for a considerable time predating the development of the frame-approach.
However, it seems to us that approaches like the frame approach can, indeed, lead to progress in linguistics, if they are not diluted too much in the course of implementation: Within these approaches, there is, as we have already said earlier on, a certain pressure for operationalizations of concepts and procedures, and it is precisely in this area that many linguistic approaches seem to have done rather badly in the past.

In the light of considerations like the one we have just engaged in, there should be no question of a mutual isolation between linguistics and artificial intelligence: A flow of ideas in both directions would seem to be promising and necessary, with artificial intelligence providing a testing ground for linguistic ideas and, in the best case, developing these ideas further in the sense of making them more precise and transparent. That it should not become the only testing ground for linguistic theories should be obvious from the entire history of applied linguistics in all its richness and diversity.

The more recent history of Systemic linguistics provides one of the most obvious examples where implementation and formalization of a linguistic theory provide a crucial instrument for theoretical development (Matthiessen & Bateman. in press; Patten & Ritchie 1987; Kasper 1987, 1988 a,b). This theoretical development, though, presupposes prior linguistic work that has reached a certain quantity as well as a certain level of explicitness, as, for example, in Fawcett (1980) or in Halliday (1985a). Without this prior linguistic work, implementation is in danger of becoming ad-hoc and impressionistic, and formalization is in danger of being empty of linguistic content. Given a certain stage of development, however, implementation and formalization will become decisive tools for further development.

2.6.7 Knowledge representation within the present approach

After discussing some more general issues in the area of artificial intelligence and knowledge representation, we shall now go on to discuss in a bit more detail the more specific issues arising within an approach such as the one outlined here. Outside of the present study, the context for this discussion is first and foremost the implementation of such an approach in the text generation system KOMET (cf. Steiner et al. 1990; Bateman & Wanner. 1990; Wanner & Bateman. 1990). Some ideas closely related to the ones presented here have been explored in publications and implementations of a conceptual system for knowledge based machine translation (Bateman, Kasper, Schütz & Steiner 1989, 1990; Schütz 1989). Work on the "upper model" derives from Bateman, Kasper, Moore & Whitney 1989, and from earlier work by Halliday, Mann, and Matthiessen. Closely related work in the areas of generating goal hierarchies and their relationship to texts can be found in Moore and Paris (1989), and, with particular reference to the notion of "register" in Bateman and Paris (1989). A representation language for driving text generation of the type we envisage here can be found in work by Kasper and Whitney (1989). We shall thus be concentrating on a particular set of ideas which have a strong internal coherence and which also have a recent history of implementation. In the present context, what gives this set of ideas its coherence is a certain way of looking at the distinction between linguistic and non-linguistic knowledge:

There is only one type of knowledge, ultimately deriving from goal-directed activities of agents in situations. A highly structured system for organizing this knowledge is language, but there are others, like various practices of members of a culture used for communication and for other purposes. The structure of language is the "cristallized" practice of members of a culture for pursuing their various types of activities. So far, then, we have mentioned two properties of knowledge:

- One of the most highly organized form of organizing knowledge is language. We can therefore use a sufficiently developed lingustic theory as a guideline to what to look for in knowledge representation in general. We shall require of whatever kinds of knowledge representation that they contain at least those types of information sufficient for a determination of lingustic structures. Note that knowledge representation in this sense necessarily includes models of s-peakers and hearers, because otherwise certain types of linguistic knowledge are systematcially underdetermined. Defaults can be used to counterbalance remaining areas of underdetermination, not, however, as an ad-hoc way out of theoretical underdetermination.
- Although language is a particularly highly structured system for organizing knowledge, it is not the only one. We therefore also require that non-linguistic ways of organizing knowledge have to be free of the particular constraints imposed by language, i.e. that types of relationships within a non-linguistic mode of knowledge organization may be different from the linguistic ones.

The resulting question then inevitably is that of how the two ways of organizing knowledge are related. As far as the "potential" of that relationship is concerned, it has been a commonplace assumption for a long time that anything can linguistically be encoded in any possible way permitted by the structure of language. Seen from this end, the structure of whatever non-linguistic way of knowledge representation systematically underdermines the structure of linguistic ways of encoding it. On the other end of the extreme, people, especially in some of the artificial intelligence traditions referred to earlier on, have tended to assume that what at best are unmarked ways of endocing knowledge is a hard-wired connection between non-linguistic and linguistic ways of knowledge representation. From this we get text generators which always encode "events" as verbs and "entities" as nouns and "qualities" as adjectives or adverbs. None of this will be sufficient for a theoretically and practically interesting text generator. The two key ideas which, in the present approach, will provide the theoretical link are *the goal structure of texts* and *the multi-functional structure of texts.*

We shall approach the question of knowledge representation from two ends, at the one extreme being "non-linguistic knowledge" and at the other "linguistic knowledge". It will be seen that the two are far from independent of each other: the linguistic knowledge, it will be seen, informs the principles according to which so-called non-linguistic knowledge is structured.

We have outlined the theoretical interface between text structure and the structure of SITUATIONS and ACTIONS in 2.4.5. At the non-linguistic end, then, we need

- knowledge about the slots of our SITUATIONS and the structure of ACTIONS which are embedded within them;
- knowledge about what the author's goals are in producing texts, and what the intended audience is.

From these types of knowledge, we generate representations such as the ones we have been discussing in this study. So far, of course, we are describing just another variant of current approaches to text generation which contain an account of speaker's goals and a model of a hearer. The characteristic features of our own approach would seem to lie more at the other end of the extreme, which is the interface of linguistic knowledge with the types of knowledged referred to so far.

Let us now briefly discuss two sets of examples (I) and (II) which should bring out some of the rich interplay of factors arising out of a functional theory of language in our context:

Example (I)

(1) *We first thought about the idea. Then we got quite excited about it.*
(2) *After we had thought about the idea, we got quite excited about it.*
(3) *After some thoughts about the idea, we got quite excited about it.*

Let us bring out some of the ways in which (1) to (3) differ, simply using Systemic theory to search for the relevant structural properties of linguistic utterances:

- If we assume a rank scale of units of texts as described in 2.4.5., then the highest ranking heads in (1) are those encoding the clause combining relations between the two clauses involved (for our notion of "ranked heads" cf. Bateman & Paris. 1989). In (2), we have a hypotactic rather than a paratactic structure, in which, according to a Halliday (1985a) type analysis of hypotactic adverbial clauses, the highest ranking head would still be the conjunction expressing clause combining, but the next highest ranking head would be the verb of the main clause, followed by the verb of the dependent clause. In (1), there would be two equally ranked heads on the second level, which would be the two main verbs. A more traditional dependency analysis of (2) would have the conjunction as a lower ranked head, but what counts in the present context is the difference as such. Example (3), of course, has the main verb as the highest head under any dependency analysis. These observations cover some aspects of the "logical structure" of units.
- In terms of experiential meaning, i.e. in terms of *constituency*, (1) is very different from both (2) and (3). But even (2) differs considerably form (3), in that (2) fully encodes a "dependent situation", whereas (3) has a covert processor of the "embedded situation".
- The fact, in turn, that (3) has a covert processor where (2) has an overt one is partly textually motivated: (3) has the *circumstance* as experiential *theme*, where (2) has the *processor*. The motivation cannot be experiential in itself, because the covert processor must be present in the semantic structure of (3), due to syntactic roles of control of English.
- In terms of interpersonal meaning, (1) and (2) are closer to each other than either one of them is to (3): they realize identical options in *mood* and *modality*, where (3) does not, for grammatical reasons, encode that type of information assuming that a PP(NP()) configuration in English does not allow these options, which is a slight oversimplification, but helps to express the point which we want to make.

How can we control these meanings? Using a functional approach to language, as Systemic theory does, the "chooser & inquiry framework" associated with the grammar will systematically address the knowledge representations to find these types of information. They are not to be found in the representation of states of affairs as such, but rather in the goal structures of the speakers.

Example (II):

(4) *We lit a fire. Because of this, the temperature rose.*
(5) *The fact that we lit a fire caused the temperature to rise.*
(6) *Our lighting of the fire increased the temperature.*

The texts (4) through (6) differ in respects similar to those in (1) to (3). We would like to concentrate here on the choice of a certain type of process realized in the verbs *to rise* vs. *to increase*. In terms of transitivity, i.e. experiential meaning, (6) expresses causation+the resulting process in its highest ranking head, making the "cause" thematically the unmarked theme. In (5), the highest ranking head encodes the causation, but dissociated form its resulting process. The syntactic control properties of *cause* in English ensure that the syntactic direct object of *cause* does not receive its participant role from *cause*, but from the affected-only verb *rise*. Still, because of these same control properties, it is part of the *rheme* of the matrix clause, rather than the *theme* of the constituent clause. Seen in the textual perspective, then, the choice of the causative verb *cause* instead of the affected-centred, ergative verb *increase* is motivated by the goal of having some *participant role* of an embedded clause as part of the thematic structure of a superordinate clause. (For an implementation of this type of analysis of causation cf. Steiner 1989). (4) is different again: It gives the causing event the status of an independent event, which is then linked to the event which it causes, but this time not at all experientially, but textually through an explicit clause combining relation and anaphoric reference (*this*).

These examples should be sufficient in the present context to illustrate the direction of an approach such as the one outlined above. We shall not go down to the level of actual tools for implementing such a strategy, because this is not the task of the present section, and because these tools have essentially been developed in a different connection. One essential component which still needs to be developed is a theoretically motivated and systematic connection between all the various connections between concepts in the upper model, some knowledge base, and the grammar itself. This will form a core of the task of a theoretically motivated development in an overall system of text generation.

We shall now give the outline of a system architecture for a text generation system incorporating an approach of the type advocated here: Assume that the system has the following components, as seen from "inside out", i.e. from "language" to "domain":

(1) Linguistic grammars covering ranks up to the clause complex, and possibly beyond, encoded in, say, Kasper's (1987,1988) extended version of *functional unification grammar*. These grammars are then used in parsing and generation, say with an extended version of PATR-II, a parser for unification based grammar formalisms, or LOOM, a knowledge representation language (as suggested in Kasper 1989) derived from KL-ONE. The idea of using KL-ONE - type knowledge representation languages in parsing is illustrated in the appendix of Brachman and Schmolze (1985), LOOM is described in MacGregor & Bates (1987). The grammars will include the system networks which we shall be discussing in section 3 of this study.

(2) The result of a parsing in (1) is the representation of a sentence, either as the more classical feature description of the type of *functional unification grammar* plus some extensions, or a labelled tree as in Steiner, Eckert, Roth and Winter (1988).
(3) Component (2) will be translated into an expression in "sentence planning language" SPL, in the way it is shown in Bateman, Kasper, Schütz and Steiner (1989), reproduced below:

```
(K1 / Know-Process
     :senser (W2 / Person
                    :mutliplicity-Q multiple)
     :phenomenon (Q3 / Quality-Ascription
                        :domain (A4 / Algorithm
                                      :identifiability-Q identifiable
                                      :multiplicity-Q unitary)
                        :range (C5 / Complex-Quality))
     :speechact (A6 / Assertion
                      :polarity positive
                      :tense present
                      :speaker S7)
     :member-set-Q (S7 W2) included)
```

Representation of : We know that the algorithm is complex.

The terms in the SPL representation are, at least in the area of *experiential meaning*, no longer grammatical terms, but rather abstracted from these. The purely grammatical relationships like constituency, dependency, linear precedence, are replaced by the corresponding upper model relationships as far as possible.
(4) A component generating ACTION and SITUATION representations out of domain knowledge (cf. 2.4.5. and 2.3.). These would also have to express concepts as well as relationships, such as constituency (part-of), dependency, linear precedence (temporal structure of ACTIONS). One type of representations which is used for the same purpose in a closely related model is the one discussed in Moore and Paris (1989) for the intentional structure of texts in the sense of Grosz and Sidner (1986).

Given these components, one could try to map the representations generated in (4) directly into those of (2). This would pesuppose that there is a relatively direct relationship between the structure of ACTIONS and linguistic structures. We have followed that approach in some detail in section 2.4.5. The primitives of (4) would be derived from the theory of goal-directed action, the values for any specific ACTION from the domain. One could, within that approach, still choose to generate constituency through an upper modell, while leaving the generation of dependency and linear precedence to the structure of the ACTION. Alternatively, one could map (4) into (3) first, trying to develop upper modell - type components for non-experiential meanings as well.

What is of interest here is not so much the implementation of such an overall structure within one particular system, but rather an account of the types of knowledge which seem necessary to model an approach of the type advocated here. The computational tools are available, but the decisive question, before concentrating on the tools, always has to be that of conceptual clarity, and it is to such questions that we shall keep returning in the sections to follow.

Chapter 3
Some variables in semantic complexity in child language seen as goal-directed action

3.1 Introduction

In sections 2.3 and 2.4, we outlined a framework for the analysis and representation of the level of *context of situation* within Systemic Linguistics, applicable to contexts which are created by some goal-directed action of human beings. We also illustrated rules and representations of this framework in several sample analyses on the level of ACTIVITY. Another analysis on that level will be undertaken in 3.2. below. Section 2.5 introduced, on a general level, some predictions derived from this framework for certain variables in semantic complexity. We mentioned three possible perspectives, under which such predictions can be made. Of these perspectives, we shall, in the remainder of this study, adopt the third: We shall apply our framework of analysis again to a corpus of child language data, but this time only in order to generate independent variables for measuring certain types of semantic complexity. The independent variables will be elements of ACTIONS, more specifically, the PLANNING and EXECUTION phases of the children's ACTIONS.

In relation to other studies of child language, we want to stress the character of our study as exploratory: We are not, at this stage, aiming towards full statistical significance; in fact, the size of the sample which we shall be investigating is too small for that, amounting only to a few hundred utterances. We are aware that there are significance measures for small data samples, but in view of their controversial predictive power, we shall refrain from relying on them. What we are aiming at is the exposition of elements of a research structure, involving a controlled corpus, independent and dependent variables, motivation of these, metrics for semantic complexity against the background of Systemic Functional Grammar and a framework for interpretation.

However, it is only in relation to the remainder of our study that the main purpose of our investigation of some child language data emerges: We are aiming at providing some independent motivation for the framework put forward in 2.3. The motivation from within Systemic theory has been given in 2.2-2.4. As usual, however, in order to motivate a given approach we have to look outside the theory itself, a process which is known as "independent motivation" (Martin 1987). We shall try to illustrate that the framework which we have outlined is not only meaningful within the theory of SFG, but that it may help to explain certain phenomena outside the theory itself, that it is independently motivated in that sense. In what follows, we shall go into some detail as far as certain phenomena in child language are concerned, and also as far as certain components of Systemic semantics are concerned. Yet, in all this, it is essential not to lose sight of our overriding goal, because it is only relative to that goal that many decisions made in our exploratory investigation can be motivated.

Let us start with a few remarks about the corpus which we shall be using: It is published in four volumes (Fawcett & Perkins 1980), and has been introduced and discussed in several places elsewhere (Fawcett & Perkins 1981; Scott 1982, 1984; Ford-Meyer, Paskay & Spruiell. 1988). The linguistic material in the corpus is controlled for sex, age, social class, and situation type (cf. Fawcett & Perkins 1980: Introduction). How do the variables which we shall be investigating relate to other studies on child language?

In a way, there has been a parallel development in linguistics and in child language studies, in that the focus of attention shifted in the course of time from phonology (Jakobson 1941; Weir 1962) and morphology (Berko 1958) through syntax (McNeill 1970) to semantics (Hayes 1970), pragmatics, and conversational and discourse structure (Romaine 1984; McTear 1985; Elliot 1981: 168ff.) This development is so well documented (for example in Reich 1986), that there is no reason to add another survey here. As far as the choice of independent variables is concerned, age has, of course, always been the first choice, but more recently, others, like social class, sex, or situation type have been included (cf. for example Romaine 1984: 82ff. and 159ff.; Elliot 1981: 168ff.). Our choice of "phase of action" can be seen in the context of this particular development. It is also this context which motivates our concentration on children who are beyond the primary phase of language development, which again is characteristic of many recent studies that go beyond the investigation of syntax.

Useful surveys of child language studies in Europe and Germany (West) in particular can be found in Levelt, Mills & Karmiloff-Smith (1981) , and in Mills (1984). There seems to be no study so far which uses Systemic Functional Grammar as its main theoretical background. As far as the investigation of semantic parameters is concerned, there are a few studies of areas related to what we shall be investigating (cf. Miller 1976; Stephany 1976; Anders 1982; Clahsen 1984). Yet, again, these studies cannot be related easily to our own explorations in so far as the independent variables are different from our own, and in so far as the dependent variables are derived from different linguistic models.

As far as the choice of independent variables is concerned, there appears to be a tradition of research within Germany, which bears a certain relationship to our own interests (cf. Klann-Delius et al 1985; Nikolaus, Quasthoff & Repp 1984): Both projects used a framework for analyzing actions and situations which is oriented towards some variant of a "Handlungstheorie" (theory of activity) to generate independent variables and research hypotheses. To that extent, but not with respect to the linguistic model used, there is a methodological relationship.

Whereas our choice of *phase of action* as independent variable would appear to be something relatively new, as far as child language development studies are concerned, our choice of dependent variables does place us in a definite tradition of research stimulated by Systemic Linguistics (cf. Halliday 1975; Wells, Montgomery & McClure 1979; Painter 1984). It is with studies like these that our investigation of dependent variables can be seen to link up directly.

In summary, then, let us state what we want to achieve in section 3 of this study:

The main goal, as we have already said above, is to give an independent motivation for the theoretical framework developed in 2.3 and 2.4. In working towards that goal, we shall be pursuing four subordinate goals, all of which could have a motivation of their own, and thus might be of interest outside the particular set up of the present study:

- We shall set up and test certain hypotheses about some areas of semantic complexity in child language. Sections 3.3 and 3.4 in particular reflect the theoretical and methodological issues connected with our formulation of hypotheses in some detail.
- We shall try to extend Systemic studies in child language to areas which have been neglected so far.
- We shall have to evaluate critically certain core areas of Systemic semantics, which will include modifications of existing Systemic tools. These modifications, again, should be of interest to the theory of SFG independently of child language studies.
- We shall try to make a modest contribution to child language studies, investigating a hitherto neglected independent variable and outlining the analytical tools for such an investigation.

It is against the background of these goals that the following investigation should finally be evaluated.

3.2 Analyzing a children's play session as goal-directed action

3.2.1 Methodological issues

It is certainly a key issue in the analysis of a sequence of human ACTIONS how a coder identifies and classifies units at the rank s/he is working on. Current standard procedures are explained in various places (cf. Cranach & Kalbermatten 1982, or Klann-Delius et al 1985: 85ff.). One standard procedure is to train a number of coders in the particular framework in which one is working and then to test the degree of consistency in coding. In the area of the analysis of goal-directed ACTION, as of now, an intercoder consistency of 70% is already considered acceptable (Klann-Delius 1985: 85). Independently of whether or not one is satisfied with this standard, one has at least to be aware of it when engaging in this kind of description. In the present study, the issue by itself is not of overriding importance, because we are only working on a pilot study, and the coding can be done by one person. The present codings were checked in various seminars in the course of working on the task with groups of students. Judging from these experiences, it is realistic to expect that the method illustrated here has every chance of conforming to the standards mentioned. Some of the theoretically interesting problems confronting the coder in this type of analysis will be discussed below, where it will become obvious that the major source of inconsistency is not the formulation of the framework as such, but the important fact that the assignemt of a representation to any segment of text on the basis of our framework is, like any such assignment in linguistic analysis, a process of interpretation. This accounts for the existence of multiple analyses of the same piece of data, just as in syntax. A somewhat more disturbing fact may seem to be that the boundaries of segments are ambiguous in some cases - a problem which occurs on any level of analysis in linguistics, but more so on the level of ACTION than on the others. Finally, section 3.2. will contain a further theoretical discussion and refinement of the notions of *temporal vs. logical structure of* ACTIONS.

3.2.1.1 Identification of elements of action. When looking at the transcript of a play session like that of the 12 B Boys (cf. Appendix 2), the question arises how we identify phases of ACTIONS, and the PLANNING phases in particular, because these are the distinguishing characteristics of ACTIONS in the present framework. The first segmentation here certainly has to be made on the basis of an intuitive understanding of what constitutes a PLANNING phase. After this initial assignment, certain further steps have to be taken which provide a sort of check up on the initial assumptions:

When we have tentatively identified a given phase as a PLANNING phase, knowing that this automatically identifies an ACTION for us, we need to find the corresponding MOTIVATION, EXECUTION, and EVALUATION phases as far as possible. In our particular data, MOTIVATION phases constitute the only major gap in that connection. We construct a first rudimentary model of what the ongoing ACTION is. In the case of our 12 B Boys play session, this gives us the list of PLANNING phases shown in Table 55, which we will designate by their goals (page and line numbers in Table 55 refer to the transcript as in Appendix 2).

The list in Table 55 does not imply that we have 21 ACTIONS in this play session. In the first place, there is duplication in the list at several places, which may either mean different ACTIONS, if the referents of the goals are not the same, which is unlikely, or else it means that the PLANNING of certain ACTIONS is either portioned or simply interrupted at certain points. In fact, what we have in our list are around 10-13 different ACTIONS as identified by PLANNING phases.

Table 55. A listing of planning phases of a play session

Temporal sequence:		Page, Line:		
1.	Road vs. Path	55,12	-	55,21
2.	Roof	57,5	-	57,13
3.	Roof	57,28	-	58,14
4.	Fencing	59,23	-	60,11
5.	Pavement	60,12	-	60,16
6.	Fencing vs. Gate	60,17	-	61,3
7.	x	61,11	-	61,15
8.	Country House	61,16	-	62,2
9.	Fencing, Path	62,16	-	62,22
10.	Fencing, Trees	63,5	-	63,6
11.	Double Gate	63,26	-	63,37
12.	Roof	64,19	-	64,24
13.	Bus Stop	64,25	-	64,29
14.	Person, he	65,1	-	65,4
15.	Bloke	66,12	-	66,15
16.	Ladder	66,16	-	66,26
17.	Inside	67,2	-	67,16
18.	x	68,7	-	68,14
19.	Window (in roof)	68,23	-	68,26
20.	White window	69,27	-	70,9
21.	x	71,4	-	71,5

3.2.1.2 Identification of hierarchies of actions. Looking at the list of lexical items designating goals of PLANNING in the play session under analysis here, we could certainly construct several different hierarchical orderings. In other words, we could assign different structures to the ACTIONS we are describing in terms of relationships between their goals. This is what we have been calling *logical structure* of ACTIONS, distinguishing it from *temporal structure.* Let us give two examples (cf. Figures 19 and 20).

The first of our possible goal-hierarchies would describe an ACTION, in which the children are building a bus stop with an inside and a roof, a road leading up to it or past it, and fencing around it. The interpretations of the branches , i.e. the relationships we have used here, are the *part of* (P) relation and the *adjacency* (A) relation (cf. section 2.6. for a discussion of relations of this type in conceptual networks). The roof would have a window and a ladder leaning against it. An obvious example of inferencing in such a graph would be informally:

((bus-stop P roof) *and* (roof P window))
→ bus-stop P window

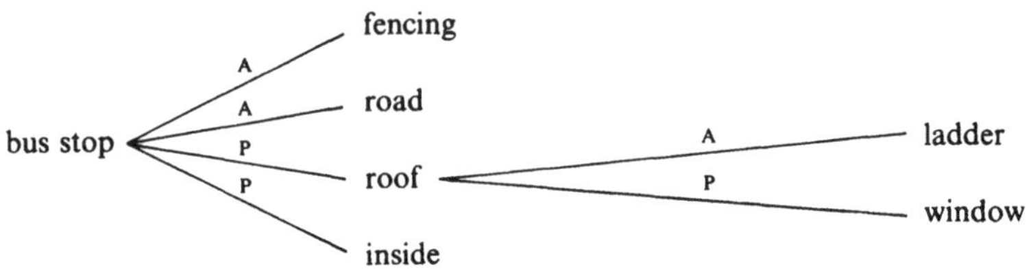

Figure 19. A possible goal-hierarchy (1)

through logical transitivity, where *P* must be read as *has a*. Obviously, *transitivity* as a logical relation has nothing to do with grammatical *transitivity* of clauses as discussed in 3.4. This type of inferencing, as is well known, cannot always be translated into natural language, as shown in the following example:

((arm P hand) *and* (hand P fingers))
→ (arm P fingers)

through logical transitivity. However, linguistically and in terms of SFG, whereas

[*attribuant associative associated*] R *an arm has a hand,*

and

[*attribuant associative associated*] R *a hand has fingers,*

are both acceptable, the direct translation of the "world knowledge inference" is at least questionable in terms of linguistic acceptability:

[*attribuant associative associated*] R ?*an arm has fingers*

In the examples above, "R" is to be read as "realizes". Square brackets enclose grammatical functions which are connected by *transitivity* features of their grammatical predicates. It should be noted that examples such as this one provide further evidence for our separation of *text* semantics and *situation* semantics as advocated in 2.3.6.

With respect to our representations, there are other interesting questions connected to inferences such as:

(bus-stop P (roof A ladder))

?→ bus-stop A ladder

Another possible assignment of structure to our goals would be the one shown in the second of our possible goal-hierarchies (Figure 20).

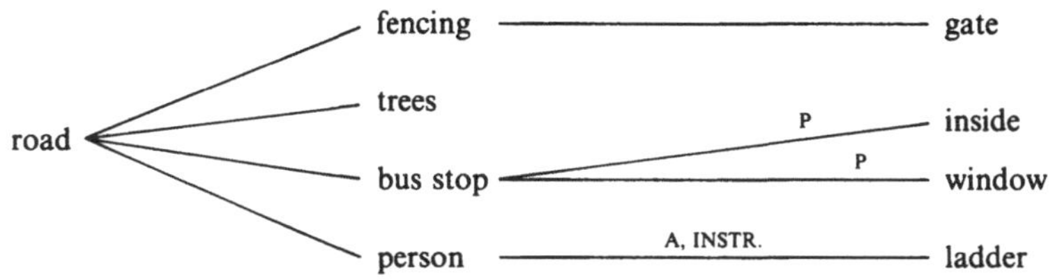

Figure 20. A possible goal-hierarchy (2)

The second of our possible goal-hierarchies would describe an ACTION, in which the children are building a road with trees and fencing alongside it, as well as a bus stop and a person walking on the road. Also, the fencing would have a gate, the bus stop an inside and a window, and the person a ladder. The concepts we are using to talk about "relationships" between the lexical items referring to the goals of ACTIONS are known in linguistics as *sense relationships* (Lyons 1977), and furthermore, we are using relationships as in various types of conceptual/semantic networks, as discussed in 2.6.5 above. In the *instrument* relationship, we are using categories of our *situation* analysis (cf. 2.3.6.), and this marks one of the specific contributions of an ACTION analysis to knowledge representation. Outlining the inferencing mechanisms in ACTION and SITUATION categories systematically should be one central aspect of future work. In the present investigation, we shall only elaborate this topic as far as it is necessary to achieve our specific goals.

With respect to the question of *temporal vs. logical sequence*, it is important not to forget that the relationship between ACTIONS of producing the goals in our representations might all be *part of*, as seen from the perspective of the AGENTS, in the cases where there are any connections. These are theoretically distinct from the relations between the goals as assigned by an interpreter. The connections between ACTIONS as seen in the AGENT'S perspective, as well as the connection between the goals of these ACTIONS as seen by the AGENT, together form the *subjective* representation of an ACTION. An *objective* representation interprets the relationships between ACTIONS and the relationships between goals from the point of view of some interpreter. How *part of* as one of these relations is interpreted more precisely has been explained in 2.4.4..

Another important question arising from our representations is that of the distinction between *conjunction* and *adjacency* in representations of ACTIONS: *Conjunction* connects two units of the same rank at the same level in a tree, whereas *adjacency* is a relationship between units involving *domination.* To transform this question from representational theory to object theory: What is the difference between building *a house and a fence* (An + Am), where the relation is *conjunction* , and between *building a house with a fence* (An(Am)), where the embedding relation is *adjacency*? For the time being, we adopt the position that *adjacency* has to be linguistically realized in PLANNING by PPs, or *relative clauses* dominated by a lexical head encoding the superordinate goal, or, alternatively, by some *adjunct* clause or some clause combination exhibiting corresponding types of *logical connection* (cf. 3.9. of this study).

Now, the analyses of goals given above describe possible, even if not plausible interpretations of our children's play session. They are possible ways of "understanding" it. In our present work, though, we do want the most plausible analysis; in other words, we need to know as accurately as possible what the children were doing, because it is on this analysis that our later linguistic work will be based. How, then, do we arrive at the most plausible reading?

3.2.1.3 Individual vs. interactive actions. In our present analysis, we are discussing interactive ACTIONS, rather than individual ACTIONS. Quite obviously, one could try to describe what is going on in the play session as a set of interlocking individual ACTIONS rather than as interactive, collective ACTIONS. This, however, would raise several methodological problems, one of which would be that we hardly ever have access to individual PLANNING through language, which will usually be an internal, cognitive process. However, for collective ACTIONS, language is the dominating medium of PLANNING, so there is a good chance that if we don't find any linguistic PLANNING for an assumed ACTION, it either does not take place at all, or it does not take place as an interactive ACTION.

3.2.1.4 Subjective vs. objective structure of actions. Our hypothetical analyses in 3.2.1.2. might be called *objective* in the sense that they do not respect in any way what is going on in and between the children *subjectively*. For example, when we assumed in our analysis above that one ACTION was superordinate, we did not check this in the text of our session. This, however, is exactly what we need to do when we want to get a picture which is reasonably adequate. In other words, whenever we want to postulate a superordinate ACTION, we require that we can identify a truely superordinate PLANNING phase, i.e., a PLANNING phase in which sub-ACTIONS are in some way mentioned as such, or in which at least two or more ACTIONS are mentioned as coordinated, so we can know that they must be coordinated with respect to some higher order ACTION. To give a few examples with references to page and line numbers:

66,12: *We need a bloke going up the ladder.*

This utterance contains the information that the two ACTIONS of building a *bloke*, or rather situating him on a ladder, and the building of the ladder are related at least by some form of local *adjacency*.

66,7–66,26 (Appendix 2) tell us that *bloke, ladder, and roof* are related as the building of a whole scene in which one person climbs up a ladder to fix a roof, that is, there are INSTRUMENT and GOAL relationships involved.

63,5,6: *we'll, we'll have the trees by yere*
and put the the fencing in front ("yere" is non-standard for "here")

This tells us at least that the building or positioning of the trees and the fencing are subjectively processed and planned by the group as in some way coordinated.

These examples should be sufficient to illustrate the difference between the structure of some sequence of ACTIONS, as it is consciously perceived by the AGENTS (subjective), and the structure of this same sequence as it is perceived by some interpreter (objective). It is obvious that from the possible conflicts between these two perspectives many misinterpretations may result in everyday situations, as well as in academic research. What we want to emphasize here is that while as analyzers, we inevitably have to be interpreters, we insist on coming as close as possible in our analysis to the cognitive reality of the AGENTS, because the semantic properties of the language used depend on the ACTIONS as carried out by the AGENTS, and not on the ACTIONS as interpreted by some observer or analyst. The extent to which our analyses of the language will yield significant discrepancies between the types of language used in PLANNING and EXECUTION phases is partly a function of the adequacy of our interpretation, which, in our present terminology, needs to be as subjective as possible, where subjective simply means "AGENT-oriented".

3.2.2 The analysis

Before considering the representations, let us re-arrange the GOALS we listed above, this time including relationships which are explicitly stated by the children at some place in the text. This will then lead us to tree diagrams which are closer to what actually happened than the diagrams which we drew in 3.2.1.2. In these diagrams of actual goal-hierarchies (Figures 21 and 22), the logical structure of ACTIONS is represented by the labelling of branches.

The relationships in our actual goal-hierarchies are all mentioned in the text, not, though, the particular types of relationships, as indicated in capitals. This,

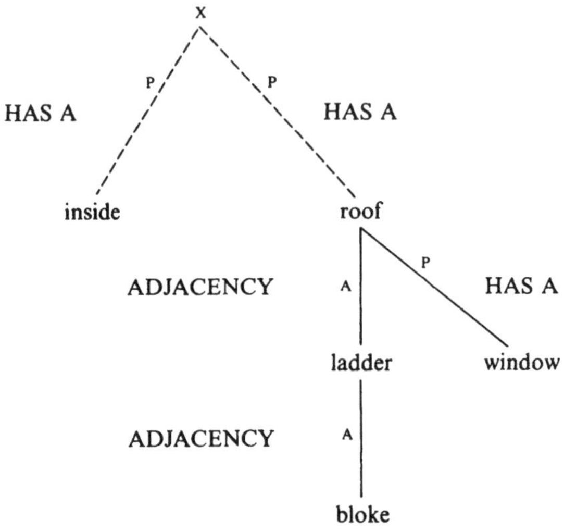

Figure 21. An actual goal-hierarchy (1)

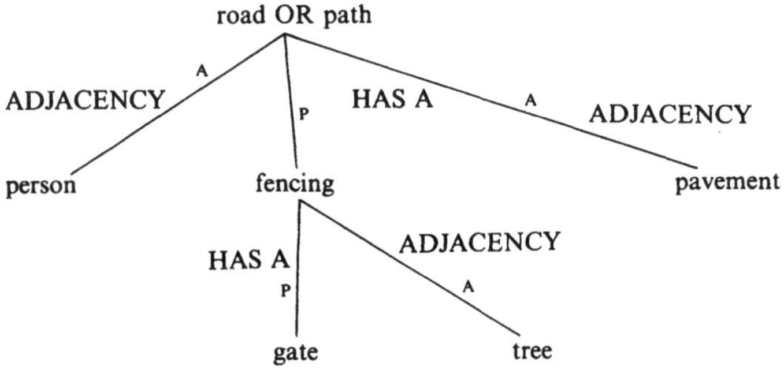

Figure 22. An actual goal-hierarchy (2)

incidentally, gives us an interesting measure for the explicitness of the structures of ACTIONS, which could be a relevant variable in an investigation which concentrates on the structure of ACTIONS (cf. the end of this section for some remarks on such an investigation).

We shall now look once more at the temporal sequence of elements of ACTION in this text, so that we have an empirical foundation for later discussions (cf. Table 56).

The list in Table 56 gives us the temporal sequence of elements of ACTIONS, together with the most important pointers to other ACTIONS. Using the numbering in our list, we now get the following representation, which contains ACTIONS, rather than elements, only (cf. Figure 23).

One point in connection with the representation in Figure 23 illustrates another interesting theoretical question: A7 is at one point mentioned as being in *adjacency* with A6 (cf. list of goals). The question is whether and how we want to represent this in a tree diagram. One obvious approach is to reduplicate A7 under A6, possibly with coindexing to express referential identity. Another possibility is to *percolate*

Table 56. Temporal sequence of elements of action

action	element	line,page	pointer
x1	EV	1,55-11,55	
A1:ROAD/PATH	PL EX	12,55-21,55 22,55-25,55	
X2	EX EV EX	1,56-18,56 18,56-24,56 24,56-4,57	
A2:ROOF	PL EX EV EX PL	5,57-13,57 15,57-18,57 19,57 20,57-27,57 28,57-14,58	
X3	EX EV EX EV	15,58-4,59 5,59 6,59-10,59 11,59-23,59	
A3:FENCING	PL	24,59-11,60	
A4:PAVEMENT	PL	19,60-16,60	ROAD(A1)
A3:FENCING	PL	17,60-3,61	GATE(A5)
A5:GATE	PL	17,60-3,63	
SIDE action		5,61-7,61	
X4	EV	8,61-10,61	
X5	PL	11,61-15,61	
A6:COUNTRY HOUSE	PL	16,61-2,62	FENCING(A3) TREE(A7)
A7:TREE	PL	23,61-31,62	
X6:	PL	1,62-2,62	

Table 56. (cont.)

action	element	line,page	pointer
A1:ROAD	EX EV	3,62-12,62 13,62-15,62	
A3/1:FENCING/PATH/ROAD	PL EX	16,62-22,62 23,62-4,63	
A7:TREES	PL EX EV	5,63-6,63 7,63-19,63 20,62-25,63	FENCING(A3)
A5:DOUBLE GATE	PL	26,63-31,63	
A3:FENCING	EX	1,64-13,64	
A1:PATH	EV EX	14,64-16,64 17,64-18,64	
A2:ROOF	PL	19,64-24,64	
A8:BUS STOP	PL EX	25,64-29,64 30,64-31,64	
A9:PERSON	PL EX	1,65-4,65 5,65-11,65	ROAD/PATH(A1)
A8:BUS STOP	EX	12,65-18,65	
A9:PERSON	EX	19,65-11,66	ROAD/PAVEMENT/
A10:BLOKE	PL	12,66-14,66	LADDER
A11:LADDER	PL EX	15,66-26,66 27,66-1,67	ROOF/BUNGALOW/
A12:INSIDE	PL EX	2,67-16,67 17,67-4,68	
X X	MO PL EX	5,68-7,68 8,68-14,68 15,68-22,68	
A13:WINDOW	PL EX EV PL	23,68-26,68 27,68-25,69 26,69 27,69-9,70	ROOF
X X X	EV MO PL EV EX	10,70-26,70 27,70-3,71 4,71-5,71 6,71-8,71 10,71	

A7 upwards to the lowest possible node giving access to A6, from where it might be percolated downwards. For this percolation, *transitivity* and some of the other relationships might be used. If we adopt that kind of solution, we have to constrain the application of such operations in a theoretically meaningful way, which is a problem that constitutes research material for the future.

Certain comments need to be made on the diagram in Figure 23:

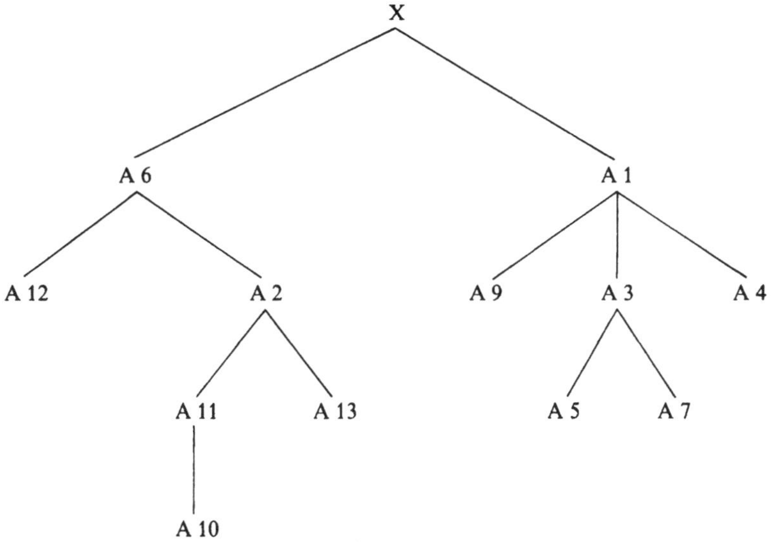

Figure 23. Actions in a play session

- The interpretation of the branches in this diagram is "*dominating node* is temporally connected to *dominated node*". This is a relatively weak interpretation of the relationship. A stronger, i.e. more constrained interpretation would be that of *is filled by* (logical structure), which would yield the tree in Figure 24. Figure 24 would be one aspect of the logical structure of ACTIONS in our play session; it would represent the *filling* relationship as realized by the *part-of* relation between goals. The remainder of the structure which we find in Figure 23 is of a different type and does not appear here.
- Even in our representation of the temporal structure of ACTIONS in our play session, there are certain ACTIONS which are not connected explicitly to the structure of activity as represented in our tree diagram: There is, for example, the ACTION of building and/or situating a bus stop (64f.), of which it is furthermore said that it is to be a bus stop *in the country*, which, lexically, points towards *country house* (61). Only, the link in PLANNING between these two is not made anywhere in the text, so there is no interactive PLANNING, and therefore we cannot integrate our *bus stop* goal with the others. Whether this was carried out as an individual ACTION, or whether it was done without any

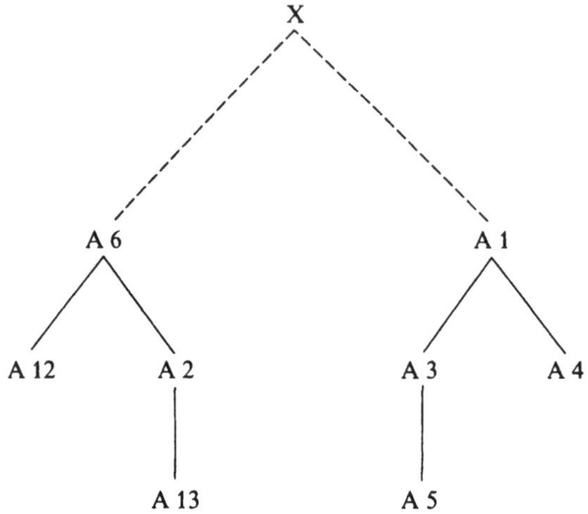

Figure 24. Logical structure of actions in a play session

PLANNING for integration, are questions which are beyond the scope of this particular analysis.

- A12 and A2 are explicitly linked in PLANNING, and A6 is explicitly introduced. However, it is not entirely clear whether A12 and A2 are consciously integrated as sub-ACTIONS of A6. A12 and A2 are linked by simple *and*-relationships and by *adjacency* (local prepositions). The relationship between A6 and (A12 *and* A2), however, is a relationship of filling:
  A6 is done by/through (A12 *and* A2).
  This relationship is not made explicit by the children, and to that extent, one may not feel justified in actually connecting up A12 and A2 in the way we have done in our diagram.
- Our second main ACTION, headed by A1, may even be linked, on the same level as A6, to yet another higher level, which would have to be something like *country scene*. However, it would again require quite a bit of guessing to make this inference. There are, though, quite a few pronominal references, most of them exophoric, which we cannot interpret with any degree of confidence, and which may very well contain that link. Also, within the ACTIONS headed by A1, the interpretation of the branches or links between the goals is not that of *part of*, but again just one of *adjacency*, except for A3 and A5. So, from a logical point of view, we are being vague at this point, because the interpretation of our links is not clear, which has important consequences for processes like inferencing

along these links. This touches on the problem of logical vs. temporal structure of ACTIONS, where *logical* is most clearly expressed in relationships between GOALS, and *temporal* through the sequence of events. It should be emphasized, though, that the vagueness in our representation is not a consequence of the framework, but entirely a consequence of the process of interpretation. The framework as such clearly constrains the types of relationships which can be symbolized by the branches in representations.

- If we now look back to our list giving the temporal sequence of elements of ACTION (cf. Table 55), we can see what a diagram would look like that was based on temporal sequence in a one-to-one fashion, i.e. including all instances of occurrences as in the list. If, on the other hand, we want to represent the logical structure of our ACTION, we get something like in the preceding paragraphs. Only in that case, we still have to decide how to handle the various kinds of logical relationships (local, temporal, causal, class/subclass, type/token, adjacency, part of etc.).

Let us summarize: In this section we have been illustrating the process and the results of the analysis in our framework for analyzing human ACTIONS. The results, i.e. the representations, might constitute a valid object of discussion even outside the present context: One might formulate hypotheses concerning the number of levels in representations, the number and kinds of right-branching vs. left-branching, vs. centre-embedding of categories, the interpretation of branches, the types of inferencing permitted along these branches, or the degree of explicitness of structure in any given ACTION. Even a superficial glance at the structure of ACTIONS of the 12 B Boys in this section as compared with the structure of ACTIONS in, for example, our cat-story (2.4.1.), or in the Heinz-story (2.4.2.) shows significant differences of organization along various dimensions. Also, the degree of divergence between temporal and logical structure, as well as differences between subjective and objective representations of the same ACTIONS might constitute interesting research material in itself. These remarks are meant as an indication of avenues of investigation. In the present context, though, we are interested in the analyses of ACTION only in so far as they yield the independent variables for our investigation of certain types of semantic complexity in the texts produced by the children under investigation. The following section will investigate one aspect of semantic complexity.

3.3 Context dependency

In the preceding section, we analyzed the 12 B Boys play session using our theory of ACTIVITY and obtaining, as a result, representations which assign each linguistic utterance in our data (cf. Appendix 2) to some phase, or element, of some ACTION. In particular, we have identified a set of utterances realizing PLANNING phases, and a set of utterances realizing EXECUTION phases. We shall now, and in the following sections, compare these two sets of utterances with respect to a number of variables indicating certain types of semantic complexity. The more specific hypotheses for the variable of *context dependency* will be formulated in 3.3.2.. Before, though, a few comments on the notion of *context dependency* might be appropriate.

3.3.1 On the notion of context dependency

The notion of a linguistic utterance being dependent on context for its interpretation has been discussed extensively in the literature. Points of particular relevance in this discussion are Bernstein (1971, 1980), Barwise and Perry (1983: 34ff.), Bierwisch (1983: 34ff), and Brown and Yule (1983: 35ff.), who give a good survey of the discussion up to around 1982. Our own approach builds in some ways on Brown and Yule (1983: 35ff.), yet differs in several respects from theirs, especially as far as the precise range of variables investigated is concerned. The criterion adopted for including a given variable in the investigation always is whether and to what extent it can be said to make an utterance dependent on context.

The apparent either/or distinction here is, of course, only a fiction: Even relatively context-independent linguistic structures, like fully lexical words, are dependent on co-text and context for disambiguation. On the other hand, even relatively context-dependent words, like deictic elements, have some general components of meaning which remain invariable across contexts. Obviously, then, context dependency is a matter of degree rather than a question of either/or.

There is an additional criterion for including or excluding a variable, which is operationalization: The criteria we are using are all tied to certain specified patterns of syntactic and/or intonational realization, which narrows down our perspective, yet leaves it controllable. We are reaching the borderline in, for example, the case of the distinction between exophoric and endophoric reference, which both are encoded, in English, by essentially the same lexico-grammatical devices, even if intonation in some classes of cases makes the distinction controllable. We shall have to return to this borderline below.

3.3.2 Hypotheses

We have outlined the theoretical basis of our hypotheses in section 2.5. On the most general level, they are connected to the fact that in the PLANNING phases of our play session, language is the dominating way of realizing the element of ACTION, which implies that in those instances where PLANNING is executed as an ACTION of its own, we even have language on the ACTION rank. By contrast, in the EXECUTION phases of our play session, we find language in its instrumental function, i.e. not as an ACTION of its own. We shall now list some more specific hypotheses as they can be formulated using the variables which we shall be investigating. Here, as in the following sections, we shall indicate functional elements of clause structure (syntactic functions) by initial capital spelling.

(H1) The percentage of fully lexical nouns as heads of nominal groups (NGs) will be relatively high if compared with the percentage of deictic elements as heads of NGs, where only NGs are counted filling one of the clause elements Subject (S), Complement (C), or Adjunct (A). It is important to observe that, at this stage, the term *Complement* refers to traditional *Objects* as well as to *Subject Complements* and *Object Complements*, which is standard at this level of delicacy in the Systemic literature. Also, at this stage, the term *Adjunct* is used as a generic term for the sub-classes *Adjunct, Disjunct, Conjunct* in the sense of Quirk et al. (1972:417).

(H2) Hypothesis (2) is identical to hypothesis (1), except that we shall be comparing fully lexical nouns as heads with pronouns, rather than with deictic elements.

(H3) The number of *valency-bound* clause elements per main verb is higher in PLANNING phases than in EXECUTION phases. More strictly within Systemic terminology, valency-bound clause elements in syntax are those realizing *participant roles* rather than *circumstantial roles*, i.e. they are assigned their semantic roles by the verb.

(H4) The number of Adjuncts per main verb (M) will be higher in PLANNING phases than in EXECUTION phases. Clauses functioning as Adjuncts are excluded here because they are counted separately under (H6).

(H5) The number of main verbs (M) from a specifically context dependent set containing *be, have, get, make, do, give, take* relative to the number of Ms not belonging to that set will be higher in the EXECUTION phases than in the PLANNING phases.

(H6) The number of clauses realizing any of the elements S,C,A of a clause will be higher per M in the the PLANNING phases than in the EXECUTION phases. In terms of valency, we are considering here clauses functioning as either arguments or as modifiers of a main verb.

(H7) The number of non-identified elements per M will be higher in the EXECUTION than in the PLANNING phases.

At the end of this section on context dependency, we shall have some remarks to make about why and to what extent the variables used in our hypotheses can be taken to indicate context dependency.

3.3.3 Coding Conventions

A few conventions for the coding of the elements which we are counting have to be made explicit at this point, because our transcripts, like any sample of naturally occurring language, offer some interesting problems as far as the identification of linguistic elements is concerned. Apart from this more technical reason, some of these questions have a theoretical significance even outside the current investigation, and therefore deserve at least to be mentioned. Finally, the child language development project whose data we are using has adopted certain coding conventions to ensure comparability of results between different investigations, and we adopt these whenever possible.

- One of the conventions which we shall adopt here concerns the treatment of false starts, ellipses, and exclamations which do not enter into the syntactic structure of the clause: The elements occurring in false starts are not counted at all. The linguistically realized elements occurring in cases of ellipsis are counted under "unidentified". If the ellipsis does not concern the internal structure of the group or phrase, then the functional elements within the group or phrase are counted, even if there is ellipsis on the rank of the clause. The elements in exclamations without any syntactic structure are counted under "unidentified". The treatment of ellipses here is theoretically unsatisfactory, in so far as endophoric ellipses should not be taken as an indicator of context dependency. It is, however, inevitable in our study because the well-known uncertainties in reconstructing ellipted elements, i.e. scoping issues, would introduce an unacceptably high degree of uncertainty into our figures. There is definitely a need for further development at this point.

- Question tags are not counted. The theoretical motivation is that they do not offer the same potential for syntactic and semantic structure as standard clauses. Furthermore, the theoretical status of question tags as far as context dependency is concerned is not clear.

- "Linkers" and "Binders", in the terminology of Fawcett (1980), are only counted as elements of clause structure, not as elements of group structure, i.e. we are concentrating on what would be called traditionally "subordinating and coordinating conjunctions" . Some *linkers, and* and *so* in particular, may realize other functions than that of a logical connector – for example that of a discourse connector. The decision as to which function they realize has to be made in each individual case. This is a decision by the analyst, which, however, is true in general of any classification. We are only mentioning *linkers* and *binders* here because the problem inevitably occurs as soon as the analyst starts work. The semantic complexity introduced by these elements will only be dealt with in our section on *logical connection* (3.9).

- The set of deictic elements recognized here consists of *here, there, this, that, these, those, now.*

- *One* and *something* are counted as nouns rather than as pronouns.

- We are assuming here a set of context-dependent verbs consisting of *be, have, get, make, do, give, take.* Their meaning is highly general in the sense that they, much more than other verbs, require co-text and context for their interpretation and disambiguation. It can be regarded as a linguistic reflex of this fact that it is essentially this set of verbs which function, in English, as relatively "empty" verbs in analytical verb constructions such as *to give an answer, to have a bath* etc. (for a discussion of the semantic properties of these constructions cf. Steiner in press).

- Sentences like *Try and get me a flat one* (p.56, line 2 of our transcript) are not counted as cases of syntactic *control*, despite their close semantic affinity to *Try to get me a flat one*. The similarity breaks down, though, if one considers pairs like (19a,b) and (20a,b):

(19a) *Try to get me a flat one.*
(19b) *Try and get me a flat one.*
(20a) *He tried to get me a flat one.*
(20b) *?He tried and got me a flat one.*

As we can see in (19a) and (20a), *to* makes the construction one of *subject control*, whereas with *and*, this seems to be restricted to imperative clauses. (20b), even if it were judged acceptable, has a finite sentential complement with an ellipted subject. The decisive fact is, though, that sentences like (20b) are hardly acceptable under the interpretation of (20a).

In general, one would not wish to discuss such an isolated case; yet it is significant in our transcripts because it occurs relatively frequently, which is the reason why we want to make our coding convention explicit here. Structures with semi-auxiliaries in general are treated as cases of embedding or *raising* or *control*, depending on the class of semi-auxiliary.

- *How* is counted as *wh-element* because of its semantic function in introducing certain classes of questions.

- *Do* and *be* as pro-forms are not counted, because in this function there is not the same degree of semantic choice as in their other functions.

- There are, in our transcripts, two interesting semantic and syntactic structures which deserve to be mentioned (predicate types are introduced and discussed in 3.4 below). The first is exemplified in (61,19):

(61,19) *(why couldn't we) have it as a country house.*

The verb *have* is the prototypical [relational, associative] verb in English. However, the only three-role variant of [associative] structures in English is generally assumed to be the one exemplified in (21):

(21) *I sold/bought a book to/from John.*

(21), though, is clearly different syntactically and semantically from (61,19). On the other hand, there is a syntactic structure similar to the one in (61,19), as in (22):

(22) *I regard it as a country house.*

A similar class of cases is exemplified by (23):

(23) *We'll have the trees by yere.*

Yere in (23) is a Welsh variant of *here*. Grammatically, (23) seems to be [relational, locational, third party agent], which is also supported by the syntax, not so, however, by the main verb. A possible conclusion is that, either we have to introduce at least two new readings for *have* in English, or else we have to admit hitherto forbidden syntactic realizations for the semantic class of [associative] processes, a decision which should only be taken as a last resort because it introduces considerable complexities into the *argument-complement* relationship, or, more generally, into the realizational patterns between semantics and syntax, which should be as narrowly constrained as possible without violating the facts of natural languages. One option that we do not have is that of just dismissing such structures as idiosyncratic; they are much too frequent in our corpus and thus indicate a relevant aspect of the semantico-syntacic potential of the language. Furthermore, the fact that these constructions are manifested in the language of twelve year old children seems to indicate that they are not typical children's language restricted to certain phases of language development: Twelve year olds are already very close to adult language in most respects.

This discussion will turn up again in our treatment of *transitivity*. For our counting in this section, it is only necessary that we state that we are counting constituents of the class of *by yere* and *as a country house* as complements rather than as Adjuncts of *to have*.

- In some cases, we find something like ellipted superordinate clauses, as in the following utterance:

(67,29) ... *because it's too big.*

The superordinate clause is nowhere realized, so that we have to make a decision about classification. In these cases, we do not count the possibly ellipted elements, mainly for the same reasons as with ellipsis in general. This is particularly compelling in cases where we have a turn boundary preceding the utterance. We do count the subordinating conjunction (*binder*).

- In a large number of cases, one has to make a decision as to whether a given word is an adverb or a preposition, and whether it constitutes a clause element of its own. Examples are well known structures like *to get out* etc. (cf. Quirk et al. 1985: 1150ff on *phrasal verbs, prepositional verbs*, and *phrasal-prepositional verbs*, as well as Charlton 1988). Our tests for constituent status are clefting, conjunction with other relevant constituents of the assumed type, substitution, modification of particle, placement of an adverb before the particle, and questioning of the candidate element. This whole area, which is highly relevant, especially for English, is well known as a problematic area, and therefore we want to make explicit here the range of syntactic tests which we are using.

- In our counting, we are deliberately using the term *embedded* in a somewhat loose but still frequently accepted sense: There are those clauses which are uncontroversial cases of embedding, functioning as Subject, Complement, or Object in clause structure. Next, there are those clauses realizing non-valency bound elements of clause structure, of which it can with some justification be claimed that they are not embedded clauses, which is reflected in their syntactic and discourse behaviour (cf. Halliday 1985a: 192ff.; Matthiessen and Thompson 1988.). Finally, there are those clauses which function as elements of group structure, such as relative clauses functioning as post-modifiers in *nominal groups*, clauses functioning as complements of adjectives, and others. These are *rankshifted clauses* in the traditional Systemic sense. While being aware of the differences between these types, we are counting them here under one heading, because their differences do not seem to be relevant with respect to context dependency, and the difference between the first two types is still not sufficiently researched. This might also be the place to remind ourselves of the fact that there are several types of hypotactically linked clauses which do not realize an element of the structure of the clause to which they are linked (cf. section 3.9. of this study). This is particularly relevant in the case of certain relative clauses which are not modifiers, cf. (24):

(24) *They told me why they had come, which was important.*

This is as far as we shall go into questions of coding conventions here. Let us emphasize once more that even those issues dealt with here which are not of major theoretical significance have to be raised in order to make our figures transparent. The various structures discussed are highly frequent in the corpus, and each decision taken with respect to their classification has a considerable influence on at least some aspect of our statistical results.

3.3.4 Results

We shall give our results here in the form of a simple table, reserving the discussion for the next section (cf. Table 57).

3.3.5 Discussion of results

We shall briefly discuss the results which we have obtained in Table 57 in order to investigate to what extent they can be regarded as theoretically significant with respect to the notion of context dependency:

Table 57. Context dependency: results

Structure	Execution	Planning
Lexical Noun as Head of S,C,or A : Deictic as Head of S,C, or A	86:35	101:18
Lexical Noun as Head of S,C,or A : Pronoun as Head of S,C,or A	86:87	101:93
Valency bound elements: Main Verb	226:128	227:111
Adjuncts (excl. clauses) : Main Verb	26:128	27:111
Main Verb from CD-set A : Main Verb not from CD-set A	72:56	58:53
Embedded Clause: Main Verb	11:128	13:111
Non-identified element : Main Verb	101:128	64:111

In this table, the following abbreviations are used:
S=Subject, A=Adjunct, C=Complement, CD=context dependency

- The number of fully lexical nouns as heads of clause elements S, C, or A relative to the number of deictic elements as heads of these elements (H1):
To recapitulate, the figures are as follows:

EXECUTION	86:55	(approx.1,5)
PLANNING	101:18	(approx.5,5)

To the extent that the deictic elements are used exophorically, this would seem to be a clear indication of a higher degree of context dependency in the EXECUTION phases. Yet, even if a large percentage of deictic elements in the EXECUTION phases were used endophorically, and not so in the PLANNING phases, which is a highly implausible assumption, we would still be faced with a very large amount of lexical cohesion in the PLANNING phases (cf. Halliday & Hasan 1976). The view underlying our choice of variables here is that fully lexical elements are less context dependent than deictic elements, which is a commonplace assumption in the literature on the interpretation of natural language utterances. To the extent that this assumption is accepted, we can regard our hypothesis (H1) about this variable as confirmed.

- The number of fully lexical nouns as heads of clause elements relative to the number of pronouns in that function (cf.H2):

EXECUTION:	86:87	(approx. 1:1 [1,0])
PLANNING:	101:93	(approx. 10:9 [1,1])

This difference is much smaller than in the case of (H1). It has to be added, though, that approximately 14% of the pronouns in PLANNING were coded as *endophoric*, whereas the EXECUTION phases showed only 10% of their pronouns as endophoric, so that the result would be further shifted in the direction predicted by (H2). There should be no illusion, though, about the reliability of the *exophoric vs. endophoric* distinction in a study such as the present one: Although both of these functions are fundamental and general to cohesion (Halliday & Hasan 1976: 31ff.; Brown & Yule 1983: 190ff.), their identification in a given piece of text is just as much a process of (necessarily subjective) interpretation, as the interpretation of the text as such.

Apart from considerations of inter-coder consistency, the results as such are not too surprising in the light of contemporary theories about discourse structure: The use of pronouns in the functions investigated here can only be taken as an indication of context dependency, to be kept separate from the dependency on *co-text* at this point, to the extent that it is exophoric. The difference between our findings about deictic elements and the findings about pronouns can partly be explained by the fact that in the case of deictics, the exophoric function is much more prominent than it is with pronouns.

- The number of valency bound-elements per *main verb*

EXECUTION:	226 : 128	(approx.1,76)
PLANNING:	227 : 111	(approx.2,04)

This figure is just one possible measure of syntactic complexity, and by itself shows a definite difference between the two phases (cf.H3). The semantic significance of this area within a Systemic approach is the following: If, in the area of *transitivity* (cf. 3.4.), a speaker encodes situations with a relatively complex structure in terms of number and types of processes and *participant roles*, then the number of roles per process is one, albeit crude, indicator of complexity and does not yet indicate whether the complexity is achieved through, say, juxtaposition, conjunction, disjunction, embedding etc.. We shall discuss the more detailed questions of types of relationships between processes and roles in the next section, so let us merely state here that the first crude measure of valency-bound elements per main verb seems to indicate that there is a clear difference between PLANNING and EXECUTION phases in our corpus.

- The number of Adjuncts (excluding clauses) per main verb (cf.H4):

EXECUTION:	26:128	(approx.0,203)
PLANNING:	27:111	(approx.0,24)

Again, taken at face value, this figure seems to be a measure of syntactic rather than semantic complexity. Also, the types of semantic complexity underlying the syntax are certainly diverse, if we think of the very different types of semantic functions realized in Adjuncts. The more specific questions will turn up in the sections on *logical connection* and *circumstances*. For the time being, we shall conclude that there is a certain difference between the two types of phases here which in the end may or may not turn out to be significant in a statistical sense.

- Number of main verbs from set A relative to those not from A (cf.H5):

EXECUTION:	72:56	(approx.9:7 [1,28])
PLANNING :	58:53	(approx. 12:11 [1,09])

In 3.3.3., we have commented on the question of whether and to what extent our set A verbs are context dependent. In addition to what has been said already, even a superficial glance at an English dictionary gives us an important indication as to the context-dependency of these verbs: all of them display a high measure of lexical ambiguity, i.e. they have a large number of readings, which can only be disambiguated through context, this time including co-text. There is the added syntactic behaviour of these verbs: they are by far the most frequently appearing *function verbs* in analytical verb constructions in English ("Funktionsverbgefüge"), which is again due to the fact that their core-meanings are highly general. Again, and as before, there is a certain amount of statistical divergence in the direction predicted by our hypothesis between the two phases of ACTIONS, but computations of statistical significance would only make sense with larger amounts of data.

- Number of embedded clauses per main verb (cf.H6):

EXECUTION:	11:128	(approx.0,08)
PLANNING :	12:111	(approx.0,1)

The comments which we have made above about the semantically multiple functions of certain syntactic structures are even more appropriate here than above: our very general notion of *embedded* underlying the present figures makes our measure a very general one, too. The difference in our figures, however, is certainly big enough to indicate that there is a difference here between the two phases of ACTION.

- Number of non-identified elements per main verb (cf.H7):

EXECUTION:	101:128	(approx.0,8)
PLANNING :	64:111	(approx.0,6)

The difference here is certainly striking and, if it could be shown to hold for larger sets of data, would be highly interesting. The language used in the EXECUTION phases has a markedly higher percentage of elements which are completely un-interpretable without context than the language used in the PLANNING phases. Given our notion of "non-identified" (cf. 3.3.3.), the semantic motivations are of various types: One obvious source are the frequent exclamations in the EXECUTION phases, another, utterances like *yes, no, oh* etc., which very often have their *Theme* in the context of situation, rather than in any preceding textual structures. So far, we seem to have here a fairly reliable measure of context dependency. On the other hand, some of the phenomena involved can also be taken as an indication of a large amount of complex cognitive planning activities, and this would seem to be indicative of language as ACTION rather than as an INSTRUMENT in terms of our theory of ACTIVITY. In our data, though (cf. Appendices 1 and 2), the *non-identifed* elements appear to reflect a large amount of context dependency, rather than planning, which will be strongly supported by the results in our section on *theme in situation.*

In summary, what is the direction in which our figures seem to point? Quite clearly, each variable with its associated figures taken by itself would underspecify any theoretically relevant notion of context dependency. The figures taken together, though, all point in the predicted direction. Now, even if it turned out in more extensive studies that one of the individual variables does not yield statistically significant differences, the probability of the general direction of results along the lines predicted by our hypotheses being a coincidence would seem to be fairly low. This will be further substantiated by the results which we shall report on in the following sections.

On the other hand – and this is just as important as the "positive" results which we have obtained – it can be seen in detail from such a study that a notion like *context dependency* is intrinsically complex: The number of syntactic and semantic phenomena contributing to it is high, and we have come nowhere near exhausting it. Furthermore, all of the syntactic and lexical structures involved realize multiple semantic functions, as can be seen in the exophoric vs. endophoric use of deictic elements or pronouns, so that necessarily each single variable taken in isolation underdetermines the decision as to whether or not a given text is context-dependent. The recognition of these general facts is important for any study of context dependency.

3.4 Transitivity

3.4.1 On the notion of "Transitivity"

The notion of *transitivity* refers to an area of central interest within Systemic Linguistics (cf. Halliday 1967-68; Fawcett 1980, 1987; Steiner 1985a; Butler 1985: 40ff.). It may be appropriate, though, in the present context to explain it briefly:

It is generally assumed within Systemic Linguistics that the semantics of the clause can usefully be covered in, at least, three functional components, the *ideational, interpersonal,* and *textual* components (cf. section 2.3.8.). At many places in the literature, these components are subdivided, yet we shall be content here with stating something like the "common core" of Systemic semantics. Each of the semantic components is internally organized into *system networks*, i.e. directed graphs (*conceptual graphs* in the sense of Sowa 1983), where the nodes represent *features* and the branches are interpreted as *if-then, and,* or *or*. We have commented on some formal properties of networks elsewhere in this study (cf. 2.3.7, 2.3.8 and 2.6). It should be noted that system networks and selectional expressions represent two different types of feature structures, system networks symbolizing the potential (grammar) and selectional expressions symbolizing the actualization (chosen paths in the system). The feature structures describing a sentence can be represented by *directed acyclic graphs*. The system networks symbolize particularly coherent areas of the semantics of natural languages, one of these areas being *transitivity*. Other areas symbolized by system networks are *time, circumstances, logical connection, modality etc*. The term *transitivity* thus covers the semantic structure of clauses in terms of *process types* and their associated *participant roles*. Essentially very similar aspects are covered in various schools of linguistics as *deep cases* (Fillmore 1968, 1977), *theta-role assignment* (Chomsky 1981; Jackendoff 1983,1987), *semantic argument assignment* (Bresnan 1982; Kaplan & Bresnan 1982) etc.. Detailed examples of system networks with their associated selection expressions in the area of transitivity will be given below. It must be borne in mind as a characteristic feature of a Systemic approach to the semantics of natural language that, while transitivity is one central dimension of the semantic structure of clauses, it is only one among a whole range of dimensions; in other words, the semantic and syntactic structure of clauses is as much a product of, say, the semantics of *modality, time, theme, information distribution* (cf. Erdmann 1990: 3) etc. as of transitivity. Also, the transitivity of clauses only covers those elements which are "valency-bound" so that the semantics of *Circumstances* represents a different area. In our approach, we shall, within transitivity, restrict ourselves to the semantics of the verb and its complements. Systemic Linguistics also has developed partial models for the transitivity of the nominal group, the adjectival group, the prepositional phrase, and the adverbial group, but these models will not be in the focus of our discussion.

While this is not the place to discuss the Systemic approach to transitivity as a whole, we shall briefly state here the most general principles underlying our particular version of it:

1. Semantic representations containing participant roles have to be locally and globally complete and coherent (cf. Kaplan & Bresnan 1982: 211ff. for the definitions of *completeness* and *coherence* in functional structures). A representation containing some verb and its participant roles is complete if it contains all the participant roles that are lexically assigned to the verb as obligatory. It is coherent if it contains only roles which are lexically assigned to the verb as optional or obligatory. One governor and its participant roles form a *local* representation, whereas *global* representations are those involving more than one governor. Henceforth, we shall use the terms *participant roles* and *roles* interchangeably in cases where there is no possible source of confusion.
2. There is a condition on the assignment of clause elements to participant roles in the lexicon and in representations such that each role must be assigned one and only one valency-bound clause element. This element may be empty, which is especially relevant in cases of *control* and *raising*, e.g. *mental* and *communication* verbs and *semi-auxiliaries* in particular. Observe that an element being empty is not the same as non-existence of an element. The condition does not hold both ways, i.e. from valency-bound clause elements to participant roles as well, because of the existence of non-referring clause elements, control phenomena, and because of raising phenomena where roles may be assigned through the process of *raising*, or rather, its SFG equivalent.
3. *Participant roles* are specific to types of process, with one characterizing role for each type of process. The characterizing roles, with the exception of the type [action], are defined by a unique syntactic realization potential (assignment of grammatical functions to arguments). The possible combinations of roles in the lexicon and in representations are thus strongly restricted (cf. Steiner et al. 1988, and Steiner 1987d for comprehensive accounts).
4. Combinations of participant roles in dictionary entries of verbs and in representations obey the "one per sent"-constraint, which says that there may be not more than one role of any given type per representation in non-co-ordinated structures.

It should be noted that the four principles listed above hold for our particular version of an account of transitivity, but not necessarily for other versions of SFG.

What are the claims as to the "psychological reality" of the Systemic concept of transitivity? In general, Systemicists hesitate to make strong claims about the psychological reality of their models. The past few years, though, have seen a certain interest by Systemicists and non-Systemicists in the question of the psychological reality of Systemic transitivity (cf. Engelkamp 1980; Fawcett. 1980; Fine 1988, and others), and certainly within an approach like our own, in which linguistic grammars are only taken as a special case of grammars of human activity, hypotheses formulated in terms of the linguistic model should be relevant to internal activities, and it is in this spirit that we shall undertake the investigations in this section and in the ones to follow.

3.4.2 Hypotheses

Taking our present theory of activity as the basis, *transitivity* is perhaps the area where hypotheses are the least straightforward if compared to other functional components and system networks. The main reason is that whether language is used as an instrument (filling elements of an ACTION, i.e. as OPERATION), as in the EXECUTION phases, or whether it is used as an ACTION itself, as in the PLANNING phases, it is always "multifunctional", in particular, the ideational function is always present. This, of course, is true in general for any of the components and the networks. Specifically, though, when we use language in internal or external PLANNING, there is absolutely no expectation that the situations and ACTIONS which are being planned have to be either *mental*, or *action*, or whatever. Note that this has nothing to do with "congruence", or "metaphor": The transitivity of a natural language encodes situations and ACTIONS which can be, and by their very essence often are, distinct from the situation in which the utterance is generated. To put it more simply: If a person is engaged in the PLANNING phase of an ACTION which is a communicative and/or mental process, there are no constraints on the classes of ACTIONS and SITUATIONS which are being planned - specifically, they do not have to be *mental* or *communication*. Observe that this is different from at least some of the other components: If, for example, in the situation of uttering a given clause I intend to give an order to someone, the congruent form, in English, will always be one type of directive, and only through some non-congruent expression, using some kind of grammatical metaphor, may I use a non-directive.

We shall investigate the following hypotheses:

(H1) The distribution of syntactically realized transitivity structures, i.e. clauses, over the different process types, per the total number of clauses will differ between PLANNING and EXECUTION phases. H1 is fairly weak, in that it only predicts that there will be some kind of difference. It makes no prediction like "there will be more *mental process* clauses in PLANNING phases than in EXECUTION phases" - predictions of that kind, although they can sometimes be heard in similar contexts, appear basically wrong in view of what has been said above. The question may be asked whether H1 in its present form is not so weak as to be of very limited value.

(H2) The distribution of actualized selection expressions over the general *types of process (action, mental, communication, relational)* per the total number of selection expressions actualized in any phase will be different between PLANNING and EXECUTION phases, i.e. we are taking the total number of actualized selection expressions in each phase to form the basis of 100%. H2 predicts that, regardless of the outcome of H1, the number of different selection expressions taken from any of the networks, which will be radically different from the number of clauses themselves, will have a different distribution across process types betwen the two phases of ACTION. In a sense, H1 pursues the question of quantitative differences, whereas H2 pursues that of qualitative differences (cf. the column "realized" in the table of results in section 3.4.5).

(H3) The number of clauses divided by the number of actualized selection expressions will be lower for the same number of instances in the PLANNING phases than in the EXECUTION phases. (H3) can be seen as containing one possible metric for overall complexity of transitivity structures, even if it does not distinguish complexity within sub-types, for example, within *action* vs. within *mental.* (H3) is a fairly straightforward deduction from the theory of ACTIVITY to the structure of language.

(H4) The distribution of percentages of actualized selection expressions relative to possible selection expression within process types should be significantly different between PLANNING and EXECUTION phases. The overall added number of percentages should be higher in PLANNING than in EXECUTION phases. (H4) actually has two parts, the first of which, again, is relatively straightforward. The second part is problematic, because the theory of ACTIVITY does not necessarily prevent the hypothesis that relatively higher semantic productivity in one area of the semantics in a given phase may be complemented by relatively lower productivity in another area, if productivity is measured as in (H4).

These hypotheses will be tested and commented upon in our section on *discussion of results*. Given the overall complexity of the transitivity component within Systemic Functional Grammar, obviously a whole range of further metrics could be developed to measure different aspects of complexity. (H1)-(H4) above should only serve here as an illustration of what the Systemic framework yields when tested for its productivity in an investigation such as the present one.

3.4.3 Networks and selection expressions

This section will provide us with the tools for our investigation in the area of *transitivity*: Networks and selection expressions. In providing these tools, however, a number of points have to be raised which are of independent theoretical and/or descriptive interest.

The network for *action* processes is taken from Fawcett (1980: 137ff.). We shall not make any changes relative to Fawcett's proposals, yet we shall, in our discussion of selection expressions, raise a few points which are interesting and/or problematic with respect to his approach. The networks for both *mental* and *communication* processes are our own proposals and represent deviations from both Halliday and Fawcett in several respects. The details will be discussed when we introduce the networks and the selection expressions. The network for *relational* is again taken from Fawcett, this time Fawcett (1987:161), and in our more detailed discussion of it, we shall see where its particular attractions lie.

Our presentation will proceed in three steps for each *type of process*: Discussions of networks, selection expressions, and notes on theoretical or empirical issues arising from them. In the case of selection expressions, it is important to observe that they represent unordered sets of features in this version of the theory, as is usually the case in SFG. There is, however, the legitimate question whether the notion of *order* of features may not be useful or even necessary here, especially in connection with the definition of a *path*. Furthermore, canonical order may also be necessary in lists of grammatical arguments, especially in the case of *participant roles*. We shall not assume canonical order in the present approach, but would like to refer to a discussion of this topic elsewhere (Steiner 1987d). A formalization of the relationship between features, selection expressions, and networks can be found in various places (cf. Patten & Ritchie 1987: 284ff.).

In Figure 25, we reproduce the central part Fawcett's *Action* network (1980: 137).

Table 58 contains selection expressions generated by the transitivity network in Figure 25. The *Instances* column is to be used for counting in analytical work.

The structure of type [natural phenomenon], which is not part of Fawcett's original network, seems to occur, in English, in three main syntactic realizations, cf. (25) to (27):

(25) *It is raining.*	S(ubject)^O(perator)^M(ain Verb)
(26) *It is cold.*	S(ubject)^M^[C(intens),{cat=adjgp,...}]
(27) *It is morning.*	S(ubject)^M^[C(intens),{cat=ng,...}]

Curly brackets here enclose syntactic feature descriptions.

There may, indeed, be a fourth type of structure that we need to account for, cf. (28):

(28) *It was snowing white flakes.*

What prevents us from adding this type of realization straight away is the fact that the status of *white flakes* as a constituent is doubtful on several criteria (commutability, clefting, questioning).

The type [affected-centred, simple], is taken from Fawcett (1980:137). We shall maintain it here, because of its intuitive attractiveness, in spite of the fact that the difference between [affected-centred, simple] clauses and [affected-centred, plus agent, overt affected, covert agent, process-facility oriented] does not seem to be an easy one to draw because it fully depends on the *degree of expectancy*, i.e. the degree of obligatoryness of a second role, whichis not easy to operationalize.

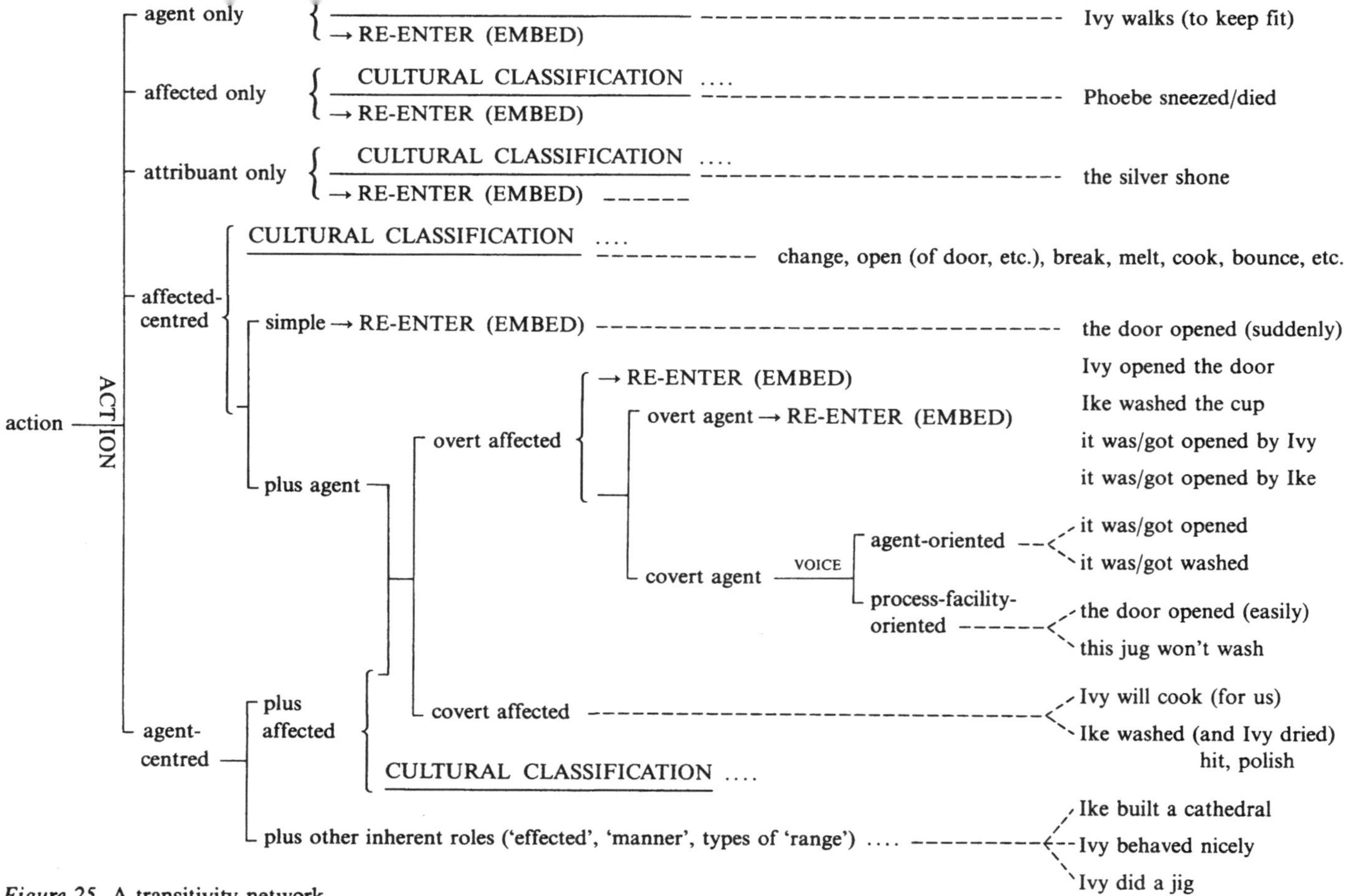

Figure 25. A transitivity network

We are grateful to Julius Groos publishers for their permission to reproduce this Figure.

Table 58. Transitivity selection expressions

Selection expression	Instances
[agent only]	
[affected only]	
[attribuant only]	
[natural phenomenon]	
[affected-centred, simple]	
[affected-centred, plus agent, overt affected, overt agent]	
[affected-centred, plus agent, overt affected, covert agent, voice:agent oriented]	
[affected-centred, plus agent, overt affected,covert agent, voice: process-facility-oriented]	
[affected-centred, plus agent, covert affected]	
[agent-centred, plus affected, overt affected, overt agent]	
[agent-centred, plus affected, overt affected, covert agent, voice: agent oriented]	
[agent-centred, plus affected, overt affected, covert agent, process-facility oriented]	
[agent-centred, plus affected, covert affected]	
[agent-centred, plus effected]	
[agent-centred, plus range]	
[agent-centred, plus manner]	

Of the clauses (29) and (30), for example, to me the first seems to realize the [affected, simple] structure, and the second the [affected-centred, covert agent] variant, whereas Fawcett has it exactly the other way round.

(29) *The door opened easily.*
(30) *The door opened suddenly.*

Observe that (30) could take a continuous aspect, increasing the expectancy of an Agent. (30) does not have an [agent] with arbitrary reference, such as the passive (30b):

(30b) *The door was opened suddenly.*

Whether or not one should admit criteria like *degree of expectancy* into the model is partly a question of the purpose of linguistic work in a given case. In general, if the task requires a high degree of consistency in analysis, then one should be careful about admitting all but the most strictly formal criteria.

In contrast to Fawcett and Halliday, we do not handle analytical verb constructions as in (31) as instances of a type [agent-centred, plus range], but rather as deriving from the *theme* and *information* systems to a large extent, with the nominal element functioning as part of the verbal group:

(31) *Ivy did a dance.*

For a more detailed treatment cf. Steiner (in press). Furthermore, the option of, say, [agent-centred, plus range] does not preclude the additional choice of [affected] on theoretical grounds, as seems to be implied by Fawcett's approach to the feature [plus other inherent roles], as can be shown by sentence types like (32):

(32) *She touches me in my very soul.*

Admittedly, (32) is rejected by some informants. To the extent that it is acceptable, it realizes the configuration [agent, affected, range].

We are now moving away from the area of *action* and on to *mental* processes. The set of networks for the area of *mental* process closest to the ones we shall be using can be found in Steiner (1985a: 183ff.). Let us comment on some differences to standard SFG accounts after presenting our networks first (cf. Figures 26 and 27):

Perhaps the most salient fact about our networks here is that an early subdistinction, which can be found in most of Fawcett's and Halliday's networks is missing: That between [emotion], [cognition], [perception] immediately dependent on the feature [mental] (cf. Halliday 1985a: 227ff. and 240ff.). The question has to be raised, though, whether there is enough, particularly formal, motivation for setting up this distinction in English. It is usually claimed that [emotion] verbs form a distinct lexical set. This argument by itself, it seems to us, is not valid as long as criteria for defining lexical sets are not made fully explicit.

Sometimes, it is also argued that there is a unique sub-system dependent on [emotion] verbs, which would be another one of the classically accepted arguments (cf. Martin 1987). The sub-system in question is that of [emoter oriented vs. phenomenon oriented], covering the distinction between (33) and (34):

(33) *I like your gift.*
(34) *Your gift pleases me.*

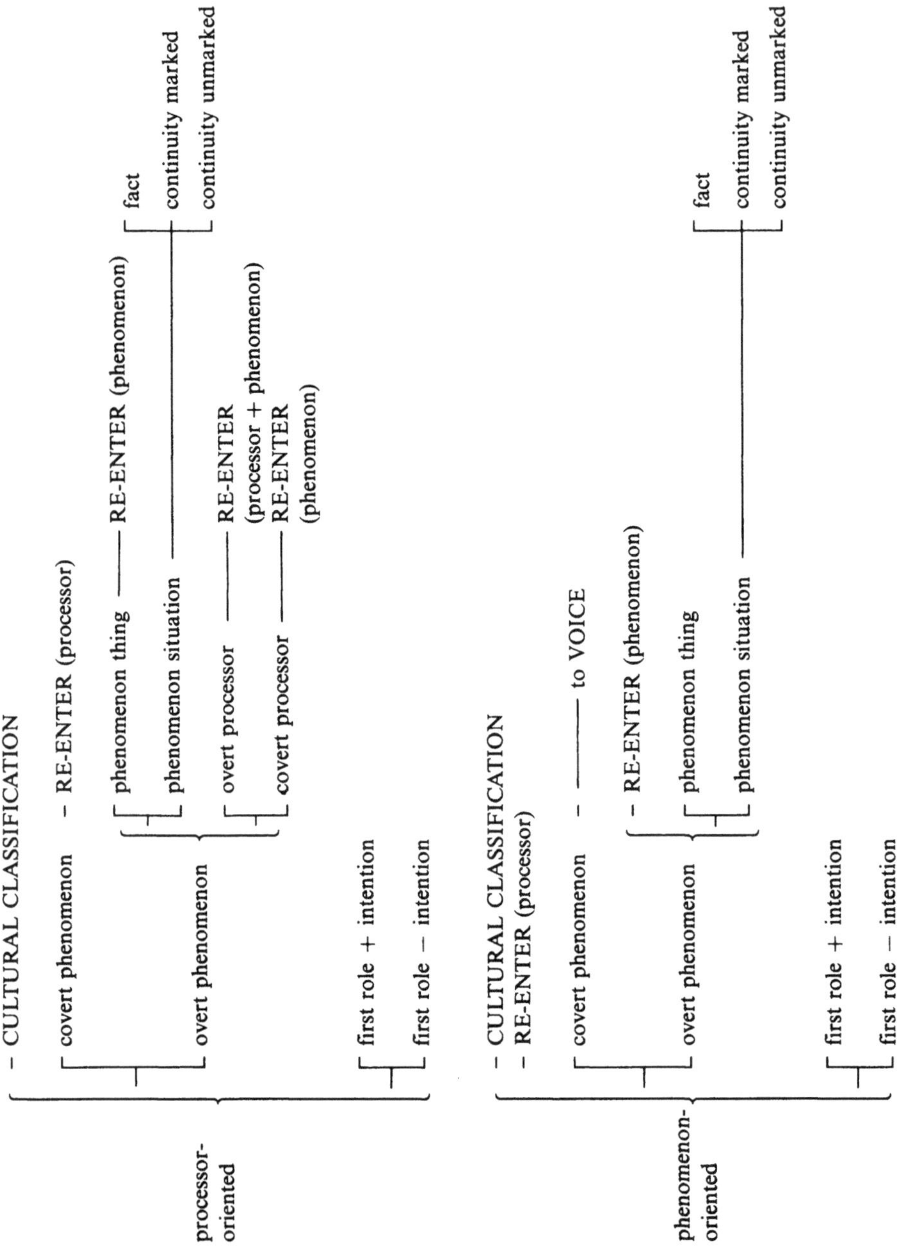

Figure 26. Mental process in English (1)

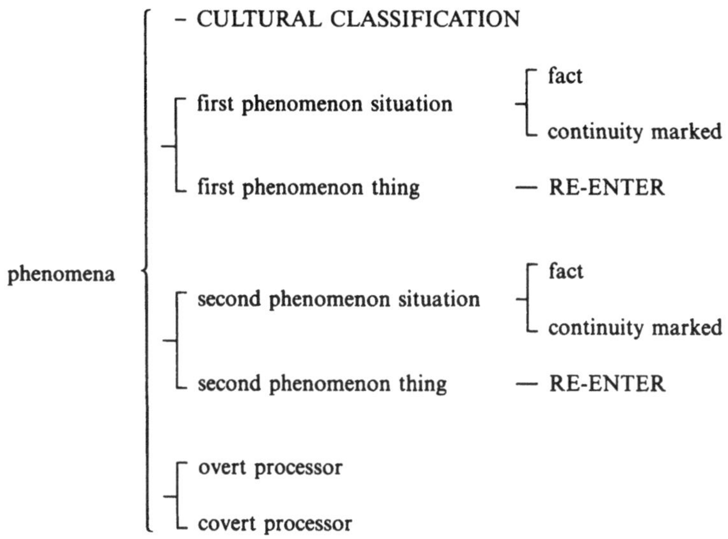

Figure 27. Mental process in English (2)

Now, apart from the fact that a very similar distinction seems to be possible with a sub-class of *relational* processes, cf. (35) and (36),

(35) *I owned a book.*
(36) *The book belonged to me.*

there are apparent counter examples even within the *mental* processes, which are not *emotion* verbs, cf. a set like *occur, influence, appear, convince, escape, strike...* as in (37):

(37) *That you are always so punctual convinced us.*

Obviously, it can be argued that many of these verbs may take additional constituents, cf. (38):

(38) *That you are always so punctual convinced us of your reliability.*

In cases like (38), however, there are reasons for claiming that the verb entry is *convince of*, rather than *convince*, in that the preposition is strictly governed by the verb. Also, with some of the verbs we are currently discussing, thematized variants seem to be the unmarked form, cf.(39):

(39) *It escaped me that you were hit by my remark.*

Rather than (40):

(40) *That you were hit by my remark escaped me.*

However, neither of these possible objections would seem to justify the denial that the option under discussion here is basically open to *mental* processes other than *emotion.* It is for these reasons that in our networks here we are holding the option of [processor oriented] vs. [phenomenon oriented] open to the class of *mental* processes in general, with the exception of our added sub-class [two phenomena].

Another consideration is that of whether one should not restrict the option of [processor+intention] vs. [processor-intention] to certain sub-types of *mental,* namely *perception* and *cognition.* Yet, it appears that there are sets of fairly typical *emotion* verbs also which seem to exhibit the same kind of semantic relationship, cf. *admire, adore, hate...* vs. *suffer, like, dislike...* which seem, even if in a vague sense, to pair like the [+intention] vs. [-intention] pairs usually accepted for the other two sub-types of *mental.* In any case, the choice seems to be fairly central in the case of [perception] and [cognition] verbs, where the imperative tests and the progressive aspect test can usually be used to differentiate the two sub-classes, but rather marginal in the case of [emotion] verbs. From a methodological point of view, it should be made explicit that in cases of this type, we are always faced with the complementary dangers of overrestriction and overgeneration of selection expressions: Quite clearly, if we keep the option of [+/- intention] open to all MENTAL processes, we overgenerate somewhat for some sub-types of [emotion] verbs. However, in this case we prefer the known danger of overgeneration to the unknown danger of losing a semantic generalization without knowing how big the loss is. Methodological questions like these always have to be respected whenever there is a choice of including or not including some feature in a network.

Another issue frequently discussed among systemicists is that of whether it would not be more satisfactory to treat *communication* verbs as a sub-type of *mental, cognition* verbs rather than as a type of their own (Fawcett, personal communication). This would then presuppose the introduction of a role *3rdpartyagent* into the *mental* networks. In philosophical terms, this would equate *telling s.o. s.th.* with *making s.o. think s.th.*, which is at least an interesting hypothesis. In semantic terms, though, it would seem to imply that this semantic class is inherently associated with three roles *3rdpartyagent, Cognizant, Phenomenon,* which would seem to force us to treat the prepositional constituents in (41-44) as complements:

(41) *He said to me "Hi lad!"*
(42) *He cried to me "Hi lad!"*

(43) *He suggested to me "Let's leave."*
(44) *?He declared to me "I shall do it."*

(44) appears to be hardly acceptable, but even the verbs of the superordinate clauses in (41)-(43) belong to a different class from verbs like *convince, persuade, warn...* which are prototypical *communication* verbs with three roles realizing their *Receiver* role as non-prepositional Object. The distinction is even more marked in a language like German, which has a large number of two-role *communication* verbs, like *rufen, schreien, flüstern...* with lexically different three-role-counterparts *zurufen, zuschreien, zuflüstern....* The point we want to make here is that what we shall treat as *communication* verbs are in no way inherently three-role processes, but seem to form a separate class with interesting semantic and syntactic correspondences between three-role and two-role processes. Above all, the control properties of many *communication* verbs are different from those of *mental* verbs in interesting ways (cf. Steiner 1987d). Incidentally, Halliday (1985: 237ff.) gives support to our own approach here.

In our approach, and in contrast to both Halliday and Fawcett, we include in *mental* a sub-type [two phenomena] to cover verbs like *mean, imply, prevent...* which seem to accept two propositional arguments. It is sometimes argued that the thematized complement in clauses like (45) is not a propositional complement, but one embedded under a non-realized noun, as can be shown by (46):

(45) *That you have finished your thesis means/implies that you'll get a PhD.*
(46) *(The fact) that you have finished your thesis means/implies that you'll get a PhD.*

If one accepted this line of argument, it would also have to apply to the second complement with many *emotion* and *cognition* verbs, such as *like, remember, think about...*, and thus force us to make some extensive revisions. This in itself, of course, is not a counter-argument. However, there seem to be additional arguments why our [two phenomena] verbs should be treated under *mental*, one of them being the possibility of introducing a *Processor* as a *Prepositional Object*, cf.(47):

(47) *That you have finished your thesis implies/means to me that you'll get a PhD.*

Again, the analysis is not uncontroversial in so far as the Complement status of *to me* is not indisputable, and in so far as a similar type of role may be possible with [relational, classificatory/identifying] predicates, cf.:

(48) *He is a great man to me.*

Whichever analysis we adopt, the consequences are fairly obvious within the general principles of Systemic semantics. Our own decision is to treat verbs as in (47) as *mental* verbs, yet verbs as in (48) as *relational* verbs, mainly because with verbs of the type of *classificatory be*, only the Subject of the clause, or rather, the first Complement of the verb, may be propositional, whereas the second one, by obvious syntactic criteria, is a *Classifier*. The same applies to *identifying* types of process, except that with them, the assignment of a unique Subject function is problematic.

Let us mention at this point that there is another candidate structure for three-role *mental* processes, exemplified in (49):

(49) *She is watching the platform for her father to appear.*

We shall analyze this reading of *mental* verbs in parallel to other *mental* verbs, recognizing that the *for-to-construction*, which seems to have fairly obvious complement status, rather than adjunct status requires some more thorough integration into Systemic semantics.

Let us summarize what we have said about our treatment of *mental* processes so far: We shall keep the choices between [processor oriented] and [phenomenon oriented] open to all *mental* verbs, as well as a second choice of [first role +/- intention], stating explicitly that we are overgenerating for *emotion* verbs. Questions arising from our notion of *canonical order* of participant roles, as implied in the term *first role*, are discussed elsewhere (Steiner 1987d). There will thus be no necessity of introducing a *3rdpartyagent* into *mental* processes, which is important for methodological reasons: In the specific approach to transitivity advocated here, we are keeping the sets of participant roles for the major types of process disjunct. In this way, we can also cover the fact that there is at least one sub-class of *communication* verbs with only two inherent roles.

From all this it follows that the only motivation which we would have for making a distinction within *mental* processes between [emotion, perception, cognition] would be one in terms of world knowledge. While for Systemic Functional Grammar as a whole, it may be debatable whether or not this type of motivation by itself is regarded as sufficient, we do not accept it as a sufficient criterion for a linguistic semantics at this point.

Two of the semantico-syntactic clause types postulated in our version of *mental* processes should be briefly commented on:

Selection expression
[processor oriented, overt phenomenon,
phenomenon thing, covert processor,
processor - intention]
[phenomenon oriented, overt phenomenon,
phenomenon thing, first role +intention]

The option of [covert processor] can, in English, be realized through certain options in the *voice* system, if we postulate such a system generalized across all the process types where it applies, which excludes important sub-types of *relational*

processes.
Sentences such as (50) are not regarded as *mental process* realizations, because they do not permit the *Phenomenon* realization for their first role, as shown in (51):

(50) *This book reads well.*
(51) **That x is the case reads well.*

(50) derives from the [action, affected centred], and, specifically, the *middle* reading of *to read.* In other words, in our approach there is a dictionary entry for a *mental* verb *to read,* which is subcategorized in the ususal way of [processor oriented, mental] verbs. There is also an [affected-centred] entry for the verb *to read* to cover what elsewhere is called the process of *argument changing* (Bresnan 1982: 166ff., and elsewhere). And, as predicted by our approach here, the *mental* reading cannot undergo argument changing, as shown in (51) above.

The postulation of a [first role + intention] type in the second selection expression above depends on the assumption that a sentence like (52) is ambiguous between [+/-intention]:

(52) *John pleased Mary.*

There is also a possible analysis of the [first role +intention] reading as [action], which at this point would be indistinguishable from a [mental, phenomenon-oriented, first role +intention] reading.

Let us now move on in our discussion to *communication* processes. The sources here are Steiner (1985a), and also Fawcett (personal communication). As compared to the *communication* network in Steiner (1985a) the one used here is less *consolidated,* for the simple reason that the former overgenerates in some cases, while some options, on the other hand, are not accounted for. So, for the time being, working with a more *displayed* network is more adequate to the present stage of our knowledge, even if it is less elegant. A brief clarification of terminology may be in place at this point:
Redundancy makes a network *displayed* in the Systemic sense, whereas the absence of redundancy makes it *consolidated.* Redundancy in the present sense is introduced into a network through multiplication of identical sub-networks with features being taken here as the limiting case of a network. From this it follows that consolidated networks are to be preferred in general, but they make any network more difficult to read. Consolidation should in general express linguistic generalizations.

Let us discuss some of the clause types classified by this network (cf. Figure 28) by giving selection expressions and sample sentences. As always in discussions of transitivity, each selection expression classifies one class of clauses.

[sender +message, covert message, overt sender, overt receiver]

A few words should be said about the justification of the primary distinctions in our *communication* network: The class of [sender +message] structures is realized by those verbs that at least have no obligatory *Receiver* in active voice, or even show a clear tendency to occur with a *Message* rather than a Receiver, such as, for example, the verbs *say* or *state*. The Receiver here, if realized, takes the form of a prepositional group. Usually, verbs of this class are not syntactic *control-verbs*, even in their three-role realization.
The class of [sender + receiver] structures is realized by those verbs which show a clear preference for Receiver as a second role (*teach, persuade, instruct*), or even have an obligatory Receiver, usually as an NP-Object. Frequently, these verbs are control verbs (cf.below). With *communication* verbs, there is often no alternation between *prepositional phrase* and *nominal phrase* as indirect Object (*dative movement*) possible, whereas this is the case with *relational* verbs like *give, send etc.*. In fact, this syntactic difference is one formal motivation for classifying the two sets of verbs differently, *give, send,..* being *relational* verbs in our system. It should be added, though, that the potential for dative movement with three role *communication* verbs increases if both Objects are NPs.

We do not, at this stage, build into our system network for *communication* processes a sub-system to account for the difference between classes of verbs like *promise* and *tell*, both triggering a kind of movement of the non-realized Subject of the embedded clause, but the first type as movement to Subject, and the second type as movement to Object. In both cases, it might be added, we have cases of control rather than raising, in the sense that the Subject of the matrix clause is assigned its participant role from its verb. It should be obvious, though, that the distinction between the two types of verb mentioned above can be built into the system in a straightforward, though not trivial way, by relying on syntactic differences, which, as in most cases, can be seen as a reflex of semantic differences.

Finally, there is a class of [sender+prompt]. This is intended to allow for the possibility of yet another role with some verbs such as *answer*, where we can get realizations such as in (53) and (54):

(53) *He answered to my question.*
(54) *He answered my question.*

The second roles in (53) and (54) certainly are not either Receiver or Message, where (53) is, admittedly, on the borderline between grammaticality and ungrammaticality. In German, for example, the stipulated role of *Prompt*, which we are tentatively introducing at this point, can even co-occur in one clause with Message and Receiver, giving us one of these rare candidates for a four role process, cf.(55):

(55) *Er antwortete mir auf meine Frage, daß er krank sei.*
?He answered me to my question that he was ill.

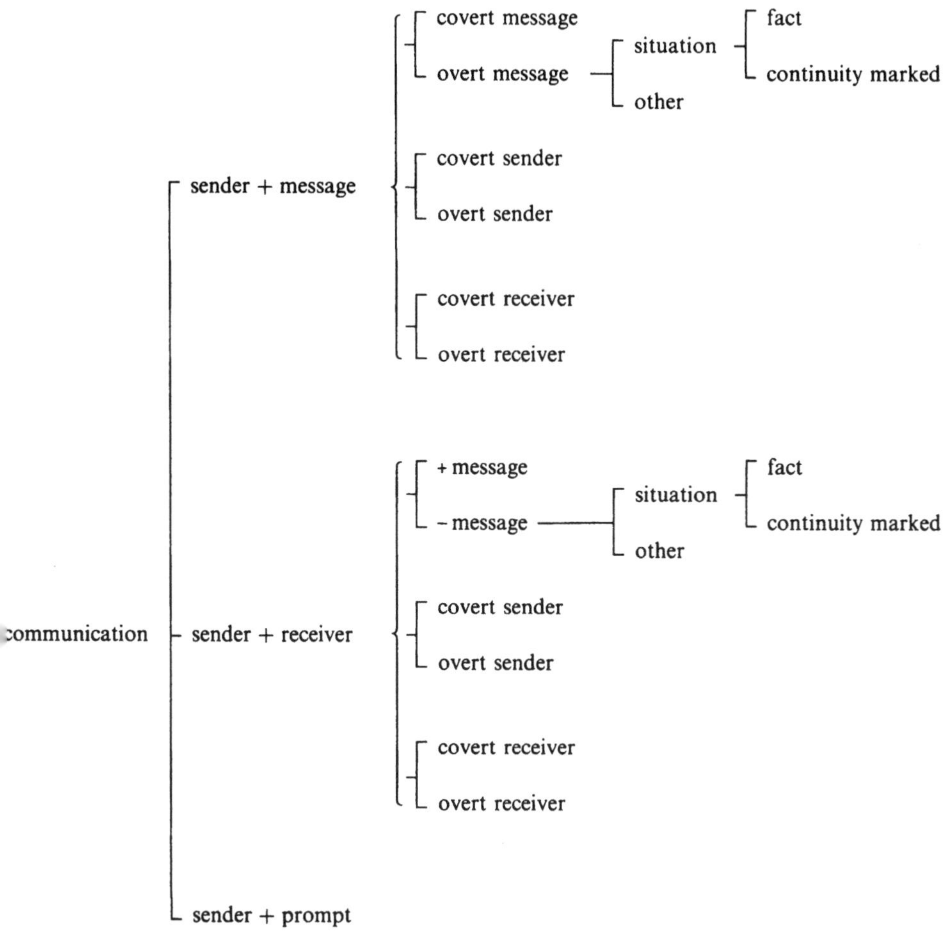

Figure 28. Communication processes in English

For English, it seems as if the role of Prompt is strongly restricted as far as admitting additional roles is concerned.

[sender+message, covert message, overt sender, covert receiver]

This selection expression will normally require some kind of *continuous form* in its realization, cf. (56):

(56) *John was shouting.*

Also, and interestingly, the presence of some Adjunct makes this a more plausible utterance, which is a question of theoretical importance: Whereas participant roles are only assigned to Complements, rather than *Modifiers*, in terms of valency, they are not always independent of Modifiers, as is also shown by pairs such as (57) and (58):

(57) *?John blackmailed.*
(58) *John blackmailed for a living.*

[sender+message, covert message, covert sender, covert receiver]

This would seem to be an instance of overgeneration for English, i.e., the network is too consolidated at this point and has to be redrawn, using the device of *zero-realizations*. In German, a type of *impersonal passive* realizes such a classification. We are leaving the selection expressions unchanged here because we want to illustrate the process by which overgeneration is created through consolidation of a network.

[sender+message, overt message, situation, fact, overt sender, covert receiver]

With some verbs of this class, such as *tell*, which belong here in so far as they require an obligatory *Message*, the selection of [covert receiver] often presupposes the choice of [situation, thing], cf. (59-60):

(59) **He told that he doesn't like it.*
(60) *He told a story.*

The following selection expression is realized in a sentence like (61).

[sender+message, overt message, situation, fact, covert sender, covert receiver]

(61) *It is sometimes said that people down here don't like gambling.*

The unrealized *Sender* in (61) has arbitrary reference.

[sender+message, overt message, situation, continuity marked, covert sender, covert receiver]

This depends on the acceptability of sentences like (62):

(62) ?*His not willing to take the blame for it was communicated.*

[sender+message, overt message, other, overt sender, overt receiver]

Some verbs, like *to say*, do not permit the selection of [other] without restriction, cf.(63):

(63) **He said the truth.*

However, cf. (64):

(64) *He did not say a word/it.*

[sender +receiver, +message, situation, continuity marked, overt sender, overt receiver]

This may require verbs with prepositions not strictly governing the complement, cf.(65):

(65) *He taught us about speaking proper English*

[sender +receiver, +message, situation, continuity marked, covert sender, covert receiver]

An example would be (66):

(66) *Speaking the French language was taught (to us) on Friday nights.*

Now, here as in some of the other cases we have highly marked selections in the *theme* and *information* networks, which may be precisely the reason why we seem to need an Adjunct.

Let us now move on to a discussion of *relational* processes. The major source here is Fawcett (1987, esp. ch.3). As compared to the corresponding networks used for example in Steiner. et al. (1988), the class of *identifying* is subsumed under *attributive*. The decisive question here is whether, in English, we have two different classes of verbs for the two types. As this does not seem to be the case, we shall follow Fawcett (1987:161), except that we include in our discussions a class of *existence* predicates.

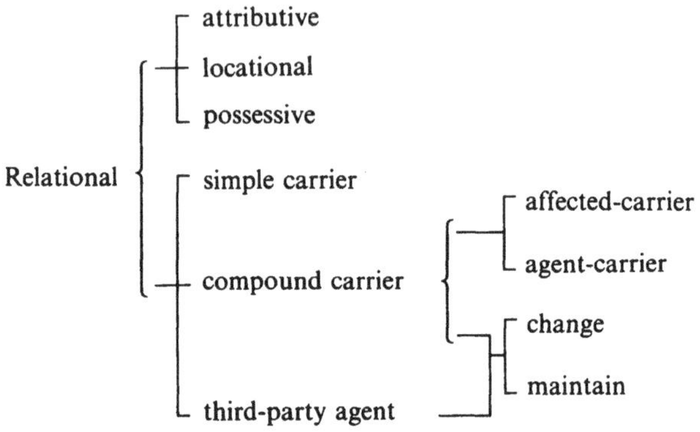

Figure 29. A maximally economical system network for relational processes in English
We are grateful to Frances Pinter Publishers for permission to reproduce Figure 29 from Fawcett (1987: 161)

In Figure 29, the role of *Carrier* corresponds to *Attribuant* in Fawcett's earlier work and in Steiner et al. (1988). Especially in connection with [relational possessive], Fawcett points out in several places that, at least in the [simple carrier] variant, they exist in [carrier oriented] and in [associated oriented] varieties, cf. (67) and (68):

(67) *I own that book.*
(68) *That book belongs to me.*

This brings to an end our discussion of networks and selection expressions. Whereas the main purpose of this section has been the presentation of tools needed for the kind of empirical research to be undertaken here, we also hope to have given an indication of theoretically interesting topics in the area of the Systemic notion of transitivity.

3.4.4 The semantic analysis of the data - coding conventions and problems

After introducing our networks and discussing some of the issues connected with our approach to transitivity, we shall now discuss some of the questions which turn up in descriptive work. The value of such a discussion will be seen in the fact that it gives us a chance of considering some theoretical problems in the light of actual linguistic data. It will also be seen that some of these problems simply do not occur as long as one restricts oneself to the treatment of self-fabricated sample sentences: natural linguistic data is in many ways more interesting and complex than one would assume when used to working with contrived examples only.

- The treatment of *tags*

We do not count any tags in this part of the analysis, the reason being that the function of tags is not the encoding of the *process* over again. In fact, tags would seem to realize features in the interpersonal component (cf. Fawcett 1980: 102f. and 108f.). Therefore, counting them as re-encoding the entire *process* which they could be said to substitute for under transitivity would give us added degrees of complexity where there are not really any, either in terms of the linguistic model (system), or in terms of production and processing (use). Note that this entails certain claims about cognitive processes going on during the production and processing of tags: one of them being that they are processed as "confirmation seekers", not, however, as encoding a *process*.

- The treatment of false starts

False starts are not counted under transitivity. This seems to be a fairly uncontroversial decision. How false starts are identified, especially as opposed to ellipses on the one hand and as opposed to repetitions with emphatic functions on the other, is more difficult. For the identification of ellipses, we refer to the treatment of that phenomenon in the literature (among many others, cf. Rath 1979: 133ff.). The identification of repetitions with an emphatic function is more difficult. One way is that of relying on the interpretation of the coder. If an assumed false start fills one whole information unit, then there are reasons for checking whether it might not be an instance of thematization and marked information focus. Otherwise, we will normally assume a false start.

- The treatment of ellipses

In general, we count ellipted elements when the antecedent is within the same utterance of one speaker. If the antecedent is not within the same utterance, we do not. This is not uncontroversial, as it could be argued that ellipsis where the ellipted element occurs in some preceding utterance does not reduce the semantic complexity of the *process*. Our primary reason for not counting it is that in these cases it is often difficult to tell precisely how many elements have been ellipted, i.e. are present in cognition. For example, whereas certain pro-forms, like personal pronouns or the predication *do* seem to have a relatively well defined scope, others do not, like, for example, the extremely frequent *yes/no* replies to questions. This is not to dispute the textual and cohesive function of ellipses and substitution, for example in question-answer pairs (cf. Halliday & Hasan 1976). However, scoping ambiguities of proforms alone would introduce such an amount of uncertainty into our figures that we have to exclude them.

- The identification of the element realizing the *process*

It is by no means always the case that the main verb of a clause, and only the main verb, realizes the semantic element of *process*. Cases in question are *analytical verb constructions, phrasal verbs, phrasal-prepositional verbs, and prepositional verbs*, several classes of "fixed syntagms", and certain classes of predicative adjectives. We shall in the following cite some cases from our data and explain how we deal with them, assuming that this definitely has consequences for writing realizational rules in Systemic Linguistics in general. In citing examples, we shall refer to page and line in our data where the examples are taken from (cf.Appendix 2).

First, let us consider an utterance such as the following:

G no/it's not worth it/really (55,19)

We are omitting stress and pauses in our examples here, yet they are part of the transcription. A slash "/" indicates the boundary of an information unit, i.e. a tone group. Abbreviations are as follows: S=Subject, P=Predicate, C=Complement, A=Adjunct

Which is the most appropriate analysis of such a sentence, cf. (69)-(71) ?

(69) [[S,it][P,'s not][C,worth][C,it][A,really]]

(70) [[S,it][P,'s not][C, worth it][A,really]]

(71) [[S,it][P,'s not worth][C,it][A,really]]

The analyses are taken only far enough to show us what the argument is about. (69) must be rejected because whereas [C,it] could be regarded as a clause constituent, especially if we substitute the pronoun by a lexical noun, [C,worth] most certainly can't. (70) likewise, is difficult to accept because [C,worth it] would not seem to have constituent status (but cf. below). (71) would seem the most plausible analysis, even if we encounter difficulties in finding evidence for a full constituent status for [P, 's not worth].

We are applying the usual substitution, questioning, clefting, and extraposition tests for the identification of clause constituents. Yet another test is based on conjunction: If *worth* was an intensive complement, (72) would have to be acceptable:

(72) **X is interesting and worth.*

Interestingly, and not quite in line with some earlier arguments concerning (70), (73) may come close to being acceptable:

(73) *?X is interesting and worth it.*

If, then, we take [P,'s not worth] to be the realization of the *process*, then it would realize the selection expression [mental process, two phenomena], which classifies it in the same way as the [two phenomena] readings of verbs such as *merit, contradict, imply*... etc..

A similar case occurs in the following example:

MB *makes sense* (60,16)

Apart from the fact that the Subject is ellipted, syntactic tests would seem to tell us that *sense* is not a constituent of its own. So, *makes sense* would seem to realize the semantic *process*. In that case, the Subject realizes a *Phenomenon*. Following this interpretation, we are faced with one of the problems connected with the notorious fuzziness of the Complement vs. Adjunct distinction, as illustrated in (74):

(74) *(The fact) that he didn't reply made a lot of sense to me.*
To me, (the fact) that he didn't reply made a lot of sense.

In (74), the function of *to me* is either that of a Complement or that of an Adjunct. There is a battery of tests which one can apply (cf. Somers 1983: 31ff.), but their results are not entirely conclusive in this case. If we decide against the interpretation of Complement, then we have one of these otherwise extremely rare occurrences of [phenomenon only] in English, (but cf. for German Steiner et al. 1988).

If we decide in favour of the interpretation as a Complement, then we are facing the difficulty that similar constituents occur in other types of process, where we do not usually give Complement status to them, cf.:

(75) *To me, he was simply acting out an act.*
?*He was simply acting out an act to me.*

(76) *To all of us, he was very attractive.*
He was very attractive to all of us.

In the fronting variants (74),(75) and (76), the constituent in question can be re-phrased as a predication on the whole clause, cf. (74a-76a):

(74a) *(It seemed) to me that ... made a lot of sense.*
(75a) ?*(It seemed) to me (that) he was acting out an act.*
(76a) *(It seemed) to us (that) he was very attractive.*

Assuming the acceptability of (74a-76a), it is doubtful whether the re-phrasing is a strict paraphrase of the non-fronting variants in (74)-(76). One of the points to be noted here is that there is an ambiguity involved as far as tense for the verb *seem* in the paraphrases is concerned: If we want to come close to a paraphrase, *past tense* is inevitable, yet there would also be the possibility of having *present tense* for *seem* in (74a-76a), and this ambiguity does not seem to exist in the non-fronting variants of (74-76). So, from this argumentation it would seem to follow that the fronted and non-fronted constituents are not necessarily of the same type, the fronted ones being clearly Adjuncts.

Accordingly, in the case of (74) we could decide in favour of the Complement interpretation, yet it should be seen that any decision like this forces one to tackle certain related questions. The splitting up of the binary Complement-Adjunct distinction as in Somers (1986) and elsewhere brings the problem out more clearly, without solving it by itself, though.

Finally, in this connection, it should be stated that in the case of phrasal verbs, prepositional verbs, and phrasal-prepositional verbs, the particles are regarded as realizing (part of) the semantic *process*, whereas in prepositional groups in which the preposition semantically governs its phrase, as in the case of directional or situational complements, it is regarded as realizing (the head of) a semantic participant role.

- The identification of problematic participant roles

Occasionally, we find realizations of participant roles and/or types of process which do not seem to be easy to identify, because they have been given little or no coverage in the Systemic literature. Cf. the following:

MB *we can use this/as a path/going from the door (55,20f).*

The types of process for the verb *use* which we can rule out immediately are *mental process* and *communication.* This verb follows a similar pattern to *treat* and *regard.* Applying the available re-expression tests, we assign the roles of *3rd party agent, Carrier, Classifier.* Note that *world knowledge* telling us that *as a path* could be regarded as some sort of Instrument, does not enter the picture at the semantic level of analysis. The role of Instrument in Systemic semantics is a *circumstantial role*, and as such cannot be assigned to a Complement.

Another interesting case can be seen in the following:

MB *this is the sort of thing that we'd need for roads/...* (55,12f)

The problem here is the classification of the verb *need.* If we realize that we can have an embedded *process* as a Complement, though, an analysis as *mental process* becomes plausible, cf.(77):

(77) *I need you to be my guide.*

Observe that *need* in this case is a main verb. In (77) we have a case of *object control*, which would violate the bi-uniqueness condition between particiapant roles and Complements, unless it was recognized as such (cf. Bresnan 1982: 163f.). Accordingly, we assume a dictionary entry for *need* which assigns two roles Processor and Phenomenon. The entry for *need* as a deontic semi-auxiliary is, of course, not covered thereby. In cases where the Subject of the propositional argument is raised to Object position of the matrix verb *need*, it leaves its participant role with the now "empty" Subject of the constituent clause. This leaves the semantic parallel between (77) and (78) intact, cf.:

(78) *I need guidance.*

- Covert participant role or different type of process?

Looking at the following examples, we can see a common problem:

MN *we put that like that/* (59,24)

G *we'll put a little bit for fencing then/* (60,17)

MB *if we're going to put the roof/* (67,2)

The question in all of these cases is: Are they cases of [relational, 3rd party agent] with a [covert location], or do we rather have a realization of an *action*-process? The question turns up, because this kind of construction is quite frequently used in South Wales, and it may have entered the linguistic system there already as an *action* type of process not requiring any location. Whatever our decision is, we are certainly faced here with one of the frequent cases where the actual usage may have to decide. Note that the principle of coding of maximal participant role frames for verbs in the lexicon does not by itself decide such cases.

- The Complement vs. Adjunct distinction

This distinction is as relevant as it is problematical in many instances. Only Complements are assigned a participant role, and thus the decision between Complement and Adjunct in instances such as below decides on the type of process and also on the participant roles to be assigned to a clause. Let us consider the following examples:

G *line the path with them or something/* (62,19)

It is not obvious that *with them* should unambiguously be analyzed as some sort of *instrumental* Circumstance, as can be seen from the possible ambiguity of sentences like (78):

(78) *He lined the paper with pencils.*

Under one interpretation, the pencils are lying alongside the paper, whereas under the other, the pencils were used to do the drawing.

At the very least, we have to assume two different types of Instruments, with one of them coming close semantically to a [relational, locational] reading.

Consider also the following sample from our data:

G *let's have it at the back/* (70,1)

This kind of structure with the verb *have* is, in fact, fairly frequent in our data. Firstly, *at the back* does not seem to be any kind of Adjunct, but rather a Complement. If that is correct, then theoretically we have either a new kind of [possessive] process, or else a [locational] with a *3rd party agent.* In fact, we counted it as [possessive], but there are good reasons for analysing it as [locational] also. It is probably just the fact that *have* is such a prototypical *possessive* verb, that we made our decision the way we did. The Complement status of the second role in this construction has already been discussed in the previous section.

- Causative constructions

Causative constructions which involve instances of syntactic embedding, are also treated as cases of semantic embedding, cf.:

MN *(right/we could have) we could have we could have*
him/ coming down the path/ (65,1f)

The analysis here is as follows: We regard *have* in this function as a verb assigning the second role *Effected* to its propositional argument, which in turn has an internal structure. Also, it would assign morphological case to the semantic *Agent* of the embedded clause, which makes it similar to a control verb. On the other hand, *him* does not seem to have full constituent status in the superordinate clause. This involves treating *have* as a causative marker semantically analogous, but not syntactically indentical, to *make* and *cause*.

These are the issues which we wanted to raise in our discussion of coding. On the face of it, the importance of such a discussion would seem to lie in making the basis for our analyses, and thus our statistics, obvious. Beyond this, though, it should be evident that most of the issues raised are of independent theoretical interest within Systemic Linguistics, and, indeed, within linguistics in general.

3.4.5 Results

In this section, we shall simply present our results in tabular form, leaving the discussion for the next section.

Table 59 on transitivity classes gives figures for the possible selection expressions in each type of process, the actually chosen paths ("realized"), and the number of instances, i.e. clauses, for each type of process.

Table 59. Transitivity classes
Percentages are given as approximations only.

	possible	realized		instances	
		PL	EX	PL	EX
action	16 (13%)	4(19%)	6(30%)	27(23%)	20(14%)
mental	34 (32%)	6(29%)	3(15%)	12(10%)	22(17%)
commu-nication	33 (31%)	2(9%)	1(5%)	2 (2%)	1(0,7%)
relation	22 (20%)	9(43%)	10(50%)	77(65%)	90(68%)
total	105(100%)	21(100%)	20(100%)	118(100%)	133(100%)

Table 60 contains figures for the number of clauses per actualized selection expression.

Table 60. Clauses per transitivity class

	Execution	Planning	
No of instances	133	118	(=133)
No of realized selection expressions	20	21	(=24,65)

Table 61 on possible and actual transitivity classes of clauses contains figures about the relationships between the number of possible selection expressions in each of the major types of process and the number of actualized selection expressions. Differently from Table 59, the basis of 100% is now formed by the potential in each type of process, rather than for all types of process together.

3.4.6 Discussion

First, let us consider our hypothesis H1 from 3.4.2., relying on the column "Instances" of Table 59 in 3.4.5.

First of all, both in PLANNING and in EXECUTION, the percentage of clauses realizing *relational* processes is very high (PLANNING: about 65%, EXECUTION:

Table 61. Possible and actual transitivity classes of clauses

Percentages are approximations only

Selection expressions			
	Potential	Realized	
		Execution	Planning
Action	16(100%)	6(38%)	4(25%)
Mental	34(100%)	3(9%)	6(18%)
Communication	33(100%)	1(3%)	2(6%)
Relational	22(100%)	10(45%)	9(40%)
Total		20	21

about 68%). Somewhat surprisingly at first sight, the percentage of *mental process* is higher in the EXECUTION phase than it is in the PLANNING phase (EXECUTION: about 17%, PLANNING: about 10%). Also somewhat unexpectedly, the percentage of *action* processes is higher in the PLANNING phase than in the EXECUTION phase (PLANNING: about 23%, EXECUTION: about 14%). Finally, the percentage of *communication* processes is quite low in both cases (PLANNING: about 2%, EXECUTION: about 0,7%).

The high percentage of relational processes is largely a consequence of our definition of relational predicates: If we took out of *relational* all those cases where an Agent is involved, the picture would be drastically different, to the effect that there would be many more action processes. However, our treatment of relational predicates is justifiable on independent grounds (cf. Fawcett 1987).

Next, we shall turn to hypothesis H2 from 3.4.2., relying on the column "realized" in Table 59 of 3.4.5. If we look at the percentages of selection expressions from different types of process realized in each of the phases, the picture comes somewhat closer to expectations:

Again, in both cases the percentage of selection expressions from relational processes is very high (PLANNING: about 43%, EXECUTION: about 50%). The number of selection expressions in mental processes is higher in the PLANNING phase (about 29%) than in the EXECUTION phase (about 15%). The number of selection expressions in action is higher in the EXECUTION phase (about 30%) than in the PLANNING phase (about 19%). Also, the number of selection expressions in communication processes is higher in the PLANNING phase than in the EXECUTION phase (about 9% as against 5%). In the case of COMMUNICATION, though, the overall number is so small that we should not rush to conclusions.

What do the differences in these percentages mean? There is a factor of uncertainty here, in so far as there are cases where an unambiguous assignment of selection expressions is difficult. We have mentioned these difficulties at length in our discussion of problems. We have also tried to state what the consequences should be for the overall theory in each case. Apart from these considerations, then, the distribution of selection expressions realized in the two phases seems to indicate clearly that in the PLANNING phases, the children make a qualitatively, yet not quantitatively more extensive use of mental process predicates, whereas in the EXECUTION phase, they make a qualitatively more extensive use of action predicates.

Next, let us consider H3 from 3.4.2., relying on Table 60 from section 3.4.5.: The number of clauses divided by the number of selection expressions would be lower in the PLANNING than in the EXECUTION phases, especially if we compute both of them on the basis of 133 clauses. This would seem to imply clearly that there is greater productivity in a qualitative aspect in the PLANNING than in the EXECUTION phases, because of the larger number of different transitivity structures relative to the number of clauses used in PLANNING. Quite obviously, serious statistical computations of significance would have to be made on a larger sample of data. Furthermore, the assumption of a linear increase in the number of different selection expressions with the number of clauses, underlying our computation of both figures on the basis of 133, is clearly untenable for larger numbers of clauses, because the number of selection expressions approaches a definite boundary for any amount of data (105), whereas the number of clauses does not. It is to be preferred, though, to a complete disregard of the number of clauses, because this would neglect the obvious fact that the probability of more selection expressions does increase with the number of clauses, although not in a linear way.

Finally, let us consider hypothesis H4 from 3.4.2. in the light of our figures in Table 61: Again, we have to remember the fact the the overall number of clauses in PLANNING is lower than in EXECUTION, which, if computed against identical bases would further shift our results in the direction predicted by H4. Even so, there seem to be two outstanding results: In EXECUTION, subjects were making qualitatively higher use of relational and action predicates than in the PLANNING phases. In the case of mental processes and communication processes, the figure is exactly the opposite: Children were making qualitatively more complex use of the mental and communication process systems in PLANNING than in EXECUTION. The second part of hypothesis H4 is not confirmed, because the greater productivity in action and relational processes in the EXECUTION phases outweighed the opposite tendency with respect to mental and communication. This can be regarded as evidence for the fact that a measure like "productivity" or "complexity" becomes much more complicated, differentiated, and to that extent more meaningful once it is operationalzed in a study such as the present one. It is also an instance of a situation where a so-called "common sense" hypothesis is not confirmed in a very interesting way.

This brings our discussion of results in transitivity to an end. Let us remind ourselves at this stage that what we are undertaking here is a model investigation, a pilot study. This explains why we are operating with a relatively small amount of data. On the other hand, experiences which have been gained in analyses of more data not published here consistently seem to point in the same direction. Also, within the context of the present study we are investigating a whole bundle of parameters other than transitivity (cf. the preceding and the following sections), and it is in that context that individual results have to be seen: Whereas probably any single result is underdetermined as far as statistical significance is concerned, the combined direction of the results in all of the individual areas that we are investigating should be fairly reliable for a prediction of the outcome of an investigation on a larger scale. On a more theoretical level, we have seen that the Systemic model lends itself easily to the formulation and testing of research hypotheses. It can be seen that a fuller exploitation of networks, features, paths and realizations will yield an even larger number of precise research hypotheses. To explore this has been one of our goals in this section as in many of the others.

3.5 Non-realized Themes in PLANNING and EXECUTION phases

This section will be relatively short and without an elaborate internal structure, the simple reason being that we are dealing with only one dependent variable which can be investigated relatively straightforwardly. We shall, in turn, comment on the notion of a "non-realized Theme" and its relevance for the present inquiry, make some necessary comments on our hypotheses deriving from the theory of activity, make the basis of our coding and counting explicit, and finish by presenting the results and discussing them.

Let us first discuss the notion of a *non-realized Theme* and its relevance for the present inquiry: The notion of *Theme* is defined as "the point of departure of the message from the point of view of the speaker" (Halliday 1985a: 38ff). It is, in a loose way, what the message is about. This, of course, is not at all the same as "given" or "new", nor is it the same as "topic", in the senses in which these terms are frequently used in different schools of linguistics (cf. Jones 1977; Rochemont 1986: 5ff; Erdmann 1990 for useful discussions), although, obviously, these concepts are related. Accepting the Systemic definition of *Theme*, one would clearly predict from the theory of ACTIVITY that in the EXECUTION phases, the Themes should be present in the immediate SITUATION of the speakers in a relatively high percentage of cases, and therefore, we would get a relatively high percentage of cases of Themes which are either realized by deictic elements, or not linguistically realized at all. The states and events acted upon and "talked in and about" are the states and events of the production of our utterances. Personal, local, and temporal deixis will refer to them in a relatively large number of cases. In the PLANNING phases, on the other hand, one would expect a relatively high percentage of linguistically realized Themes, precisely because, at least in interactive PLANNING, the possibilities of exophoric deixis in that phase should be considerably reduced. The states and events encoded in utterances in PLANNING phases are, because of the very nature of this phase, projected and possible, rather than present and actual, and as long as the PLANNING is interactive and therefore predominantly linguistic, one would clearly expect linguistically realized Themes - they are not available as reference points in the situation in which the utterance is produced.

As we have already seen in our discussion of context dependency, these hypotheses receive definite confirmation from our data on deictic elements. As, however, the distribution of deictic elements in the two phases is only one of several factors interacting with the distribution of Themes, we shall consider the fuller picture in the following.

Which are the variables interacting with the notion of Theme as we are using it here? The constant independent variables are age, sex, social class, and situation type. The only changing independent variable is *phase of* ACTION, and it is precisely this variable which should cause differences, if the predictions of the theory of activity go in the direction we suppose. Our dependent variables in this section are computed on the basis of utterances rather than clauses. Of course, Theme and Rheme are defined on the basis of the clause rather than the utterance, and they are also identified for the clause in our study, i.e. we assign Themes to clauses in utterances. For reasons of compatibility of figures with those in certain other sections, we will tabulate our results on the basis of utterances rather than clauses. This also opens the way for us to discuss the following characteristics of spoken language, which any study such as ours has to consider:

In counting utterances, we have followed the rules for calculating mean length of utterance (MLU) which have now become standard in child language development studies (Brown 1973: 54; Reich 1986: 75), and have added, or emphasized, the following rules which were mainly made necessary because of the particular nature of our data:

- *Yes/No* were counted as utterances, but not as either *Theme in situation* or *Theme in co-text*, although it could be argued that this is exactly what they encode. The means for determining this, however, are somewhat vague.
- Our transcripts show simultaneous utterances printed like sequential utterances with some bracketing in the margin. An utterance having another utterance running parallel for part of or all of its time, was still only counted as one.
- Sounds such as *oh* and *ah* were not counted, although it could again be argued that they are utterances consisting only of a Rheme and having their Theme in either the cognitive or external situation. Still, for our purposes, we considered it too much of an open question whether we should still regard those as realizations of the linguistic system.

Let us now inspect a bit more closely our dependent variable "Theme in Situation or in preceding utterance":

It may seem strange to count together the cases where the Theme is in a preceding utterance and where it is in the situation. The simple reasons is, however, that these two kinds of linkage can in many cases not be differentiated easily and unambiguously. It could be argued that under these conditions a high score in this category might just mean a high degree of cohesion by anaphoric reference through ellipsis. This, however, is very unlikely: when exophoric and endophoric reference are counted separately, accepting the ambiguities in identification, exophoric reference is much more frequent in EXECUTION than in PLANNING phases. Observe also that in our results below the number of non-Theme ellipses is higher in PLANNING than in EXECUTION phases, and in these cases it does tend to be endophoric rather than exophoric. Exophoric ellipsis of non-Theme elements seems to be extremely rare as a whole. Finally, in accounting for the role of Theme-ellipsis, the important and statistically significant role of the imperative in English should not be overlooked: The subjectless imperative in English requires Theme-ellipsis, and is frequent in EXECUTION, but very rare in PLANNING phases. As we have said already, under the heading of *ellipsis* in our table of results below, we only count ellipsis of non-Theme elements. For the identification of ellipses, we would like to refer again to Halliday/Hasan (1976:142ff.), and also to Rath (1978:133ff.). False starts and anacoluthons, in contrast to ellipsis and complete repeated utterances, were not counted. We will not give explicit procedures here for identifying these, except for saying that if you have good positive criteria for the identification of *Theme in situation* and the various kinds of ellipsis, then it is possible to use these as reliable negative criteria for the identification of false starts and anacoluthons.

Table 62. Results: theme

	Utterances as described	Ellipsis	False starts & anacoluthon	Theme in Situation or preceding utterance
EX	142	8	17	96
PL	116	18	27	22

Let us briefly discuss the findings that we have tabulated in Table 62: The most striking difference is probably in the figures on *Theme in Situation or in preceding utterance*: In the PLANNING phases, we find that approx. every 5.27 utterances there is an instance of a Theme in situation or preceding utterance. In the EXECUTION phase, we find one approx. every 1.48 utterances. In the PLANNING phases, we find ellipses other than Theme ellipsis every 6.4 utterances, whereas in the EXECUTION phase the equivalent figure is 17.75. That is, we find a far higher use of non-Theme ellipsis in the PLANNING phases than in the EXECUTION phases, which is generally taken as a measure of cohesion. Assuming that the same tendency carries over to Theme-ellipsis, the tendency under *Theme in situation or preceding utterance* would become even more marked, because one would expect them to be the reverse taking into account the anaphoric function of ellipsis only.

Finally, and somewhat surprisingly, false starts and anacoluthons seem to be more frequent per utterance in the PLANNING phases (one approx. every 4.29 utterances) than in the EXECUTION phases (one approx. every 8.35 utterances). Whether or not this has to do with the increased overall complexity of utterances in the PLANNING phases as measured under context dependency and mean length of utterance (cf.below), is not clear. It would then provide a confirmation of earlier findings of Goldmann-Eisler on the complexity of linguistic productions (cf. Goldmann-Eisler 1958). Still, it is not something which one would have predicted straightforwardly from the theory of activity.

The investigation of the *Theme*-variable, while being intrinsically less complex than, for example, the overall area of *transitivity*, has yielded a very clear result. We shall now proceed to investigate another, even simpler, variable, which, however, is one of the most longstanding variables in child language development studies.

3.6 Mean length of utterance

The measure of "mean length of utterance" has been extensively discussed in the literature on child language development studies. A useful source outlining its history and its operationalization is Reich (1986: 75ff.). We shall very briefly comment on our guidelines for coding, give our results in Table 63, and then make the necessary comments in the context of the present study.

The guidelines for counting are the same as under "Non-realized Themes in PLANNING and EXECUTION phases", except that this time false starts and anacoluthons are not counted at all, neither as utterances, nor the morphemes.

From the results it is obvious that the number of morphemes per utterance is clearly higher in the PLANNING phases than in the EXECUTION phases. In child language development studies, the *mean length of utterance* is usually taken as a crude but reliable measure of overall complexity, and we shall also take it as such. It can be seen that the results point in the same direction as those under context dependency and under "non-realized Theme in PLANNING and EXECUTION phases". They confirm the predictions of our theory of ACTIVITY for the structure of language in different phases of an ACTION. It should be absolutely clear that there can be no value judgement in terms of "better" or "inferior", as the theory of ACTIVITY exactly predicts that the language needed in different phases has to have different qualities in order to serve its respective functions. In a broad way of speaking: someone who always used exactly the same kind of language as measured by our variables would not talk in a functionally adequate manner.

While the results for mean length of utterance are straightforward and unambiguous, their restricted meaning should be seen clearly: As we have shown in the preceding sections, and as we hope to show in the sections to follow, semantic complexity is an intrinsically complex notion, and is only indirectly reflected in morpho-syntactic properties. Still, in the present state of child language development studies, a measure like mean length of utterance deserves to be taken into account, if only to permit a comparison with other studies in the area.

Table 63. Results: mean length of utterance

	EXECUTION	PLANNING
Utterances	142	116
Morphemes	869	843
Morphemes per utterance	approx. 6.12	approx.7.27

3.7 Circumstances

In this section we shall investigate the semantic complexity in PLANNING vs. EXECUTION phases in the area of *Circumstances*. This area of the semantics of natural language has received some, but still quite limited attention within the literature on Systemic Functional Grammar. It is therefore inevitable that we make a number of comments on theoretical as well as on descriptive issues. This we shall do predominantly in the section on "theoretical problems". We shall then give our results and, finally, discuss them in the light of our theoretical remarks and in the light of expectations and hypotheses derived from the theory of ACTIVITY.

3.7.1 Hypotheses

We shall only test three rather general hypotheses, commenting on possible additional ones in our discussion section. The hypotheses are:

(H1) The number of clauses per Circumstance will be higher in the EXECUTION than in the PLANNING phases.

(H2) The number of clauses with more than one Circumstance will be higher for the PLANNING than for the EXECUTION phases.

(H3) The percentage of *contingency*-Circumstances will be higher in PLANNING than in EXECUTION phases, where *contingency* has the sub-types of *cause, reason, purpose, result, condition, concession.*

3.7.2 Theoretical problems

- Adjunct vs. Disjunct vs. Conjunct

We begin by relating SFG concepts of Circumstances to those developed in the most widely accessible grammar of modern English, that of Quirk/ Greenbaum/ Leech/ Svartvik (1972, 1985). The whole area of *Adverbials* in a wide sense is a very complex and difficult area on many counts. One standard view (cf. Quirk et al. 1972: 417ff) draws a three way distinction, partly on syntactic and partly on semantic grounds. What is commonly called *Circumstances* in the Systemic literature, is realized in Adjuncts in terms of Quirk et al. What is called *Disjuncts* in Quirk et al (1972: 507ff) would appear to be realizations from the interpersonal component, and within this from *modality*, understood in a broad sense (cf. Halliday 1985a: 85ff). It has to be said, though, that Disjuncts in the sense of Quirk et al. would seem to realize a far broader range of meanings than covered by Hallidayan *modality*. *Conjuncts* in the sense of Quirk et al seem to be fairly well covered by Systemic views on the *clause complex* (Halliday 1985a: 192ff.), and seem to be realizations from the textual and logical components of the semantics in a Systemic sense. We shall cover this area in the present study's chapter on *logical connection*. Because of uncertainties of operationalization, we shall not draw a four way distinction here as in Quirk et al. (1985a: 566ff.), who include a class of *Subjuncts* in their classification.

As we shall see, and as is generally known, the distinctions between the three classes set up by Quirk et al. 1972 are not easy to draw in all cases. There are considerable areas of ambiguity, such as those illustrated below:

Consider the following example from our 12 B Boys play session (page and line number are given in brackets after the citation):

MB *this is the sort of thing that we'd need for roads/ because it's the only black one we got* (55,13)

The constituent *...because it's the only black one we got* is certainly not an Adjunct here, although it might conceivably pass either test (2) or (3) of Quirk et al. (1972: 421f.). We should add that it seems to be neither an Adjunct in the main clause, nor in the relative clause. What it means is *...and I'm saying this because it's the only black one we got.* From this perspective, it would seem to belong with the Disjuncts, although it does not fit easily into any of the classes mentioned. It does satisfy the test for Disjuncts as given by Quirk et al. (1972: 423f.). Accordingly, we count it as such, assuming that we'll have to add to the classes of Disjuncts.

Let us consider some additional examples from our data:

G *no/it's not worth it/really/* (55,19)

Again, *really* seems to be clearly outside the scope of negation. We classify it as an *attitudinal Disjunct* in the sense of Quirk et al.

G *I got a red flat one/if you want a red flat one* (56,12f)

...if you want a red flat one does not seem to be an Adjunct. The tests by Quirk et al indicate that it is a Disjunct, but then, we encounter difficulties in classification. We therefore count it as an inferential Conjunct, being aware of the uncertainty of the classification.

In the 12 B Boys play session, we have between 10 and 15 cases which display Circumstances semantically depending on ellipted or inferred clauses, which is quite a considerable number relative to the overall figures. Going through the available tests and stating their limitations clearly, thus pointing to areas of future work seems to be the only reasonable solution to adopt.

- Ellipsis

We have already stated our general principles for dealing with ellipses in the sections on context dependency, and in some of the other sections. In this section, we have somewhat loosened our restrictions on counting in the following way: We have counted constituents of elliptical sentences if they occur within the utterance of the same speaker producing the antecedent clause, or if they were answers to questions which demanded obvious cases of ellipsis from a communicative point of view. We also counted "Theme in context/co-text"-utterances, such as the following:

MB *exactly/* (58,14).
MN *we put that like that/*
G *right* (59,24f)

The complementary phenomenon can be seen in "Rheme in context/co-text"-utterances, which were also counted, cf.

MB *...it'll go down 'ere/*
MN *no*
MB *what* (60,8ff)

However, it should be said that we did not count pro-forms such as the following:

MB *but a bungalow only has a flat roof/*
G *doesn't*
MN *doesn't* (66,16ff).

Our reason for not counting those is that there is considerable controversy in the literature as to whether these pro-forms include the Adjuncts or not (cf. Quirk et al. 1972: 427 vs. Somers 1983: 41ff.). We tend to assume that pro-forms, by nature of their definition should not necessarily include the non-valency bound elements in their domains, but it would be unwise to make a decision at a point when there still is so much controversy.

These slight modifications seemed necessary because otherwise, too many cases of Circumstances would have been lost in the counting. Needless to say, the whole question of ellipsis introduces some degree of uncertainty into our statistics. The only way of counteracting this would seem to be that of making our principles for counting as explicit and restrictive as possible.

- Ambiguities between Post-Modifiers and Adjuncts

The ambiguity mentioned here is illustrated by the following utterance:

MB *use it as a wall/for the fencing/it'll go down 'ere*

Now, it is well known that *pp-attachment* as in *for the fencing* provides a standard source of ambiguity in our area. The fact forcing us to think about categorization is that *for the fencing* receives an information unit (tone group) of its own, pointing to the fact that it might rather have been an Adjunct. There is no way to be sure, yet we counted this as an Adjunct. Fortunately, we had very few cases of that class in our data, and our decision was made with the help of *information distribution*, e.g. assignment of information units to structures.

- Conjunctions, relative pronouns, "wh-binders"

All of these words may either integrate one clause into another as a clause element, or as element of a group (cf. also the treatment of the *Comp* node and trace theory in Government & Binding Theory, as illustrated in Chomsky 1981, or in Block 1986: 27ff.). The question relevant for us at this point is, to what extent these words also function as (part of) elements of the clause which they "subordinate" or "coordinate". We are adopting the following counting conventions, which, quite obviously, express a theoretical commitment to certain principles regarding the status of these word classes within the clause in which they function.

Relative pronouns and "question"-pronouns (*why, when, where*...) function as elements of their clause while they may have, at the same time, the function of "binding" the clause into another one. They are, therefore, counted as Circumstances, when they function as such. Co-ordinating conjunctions ("linkers", cf. Fawcett 1980) are counted as Circumstances whenever they have that function (paratactic *therefore, yet, however*...). Binders, or subordinating conjunctions (hypotaxis), are not counted within the clause they bind i.e. the subordinated one, if they do not have constituent status within these clauses.

- Differences in figures as against context dependency

From what we have said in this section, it is clear that some differences to the counting of A-elements under context dependency are to be expected: This is due to the treatment of ellipsis, and to the fact that we are separating strictly here Adjuncts, Disjuncts, and Conjuncts.

3.7.3 Results

We shall below reproduce our coding sheet which contains types and sub-types of Circumstances as well as numbers and percentages of the instances found in our corpus (Table 64). The appearance of our coding sheet should not lead us to the unjustified conclusion that we are dealing with a system network here: There are theoretically no co-occurrence restrictions between types of Circumstances, so that all we would have here is an AND-connection. Between sub-types, there may be such restrictions, but again, in the present state they are not extensively researched so that we do not intend to make any definite claims about constraints between sub-types. The present inability to establish a well-motivated system network points to the theoretical status of Circumstances on the one hand, and to a lack of specifically detailed research on the other.

3.7.4 Discussion

This discussion will give a brief interpretation of our findings, which have to be seen against hypotheses H1-H3 in 3.7.1. Furthermore, they are indicative of certain tendencies, yet do not have a more definitive status, mainly for two reasons: First, the amount of data covered is far too small to permit more than statements about trends. Second, the definitions of some classes of Circumstances and of such phenomena as ellipsis and even Adjunct/ Disjunct/ Conjunct are still not far enough operationalized to avoid ambiguity in all cases.

- The number of clauses per Circumstances.

As we can see in Table 65, the children produce 1 circumstances every 2,07 clauses in the PLANNING phases, but only every 3,84 clauses in the EXECUTION phases. This certainly means that the overall complexity of *circumstancial* elements is higher, at least in so far as sheer frequency is accepted as a measure. Taking into account the fact that in most versions of Systemic Grammar, Conjuncts and Disjuncts would be generated from the *modality* network and from the *logical relationship* network, rather than from Circumstance, the discrepancy with regard to Circumstance would even be slightly higher. We can therefore regard hypothesis H1 of this chapter as confirmed.

- Multiple Circumstances

As we can see in Table 65, in the EXECUTION phases only about one fourth of the clauses had any Circumstances at all, whereas for the PLANNING phases the equivalent figure is 41%. Also, in the EXECUTION phases, only 0,5% of all the clauses had two Circs. In the PLANNING phases, a third of all clauses had one Circumstance, yet 7% had two Circumstances, and there was one occurrence of a clause with more than two Circumstances. It should be said here that multiple

Table 64. Circumstances

Type	Subtype	Instances	
		PL	EX
	position	15(23%)	6 (12%)
space			
	distance	1 (1,5%)	1 (2%)
	position	5 (8%)	10(20%)
	duration	0	1 (2%)
time	frequency	2 (3%)	0
	others	0	0
	manner	6 (9%)	8 (16%)
	means	0	0
process	instrument	0	0
	agentive	0	0
respect		0	0
	cause	0	0
	reason	3 (4,5%)	2 (4%)
	purpose	13(20%)	1 (2%)
contingency	result	0	0
	condition	2 (3%)	2 (4%)
	concession	0	0
	emphasis	0	0
modality	approximation	0	0
	restriction	5 (8%)	0
	amplification	2 (3%)	1 (2%)
degree	diminution	1 (1,5%)	3 (6%)
	measure	1 (1,5%)	0
disjuncts		4 (6%)	5 (10%)
conjuncts		6 (9%)	10(20%)
Total		65	50

Table 65. Circumstances per clause

	PL	EX
No of clauses per Circ	2,07	3,84
% of clauses with 0 Circ	59%	74,75%
% of clauses with 1 Circ	33,3%	24,75%
% of clauses with 2 Circ	7%	0,5%
% of clauses with ¿2 Circ	0,7%	0%

Circumstances are only given when they are Circumstances of the same verb, i.e. a Circumstance in an embedded *circumstancial* clause is of course not counted as Circumstance of the verb in the superordinate clause. Again, in so far as these

Table 66. The most frequent classes of Circumstances

	Pl	Ex
The 3 most frequent classes of Circ	position,(23%) space purpose (20%) manner (9%) conjuncts(9%)	pos,(20%) time conj(20%) manner(16%) pos,(12%) space

Table 67. Classes of Circumstances

% of all Circs in:	Pl	Ex
space	24,5%	14%
time	11%	22%
process	9%	16%
respect	0	0
contingency	27,5%	10%
modality	8%	0
degree	6%	8%
disjuncts	6%	10%
conjuncts	9%	20%
* All percentages given are approximate values		

figures are accepted as measures of *circumstancial* complexity, there seems to be a clear difference between the two types of phases and hypothesis H2 must be regarded as confirmed.

- The most frequent classes of Circumstances

Within the PLANNING phases, *space position circumstances* are the most frequent (23%), next we find *purpose* (20%), and then *manner* and *conjuncts* with 9% each of all the *circumstances* (cf.Table 66). Within the EXECUTION phases, *time position* and *conjuncts* are the most frequent classes (20% each), then *manner* (16%) and *space position* (12%). We shall not interpret the figures in great detail, yet it should be recognized that the frequency of *purpose circumstances* looks like an unusually straightforward case of indication of the phase of ACTION, and hypothesis H3 can be regarded as confirmed. Also, such figures should be taken within their proper context: Whereas the higher percentage of *contingency* in PLANNING over EXECUTION phases (27,5% over 10%) would seem to indicate a higher linguistic realization of logical relationships within clauses, the reverse tendency can be observed for *conjuncts* (9% in PLANNING and 20% in EXECUTION), where it has to be borne in mind that many types of *conjuncts* realize logical relationships between sentences. So, what may be achieved through *experiential structures* in the

PLANNING phases may in the EXECUTION phases be achieved through cohesive devices. A closer look at the figures tells us that still the number of overt logical relationships is higher in the PLANNING phases than under EXECUTION, yet one should certainly beware of hasty generalizations (cf. Table 67).

One fact that is clearly illustrated here should be borne in mind: SFG is a semantically oriented linguistic theory. Still, being a linguistic theory rather than, say, a psychological theory, it divides its field of study according to linguistic, i.e. formal criteria. It is this very fact which leads to the distribution of what seems to be semantically a unified phenomenon, logical relationships in this case, over a range of different semantic components, like Circumstances and *logical connection.* This is probably nowhere brought out more clearly than in an empirically-based study such as the present one.

3.8 Time

3.8.1 Introduction

Time, like any other concept in the semantics of English, or any language, is more complex and its syntactic realizations more diverse than it would appear at first sight. In these introductory remarks we shall try to characterize some of these complexities within the theoretical framework of Systemic Functional Grammar.

Somewhat surprisingly, the semantics of *time* has so far received less coverage within SFG than other core areas of the semantics of natural language. Halliday's "The English Verbal Group" (cf. Kress 1978: 136ff.) gives an account of options in *time* as realized in the verbal group, which is repeated and extended in Halliday (1985a: 175ff.). We find Halliday's most recent views on *time specification*, even if not under that name, in his discussion on Circumstances in (1985a: 137ff.). *Time* as realized inter-sententially is dealt with in (1985a: 192ff.)., in his treatment of the clause complex. Fawcett states the problem in general, making some useful general observations (1980: 154ff.), but does not seem to go beyond Halliday's approach. In the Systemic literature on cohesion, *time* is usually covered in so far as it is realized by cohesive devices between sentences, as in Halliday & Hasan (1976). Apart from Halliday in Kress (1978) and Halliday (1985a), the third major source for a treatment of *time* and tense within SFG is still Hudson's (1971) "English Complex Sentences" , which covers fairly extensively the realizations of *time* for non-finite clauses (1971: 109ff.), Complement clauses, or *nominal clauses* in his terminology (1971: 201ff., cf. also p.244 for an extended system network). However, whereas Hudson's work can be said to have a level of detail which is hardly surpassed in Halliday's (1985a) account of *time* and *tense*, it is too strictly syntax-oriented to function as our primary starting point within the present context. We shall have to evaluate critically, though, to what extent Halliday's (1985a) approach gives a

semantic rather than syntactic account of *time*.
As this particular study is situated within the model of SFG, we shall not try to discuss alternative theoretical approaches to the linguistic problem of *time*. The major alternative which comes to mind here would seem to be that of a "logical" approach to *time* (cf. Reichenbach 1966: 287ff., or Lyons 1977 Vol.1: 161ff.). It is, in particular, the complex interaction between Reichenbach's "point of speech, point of reference, and point of event" which would seem to receive too little attention within SFG-accounts of *time* (but cf. Matthiessen 1989).

What the SFG approach does seem to be particularly good at, is the recognition and the modelling of the complex interplay between linguistic levels and ranks, as well as that between semantics and realization as linguistic phenomena. We shall now outline these in general as the problems of "distinct levels, intra-element vs. inter-element realization in syntax, and the problem of different ranks".

- Distinct levels

Time is a concept from the semantic level of language, and as such it has to be kept conceptually distinct from terms like *tense, temporal adverbial, temporal conjunction* etc., which are clearly phenomena on the level of lexico-grammatical form. A first step in this connection has to be that of getting a realistic impression of what the complexities are on each of these two levels. We shall try to contribute towards this goal in the present section. The next step, which is that of modelling the complex interplay between these two levels can only be approached here in general terms.

-*Time* as realized within and between elements of clause structure

Restricting ourselves to the clause as the domain of realization for the moment, the most immediate idea is that *time* is realised by the tenses within the *verbal group*, assuming that we operate with the notion of a verbal group, like Halliday, rather than treating the elements of the verbal group as elements of the clause directly (like Fawcett 1980). The *tense* feature would then simply be percolated upwards from the verbal group to the clause. This, however, seems to be missing out the important fact that *time*, as a semantic phenomenon, seems to be realized, in clause structure, in the verbal group and in other groups functioning as Adjuncts, Conjuncts, Binders, or even Complements in clause structure (see below for examples). It is more adequate to say that *time* is realized through the interaction of elements in the verbal group and the elements of clause structure just mentioned.

-*Time* as realized on different ranks

It is possible and even necessary to make statements about *time* on different ranks. Talking about *time* as realized in groups and in the clause is only part of the picture. *Time* is also a phenomenon in discourse and text, with semantics and form of *time* being related, yet not identical to those at clause rank. We shall confine ourselves here to the ranks of the group and the clause, simply because this is a first step. Later, when we are investigating clause connection, we shall begin to go beyond those ranks.

Another issue that needs to be mentioned here is that of *time* vs. *aspect/aktionsart*: Whereas *time* as a semantic phenomenon has to be analyzed into its levels (semantics vs.syntax) and ranks (group, clause, sentence, text), it has, as a whole, to be separated from related phenomena like *aspect* and *aktionsart*. About aktionsart, we shall have more to say in a later section. Aspect will be disregarded for the time being, not because it is considered unimportant, but simply because the predictions of the theory of ACTIVITY do not refer to it at this stage. Needless to say, this separation is one for methodological reasons only. Halliday (1985a: 157ff.) appears to handle *aspect* under the general heading of *time*, which, as we shall see, leads to certain counter-intuitive semantic features in the network.

After these opening remarks, we shall in the following adopt and modify existing SFG approaches in a way sufficiently detailed to permit application to the data which we shall be analyzing.

3.8.2 A network for time as expressed in the verbal group

The system network for *time* in Figure 30 is an alternative notation for the account given in Halliday (1978: 153 and 1985a: 180f.). It expresses the options within the finite verbal group, and thus includes the more restricted options of the non-finite/modalized verbal groups and the verbal groups after past projection-verbs, i.e. indirect speech, cognition and perception . Also, these options are only open to indicative (including interrogative) clauses, which means that imperatives are excluded at this stage. It will be seen that this network symbolizes a wider range of options than is actually realized by our 12 B boys, which however, is true of all the system networks we are using.

- Discussion of problems

In the system network in Figure 30, system 1 is of particular interest in so far as it is through options in this system that the speaker situates the utterance relative in time to the communicative situation, i.e. the "here and now", which is close to Reichenbach's (1966: 287ff.) relationship between *point of reference* and *point of speech*. If options are chosen in system 1 only, point of reference and point of event are non-distinct. This applies only for independent clauses. Clauses which themselves function as elements in the structure of some other clause may be temporally situated relative not to the situation of the superordinate utterance, but to the situation encoded in the utterance which they are situated in. In that case the realizational rules change: a given *time* feature is no longer realized by the same tense as in the case of a *present* clause. Depending on the *time* of the superordinate clause, the options available may be limited and distinctions may be neutralized in realization, cf.:

(79) *I didn't go to the shops because I will not need anything.*
(80) *I didn't go to the shops because I wasn't going to need anything.*

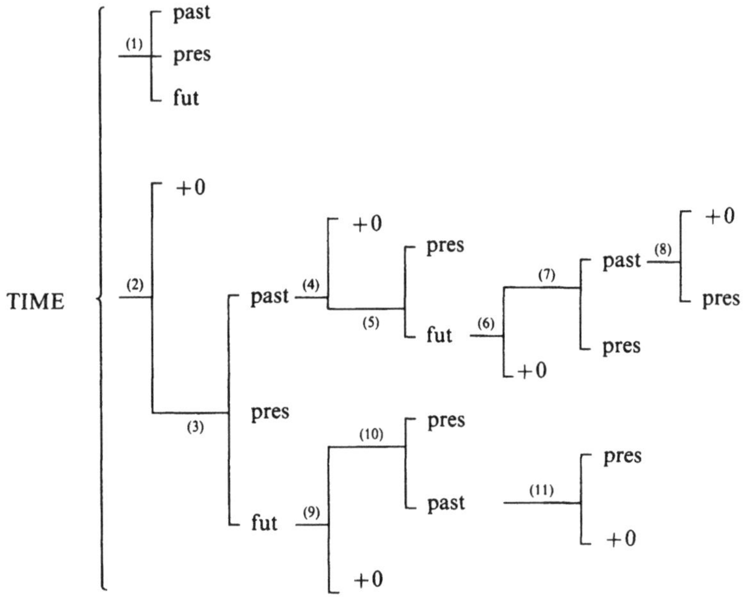

Figure 30. A network for time

In clause (79), the *reason* clause is situated in time relative to the situation of the utterance of the main clause. In (80), however, it is situated relative to the situation encoded in the main clause. This phenomenon needs further investigation. It is also different from the case of *projection*-clauses.

Selection expressions and examples for our system network are given in Figure 31 from Halliday (1985:180f.).

This also seems to be the place for commenting on some further difficulties arising from the application of the time network to our data:

- Some of the tenses captured by Halliday would clearly seem to have a wider range of meanings than indicated in the network, as is illustrated the following examples:

MN *then we're doing a yellow or blue/* (68,12)

According to Halliday (1985:180f), we are forced to code this as sit[pres+pres], to be read as *present in present in speech situation*, although the meaning would seem to be rather sit[pres+fut], even in the absence of the lexical item *then*. The same applies to the following example:

MN *we're only doing one layer of white* (68,9).

TENSE			Non-finite, and finite modal, tenses (12): read as far as β			Finite non-modal tenses (36): read as far as α	
ϵ	δ	γ	β	α			
						past	1
			(none)	I		present	2
						future	3
						past	4
			past	II	in	present	5
						future	6
						past	7
			present	III	in	present	8
						future	9
						past	10
			future	IV	in	present	11
						future	12
						past	13
		past	in future	V	in	present	14
						future	15
						past	16
		present	in past	VI	in	present	17
						future	18
						past	19
		present	in future	VII	in	present	20
						future	21
						past	22
		future	in past	VIII	in	present	23
						future	24
						past	25
	past	in future	in past	IX	in	present	26
						future	27
						past	28
	present	in past	in future	X	in	present	29
						future	30
						past	31
	present	in future	in past	XI	in	present	32
						future	33
						past	34
present	in past	in future	in past	XII	in	present	35
						future	36

	Finite non-modal tense
1	took / did take
2	take(s) /do(es) take
3	will take
4	had taken
5	has taken
6	will have taken
7	was taking
8	is taking
9	will be taking
10	was going to take
11	is going to take
12	will be going to take
13	was going to have taken
14	is going to have taken
15	will be going to have taken
16	had been taking
17	has been taking
18	will have been taking
19	was going to be taking
20	is going to be taking
21	will be going to be taking
22	had been going to take
23	has been going to take
24	will have been going to take
25	had been going to have taken
26	has been going to have taken
27	will have been going to be taken
28	was going to have been taking
29	is going to have been taking
30	will be going to have been taking
31	had been going to be taking
32	has been going to be taking
33	will have been going to be taking
34	had been going to have been taking
35	has been going to have been taking
36	will have been going to have been taking

	Non-finite, and modal tenses: (perfective, imperfective; modal
I	to take, taking; can take
II	to have, having; can have + taken
III	to be,being; can be + taking
IV	to be, being; can be + going/about to take
V	to be, being; can be + going to have taken
VI	to have, having; can have + been taking
VII	to be, being; can be + going to be taking
VIII	to have, having; can have + been going to take
IX	to have, having; can have + been going to have taken
X	to be, being; can be + going to have been taking
XI	to have, having; can have + been going to be taking
XII	to have, having; can have + been going to have been taking

Figure 31. Tense in Halliday (1985)
We are grateful to Edward Arnold publishers for permission to reproduce Figure 31

A parallel problem with a different tense is illustrated in the following example:

MB *let's put the ladder on/after we've done the roof* (66,25f)

This particular clause is not counted because the main clause is a form of imperative, yet the point remains that the sit[pres+[pas]] really is sit[fut+[pas]]. For the notation, it is important to observe that each predicate receives its own pair of parentheses, whereas complex tenses within one clause do not receive internal bracketing, but are simply connected through the usual "+" symbol. Observe also that, as different from some other system networks, the features in *time* are strictly ordered in selection expressions.

The same problem with yet another tense is illustrated in the following:

MN *and you put them all the way round/*
and they are up like that/(57,28f)

Whereas our network forces us to code sit[pres+0], the chances are that the semantic structure is sit[fut] for each of the two clauses.

- The interaction of Conjuncts or Adjuncts with tense.
Let us again start out by considering two examples from our data:

MN then we're doing a yellow or blue (68,12)

MB ...
we'll do a white bottom/
...
then a different colour next/
then a different colour next/... (58,7ff)

In the first case, we are forced to code as sit[pres+pres], whereas the semantic structure on text level would seem to be sit[fut[fut]], because the clause immediately preceding (68,12) has already established future reference. This, of course, implies a deviation from our notation so far, treating a clause and its antecedent as a semantic unit, and it is only used here for the sake of illustration. In the second case, we have to code sit[fut] three times over (remembering our rules for dealing with ellipsis), whereas the appropriate analysis would seem to be something like sit[fut[fut[fut]]], although again we would be violating our principle of restricting ourselves to the domain of one clause at a time. This, of course, has to do with the difference of *time* as a phenomenon on clause rank and on text rank.
Now, part of this problem is, of course, solved in the separate treatment of *logical connection* or *clause combining*, yet as long as we do not integrate both of these descriptions, our analyses remain fragmentary from the perspective of textlinguistics.

- Let us finally return here to the question of clause embedding and clause combining, which is made even more complicated by the phenomenon of ellipsis, where they occur together. Cf. the following passage:

MB	*won't it/I've just knocked a cheese sandwich/*	
G	*why/*	
	oh/because it's too big/	(67,27ff)

Now, because of our particular rules for dealing with ellipsis, the third line here is not counted as a continuation of the second clause in the first line, but this is just accidental. If we have to count such cases, what is the *time*?
If we treated its tense as functioning relative to the tense of the superordinate clause (cf. for a discussion of *superordination* below), then the structure would be something like: sit[pres+pas[pres]]. This, however, would not seem to be uncontroversial. In one perspective, the adverbial clause seems to establish *time* and tense relative to the context of situation directly, i.e. sit[pres].

Independently of the complexities introduced by ellipsis, there seem to be two areas that have to be explored further:

- Most *projection* clauses (cf. Halliday 1985a: 227ff.) would seem to establish *time* relative to the clauses in which they are embedded, although even there this is not an absolute rule, cf.:

(81) *He said that he didn't like it.*
(82) *He said that he doesn't like it.*

- In non-projected adverbial clauses, both possibilities would also seem to exist, but with possibly different mechanisms involved, cf.:

(83) *I've just knocked a cheese sandwich because it's too big.*
(84) *I've just knocked a cheese sandwich because it was too big.*

Of course, in establishing *time* relative to a preceding utterance one also establish it recursively with reference to the context of situation (cf. van Eynde 1988; Rohrer 1985).

Another interesting case, which illustrates the basic fact that the *time*-line as such is not absolute, but moving, at least within the context of an ongoing action, is illustrated in the following:

MN *look/ if we put that/like that/-*
there you are (64,13f)

The question here is that of which *time* to assign to the *if*-clause. What seems to be happening here is that MN starts a conditional construction, but goes on working at whatever he is talking about and thus ends up realizing the state of affairs which he was going to predict after the short pause indicated by "-". So, the selection expression would seem to be something like: sit[fut +0 [fut]], with the second [fut]=[sit[pres+0]] with respect to the changing *time*-line. This class of cases, which can be expected to be a not infrequent case in ongoing actions, is not covered in any obvious way by the treatment of *time* within Systemic Linguistics so far.

3.8.3 Time Specification

As has been stated above, *time* is not realized through tense alone, but through the interaction of tense with *time specification* as realized in Adjuncts and Conjuncts. Now, each of these are treated separately elsewhere, but their function of realizing options in *time* would only seem to become obvious when they are seen in their interaction with tense. We shall make an attempt at doing so here, without any claim to comprehensiveness or originality.

The interaction of tense with temporal Adjuncts or Conjuncts on clause rank has, to my knowledge, been rather neglected within SFG. We shall take up here an approach followed by Crystal (1966). For the moment, we shall use Halliday's and Crystal's classification side by side without trying to integrate them. Crystal's classification makes reference to tense, classes of Adjuncts/Conjuncts, and even the transitivity of the verb, so that the two analyses do not just complement each other. As, however, it seems obvious that both classifications capture important facts about the realization of *time*, we shall use them both with a view to integrating them into one description at a later stage.

It has to be said that Crystal's classification of *time* as expressed by tense + time specification causes difficulties in the context of our particular task. Some of these difficulties are specified in the following:

- Crystal's classification (Crystal 1966:24ff.) does not seem to give us a way of handling verbal groups with modal auxiliaries. They appear to be excluded, and accordingly we cannot count them. We are counting them, though, within the Systemic approach.
- Also, Crystal's classification does not seem to provide for non-finite verbal groups.
- The operationalization of Crystal's semantic distinctions is not always clear. For example, he includes, under the heading of *specific perceivable activity taking place* (1966: 24), examples like *I'm enjoying this*. It is certainly not immediately obvious why one should classify this as an *activity* in the first place, and as a "perceivable" activity in addition. This is quite a general problem with Crystal's classification and inevitably reduces the reliability of any conclusions one might draw from statistics using that classification. In the same connection, Crystal appears to be using the term *activity* to refer to *states* as well.
- Some tenses do not seem to be covered at all, as for example the very frequent constructions using *going to*.
- Some obvious cases seem to be missed in Crystal's classification, as for example the realization of *future time* by simple present tense, cf.:

MN *and you put them all the way round/*
and they are up like that/ (57,28f)

This is a gap which Crystal's approach shares with the Hallidayan so far, and thus it causes quite a few difficulties for a strictly semantically based approach.

Another case which is missed out by Crystal (1966) is the possible realization of *past in future time* by the *present perfect*,cf.:

MB *let's put the ladder on/ after we've done the roof/* (66,25f)

Drawing a conclusion from our statements about Crystal's approach, it is obvious that our using it can only be seen as a step on the way to a more satisfactory scheme for dealing with the interaction of tense and adverbials, or *time* and *time specification.*

3.8.4 Conventions and rules for counting

In considering *time*, we are not including clauses that are elliptical or incomplete, except in cases where an elliptical clause is a direct answer to a question, and substitution therefore relatively reliable. We are also counting elliptical clauses which have as antecedents of their ellipted elements structures in the same utterance of the same speaker.

Apart from the question of ellipsis, there is another individual structure which we have to comment on, because it is particularly frequent and its treatment is not immediately obvious. cf. the following utterance (56,1):

MN *ah/I got an idea/ I got an idea/*

The question here is what tense and *time* to assign to *got*, and also *have got*, where they occur with clearly simple present reference i.e. synonymous with *have*. In all of these cases, we coded as simple present, i.e. sit[pres+0], rather than as *past in present*, i.e. sit[pres+pas]. For an approach based on meaning, this seems to be the preferable alternative.

A further convention which follows directly from Halliday's general approach is that at this stage imperatives are excluded from counting.

3.8.5 Hypotheses

We shall list here the hypotheses which we derive from the theory of activity for the complexity of *time* structures in PLANNING and EXECUTION phases respectively. These hypotheses are mainly based on the fact that in PLANNING phases, the agents have to encode future and/or hypothetical situations linguistically to a much greater extent than in EXECUTION phases. For the predictions, we continue to rely on the system network and the feature notation which we have been using in this section. Again, as in the other cases where we generate hypotheses, there would be scope for many more, and especially more detailed predictions. These, however, would be outside the scope of a pilot study such as ours.

(H1) The overall complexity of *time* structures as measured by the number of different selection expressions divided by the number of instances (clauses) is higher in PLANNING than in EXECUTION phases.

(H2) The number of selection expressions which have a feature for (epistemic) modality is higher in PLANNING than in EXECUTION phases.

(H3) The number of selection expressions which encode the *situation of utterance* (Davies 1979), or the *reference point*, as *present* in the *situation of performance* (*point of speech*) is higher in EXECUTION than in PLANNING phases.

(H4) The feature [future] as dependent on the feature [present] will occur more often in PLANNING than in EXECUTION phases. (H4) is necessary, because [pres+fut] can be expected as quite a frequent encoding of future states of affairs in our corpus, yet this is not recognized in the formulation of H3.

(H5) The feature [past] will be found less frequently in PLANNING than in EXECUTION phases. This feature, in fact, should be significantly more frequent in EVALUATION phases than in any other phase; however, this is not within the scope of our present investigation.

(H6) Complex selection expressions with embedding of features will be more frequent in the PLANNING than in the EXECUTION phases.

(H7) The number of features per selection expression will be higher in PLANNING than in EXECUTION phases.

In the section on the results and in the discussion section, which follow below, we shall evaluate to what extent our hypotheses are confirmed.

3.8.6 Results

We shall in the following list selection expressions for TIME, based on tense, which are derived from our system network. The rules for deriving selection expressions from a system network are standard in Systemic Linguistics and thus do not require further elaboration (cf. Fawcett 1980: 20; Cummings 1987). The following notational conventions should be mentioned, though, because our own notation for TIME has been developed for our particular purposes:

As a first feature, we shall always have SIT for *situation* which is the name of the system, as it were. It means that any TIME expression is situated relative to a situation. Furthermore, there may be a feature *modality*, which functions in the same way as any other feature, but which we have not included in the network at this stage. A clause like (85):

(85) *You may be right*

is coded as: sit[modality+pres+0], which means that the clause encodes some modality in a situation and a present *time* relative to that modality. Of course, modality itself is internally complex in that it can be subclassified in several degrees of delicacy. This could be expressed here as nested attribute-value pairs within modality, in which case special notational conventions would have to be developed for handling "cascading" and modification of modals. We will not do this for the time being because it is not necessary for our investigation. The tense on the modal itself is at the moment generalized into the feature [modality], which, again, is appropriate within our particular investigation.

There may also be the feature [non-finite] , as illustrated in the following example:

MN *we could have him/ coming down the path* (65,2)

sit[modality+pres[non-finite+pres]]

This expresses embedding at the same time. Note that a tense, however complex it may be in terms of our system network,does not receive internal bracketing. Internal bracketing symbolizes syntactic embedding or hypotactic clause combining (in terms of Halliday 1985a, who does not treat adverbial clauses as cases of embedding). If we wanted to use attribute-value pairs expressing subclasses of, say, modality, we would have to use a different way of bracketing, for example:

sit[modality(modality=possible)+pres[non-finite+pres]]

Admittedly, a featurization based approach to modality must offer solutions to the problems of scope of negation and modification of modals, as exemplified in (86) and (87):

(86) *He may not be likely to do it.*
(87) *This may well be the case.*

Cascading of modals as such presents an additional problem. Any featurization approach has to tackle these issues, which are, to the best of our knowledge, neglected in SFG. In the context of our particular tasks here, however, we can afford to continue with our empirical results in Tables 68 and 69.

Table 68. Time in planning phases

Time: PLANNING	
Selection expression	Instances
sit[pres+0]	43
sit[pres+fut+0]	15
sit[modality+pres+0]	17
sit[modality+pres[non-finite+pres]][1])	2
sit[pres+fut[non-finite+pres[pres+0]]][2])	2
sit[pres+[pres]]	7
sit[fut]	16
sit[past+pres]	1

[1]) Cf.: MB *we can use this/as a path/going from the door/* (55,20)
[2]) Cf.: MB *we're going to have to have a little ledge/to show... that it's the roof* (57,10ff)

3.8.7 Discussion

Tables 70 and 71 give us the summary of results for the number of instances of each *time* constellation and for the number of selection expressions for different types of *time* structure, respectively.

What, then, do Tables 70 and 71 tell us about semantic complexity in PLANNING and EXECUTION phases?

Table 69. Time in execution phases

Time : EXECUTION	
Selection expression	Instances
sit[pres+0]	68
sit[modality+pres][1])	4
sit[past+0]	5
sit[past+pres]	1
sit[pres+0 [pres+0]][2])	4
sit[pres+0[modality+pres]]	2
sit[pres+pres]	5
sit[fut + 0]	1
sit[pres+past]	1
sit[pres+0[pres+pres]]	3
sit[pres+fut]	1

[1]) Interestingly, and as expected, 2 out of these 4 cases are cases of deontic rather than epistemic modality, cf.:
G *you have to move that one along one/* (64,6)
[2]) cf.: G *oh/ I see what you mean/* (56,31)

First, it appears not to be the case that the overall complexity in terms of the number of different semantic structures is higher in the PLANNING phases. In fact, in the EXECUTION phase, the children used a new semantic structure approx. every 8,5 instances, whereas in the PLANNING phase, they only used a new structure every 9,4 instances. (H1) is, accordingly, not confirmed. This gives us the insight that the linguistic encoding of ongoing activities, which is typical of the EXECUTION phases, may require a degree of complexity as defined in (H1), which is considerably higher than originally expected. More precisely, it can be seen from our figures that the added complexity in EXECUTION phases lies in those areas where the PLANNING phases are relatively non-complex.

If we look at the frequency of individual semantic types in terms of instances, we get something which is closer to initial assumptions (Table 70):

18,9% of all instances in the PLANNING phases are modalized, whereas in the EXECUTION phases, there are only 7% of modalized instances, a high percentage of which are cases of deontic rather than epistemic modality. (H2), then, can be regarded as confirmed.

Next, let us look at the number of instances in which the utterance situates the proposition encoded in the present relative to the communicative situation: That number (PRES as first feature in SE) is 66% in the PLANNING phase, but 85% in the EXECUTION phase, which conforms in a straightforward way with predictions from the theory of ACTIVITY (H3). Correspondingly, the proposition encoded is placed in the future in 15% of the instances in the PLANNING phase, but only in

Table 70. Time: results (1)

Number of instances	PLANNING	EXECUTION
Modality in SE	19 = 18,9%[1])	6 = 7%
Modality as first feature in SE	19 = 18,9%	4 = 4,5%
PRES in SE	86 = 85%	89 = 90%
PRES as first feature in SE	67 = 66%	84 = 85%
FUT in SE	32 = 31%	2 = 2,5%
FUT as first feature in SE	16 = 15%	1 = 1,5%
PAS in SE	1 = 0,9%	7 = 7,5%
PAS as first feature in SE	1 = 0,9%	6 = 6,5%
Cases with one embedded set of features	9 = 8,9%	12 = 12,5 %
Cases with more than one recursion of *time*	2 = 1,9%	0
No of features per SE	24:9=2,66[2])	21:11=1,9

[1]) Percentages are approximate figures only
[2]) The numbers here do not include the feature SIT, which is, by definition, always present. They do, however, include the feature [non-finite] which is not truly a semantic feature. If we discount the cases of non-finite, the figure for PLANNING is only 21:9=2,3, whereas the figure for EXECUTION remains the same. The children used non-finite in four instances in the PLANNING phase, whereas they did not use it at all in the EXECUTION phase.

1,5% of instances in the EXECUTION phase. In this case, we also have to look at instances when the children were using [future in present] (H4), and then the figures are even 31% in the PLANNING phases and only 2,5% in the EXECUTION phases.
Table 71 also tells us that the number of instances in which [past] was used is lower in the PLANNING phase than in the EXECUTION phases, where they are low in both, compared to the overall frequencies of tenses, which conforms with (H5). Somewhat surprisingly, the number of cases of embedding of tense as a whole is slightly higher in the EXECUTION phases than in the PLANNING phases, whereas multiple embedding (actually to a depth of 2) occurs in PLANNING phases only. (H6), therefore, is only partly confirmed.
Finally, the overall complexity of *time* as measured by the number of features per

Table 71. Time: results (2)

Number of SE	PLANNING	EXECUTION
Overall	9	11
FUT in SE	4	1
FUT as first feature in SE	1	1
PRES in SE	8	9
PRES as first feature in SE	5	7
PAS in SE	1	3
PAS as first feature in SE	1	2
MODALITY in SE	2	2
MODALITY as first feature in SE	2	1

SE is higher in the PLANNING phases than in the EXECUTION phases (2,66 vs. 1,9), which is, what one would expect according to (H7).

Table 71 tells us something about complexity if we focus on numbers and types of SEs without regard to the number of instances of each: Here the only significant difference would seem to lie in the fuller exploitation of *future* time in the PLANNING phases. The overall figures in this perspective, though, are certainly too small to permit even the cautious conclusions which we drew with respect to instances per type.

As we have already said in our discussion of problems with Halliday's and with Crystal's approaches respectively, Crystal (1966) has so many ambiguous definitions that it would not mean very much to cite any figures. We shall discuss some tendencies which seem to emerge from working with Crystal's approach:

Both PLANNING and EXECUTION phases carry an overall majority of *time* expressions for *contemporaneous* processes and activities. The majority, however, is much greater in the case of the EXECUTION phases. Only in the PLANNING phases do we find some instances where [pres] is used to express *future*. Furthermore, apart from the fact that PLANNING phases show a much higher degree of some [FUT]-tense and modality altogether, the PLANNING phase shows 6 cases of the use of *would* to express "conditional activity" (Crystal 1966: 28), whereas the EXECUTION phases do not show a single one of these cases. In all of the other areas the results of counting along lines suggested by Crystal do not show anything very different from what we know already from using the pure SFG approach. However, it would seem that this lack of additional information gained from using a Crystal-type approach, is more a consequence of imprecise operationalizations of categories than a result of the actual properties of language. With all the areas

that a Hallidayan approach does not attempt to cover in principle (cf. above), one would clearly expect significantly new information from an approach based on the interaction of *time* and *time specification.*
It will be seen that some of the questions we have been dealing with in this section on *time* will re-emerge in connection with our treatment on *logical connection.*

3.9 Logical connnection

The concept of "logical connection" is complex, just like any other semantic phenomenon. We shall restrict ourselves here to logical connection where and only where it is in some way structurally realized, either by some structural marker like hypotaxis in itself, and/or by lexical items, like certain classes of *linkers* and *binders*. We shall not try to cover cases where some logical relationship between clauses or sentences may be inferred during processing of an utterance, yet without any formal marking. This is not to deny that processes such as this kind of inference actually take place. However, they are difficult to determine with any degree of certainty, and they seem to be a matter of interpretation rather than semantic structure. For these reasons, we shall stick with the restriction just stated.

Next, logical connectors may occur between sentences, clauses, phrases, or words. We shall restrict ourselves to connectors between sentences and clauses here, not because the different ranks of connection are entirely unrelated, but rather because it seems prudent to split up the whole complex phenomenon into smaller modules, each of which by itself is, at this time, easier to control in a reliable way. In other words, we are specifically interested in the ways in which the children use various types of clause complexes. The present section, then, links up with SFG accounts of logical connection such as in Halliday (1985:192ff), but also those in Mann and Thompson (1987a and 1987b), Matthiessen and Thompson (1988), and related accounts such as Grosz and Sidner (1985 and 1986). None of those mentioned, though, is as strictly limited to cases of structural and/or lexical realization of logical connection as our own approach here.

Let us make some brief comments about coding conventions which are different from those in other sections and are motivated by the nature of the particular variable we are investigating here. As for the rest of the conventions, they are taken over by default from those in the preceding sections.

- Tags and pro-forms are not counted when they stand alone in an utterance.
- One word utterances are not counted, because their potential for the kind of linkage we are investigating is severely restricted. Accepting the basic premise of SFG that there can only be meaning where there is choice, it would be counterintuitive to count these utterances.
- It is well known that *linkers* like *and* and *so* have other functions apart from being logical connectives. They frequently function as discourse linkers without

their logical meaning. However, it is often highly doubtful to what extent these two functions can be neatly separated. For this reason, we count every instance in these cases. In the particular set of data that we are investigating here, the instances of possible discourse linkage as distinct from *logical connection* seemed to be very few.
- In those cases where an overt linkage of some sort is given, we only count the relationship once, whereas in the case of two clauses without any overt linkage, we count each clause.

Figure (32) summarizes most of the possibilities for logical connection as given in Halliday (1985a: 192ff.) in a system network. Halliday goes into some more delicate distinctions, which we shall not cover in our present chapter.

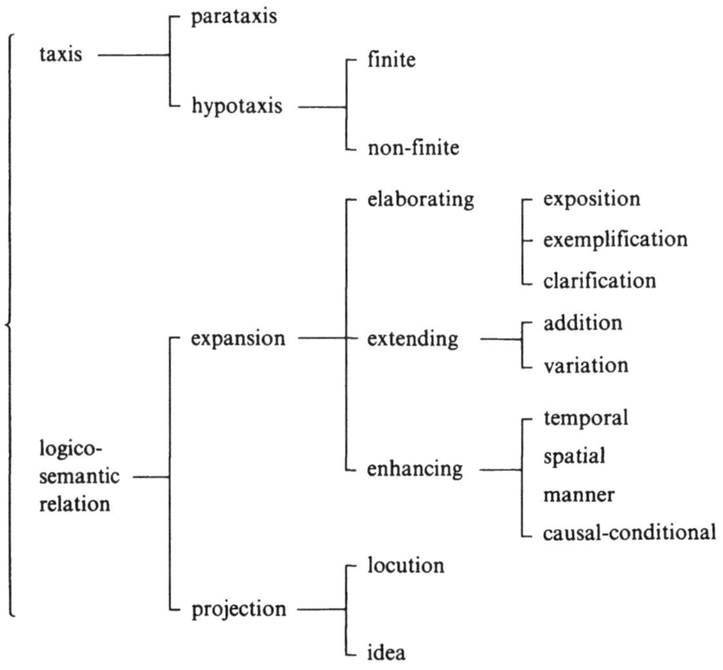

Figure 32. Logical connection

Below, we shall list the hypotheses which we derive from the theory of ACTIVITY for the complexity of logical connection in PLANNING VS. EXECUTION phases:

(H1): As the PLANNING phases require a higher degree of independency from the context of situation, i.e. the "logic" between elements in a situation can be inferred to a lesser extent than in the EXECUTION phases, the overall amount of explicit linkage between clauses and sentences in the PLANNING phases should be higher than in the EXECUTION phases.

(H2): The number of *causal-conditional* selection expressions (SE) should be higher in the PLANNING phases, because PLANNING is in part exactly the making explicit of causes and conditions of alternative and projected courses of ACTION.

(H3): The *temporal* SEs should be higher in PLANNING phases, because of the explicit PLANNING of temporal structures of ACTIONS.

(H4): Both the number of *extending* and *elaborating* SEs should be higher in PLANNING phases than in EXECUTION phases.

(H5): If the PLANNING phases reflect the nature of the PLANNING phase itself in the language, then one might also expect the number of *projections* to be higher in the PLANNING phases. This inference, though, is somewhat doubtful, because the mere fact that the language in the PLANNING phases realizes planning does not necessarily mean that the projected events and/or states of affairs are of the same kind. In other words: It is not necessarily the case that someone who is engaged in some sort of PLANNING phases also has to use a high number of *projection*-verbs.

Table 72 gives us the results obtained through analyzing the utterances of our subjects in PLANNING and EXECUTION phases for logical connection.

To what extent do the results confirm, or disconfirm, the hypotheses listed above?

As assumed in our first hypothesis (H1), the overall amount of explicit linkage is higher in the PLANNING phases than in the EXECUTION phases: in the PLANNING phases, we find some kind of explicit linkage in 42% of all cases, whereas we find this linkage in only 22% of all cases in the EXECUTION phases.

Within the limits given by the overall small size of our sample, our second hypothesis (H2) is also confirmed: Taking paratactic and hypotactic linkage of the causal-conditional type together, the PLANNING phases show linkage in 9,2% of all cases, whereas the EXECUTION phases show linkage in 6,2% of all cases. The difference derives from the figures under hypotactic linkage, because as far as paratactic linkage is concerned, the figures in the EXECUTION phases are even slightly higher.

As far as temporal connectors are concerned, the PLANNING phases (9,2%) display a higher percentage than the EXECUTION phases again (2,5%) (H3).

Our fourth hypothesis (H4), predicting more *extending* types in PLANNING than in EXECUTION is confirmed straightforwardly (16% as against 3,7%).

Somewhat surprisingly, the percentage of projection relationships is higher in the EXECUTION phases than in the PLANNING phases (6% vs.3,2%), which means that (H5) is disconfirmed. This tendency is, indeed, remarkable. It does, however, confirm an insight which we had at several places before in this study, as in the section on *transitivity*, where we investigated the percentage of *mental* predicates in the two phases:

Language does have the twofold nature of being an instrument and a reflection of activity at the same time. To the extent that it encodes some state of affairs, there

Table 72. Logical connection: results

Selection expression	Planning	Execution
No linkage	57 (58%)[1])	104 (78%)
embedded expansion	4 (4,1%)	2 (1,5%)
[[taxis, hypotaxis][logico-semantic relation, expansion, enhancing, causal-conditional]]	7 (7,1%)	5 (3,7%)
[[taxis, parataxis] [logico-semantic relation, expansion, enhancement, causal-conditional]]	2 (2,1%)	3 (2,5%)
[[taxis, parataxis] [logico-semantic relationship, expansion, extending, addition]]	15 (16%)	5 (3,7%)
[[taxis, hypotaxis] [logico-semantic relationship, projection, idea]]	2 (2,1%)	8 (6%)
[[taxis, parataxis] [logico-semantic relationship, expansion, enhancing, temporal]]	8 (8,1%)	3 (2,5%)
[[taxis, hypotaxis] [logico-semantic relationship, expansion, enhancing, temporal]]	1 (1,1%)	0 0
[[taxis, hypotaxis] [logico-semantic relationship, projection, locution]]	1 (1,1%)	0 0
	97	133

[1]) Percentages are rough figures

is, indeed, no necessity whatsoever that it be the same state of affairs (situation) within which an utterance is produced. It is the very essence of language that it can encode some *situation* which is different from the situation of its production, and to that extent hypotheses like H5 are simply ill-founded.

Apart from (H5), though, our hypotheses have been confirmed, and it is this which should provide motivation for future research along the lines indicated here.

3.10 Aktionsarten

3.10.1 Introduction

In this section, we shall investigate a semantic classification of predicates which so far has been largely neglected within SFG. We shall refer to it as the classification of predicates, or rather, as we shall see, clauses, into "Aktionsarten".

The term *Aktionsarten* in itself is not without problems as a linguistic term, especially to the extent that it is juxtaposed to the term "aspect". Traditionally, both *aspect* and *Aktionsart* may be used to refer to a semantic classification system for certain properties of the process or state realized in the verb phrase. Where there is some grammatical or morphological marking, as in the Russian aspectual verb forms, or as in the English verb phrase, the term *aspect* is usually preferred, and it is to that extent the more "syntactic" term. Where the criteria are to some greater extent based on selectional restrictions between the verb, its Complements, and its non-valency bound clause elements, *Aktionsart* is usually used as the wider term, which may or may not include *aspect*, depending on the author (cf. Conrad 1985: 19). We are using *Aktionsart* here, because we want to include as realizations relationships between verbs, Complements, and Adjuncts, in addition to morpho-syntactic realizations.

What we are referring to in this section is the semantic classification of predicates, as it is represented in Vendler (1967), and Ikegami (1981). *Predicates* here is used somewhat loosely, because the classification seems to be one of clauses, rather than only predicates, as we shall see below. Furthermore, the classification can be made more detailed, so as to include features like *resultative, causative, durative (inchoative, mutative, iterative), punctual* as shown in the work of Comrie (1976), Bache (1985), and Lyons (1977 Vol.2: 703ff.). Some of the suggestions which we shall put forward here have previously been formulated in the context of machine translation to capture the interaction between SFG *transitivity* and a system for semantic features such as the one proposed in Zelinsky-Wibbelt (1988).

The interaction of a system for Aktionsarten and an SFG classification of clauses according to transitivity is complex and not without problems: The approach to Aktionsarten from which we shall be starting has its roots in philosophy rather than in linguistics, whereas SFG is one of the "functionalist" schools of modern linguistics. This implies that the criteria for the identification of classes used in each approach are very different. What provides the methodological link is the fact that the object is natural language in either case, with the immediate consequence that operationalizations are usually formulated so as to include linguistic material (paraphrases etc.) as criteria for decisions to be made, or, at the very least, as examples.

The primary motivation for arguing for an inclusion of the phenomenon of Aktionsart in SFG models is that the semantic phenomenon as such, which is realized linguistically in different ways (in the auxiliary complex, in the selection of verb classes, in the choice of sub-classes of Adjuncts and Subjects, etc), apparently cannot be handled economically in the SFG model by, say, a combination of information from *transitivity*, *time*, and *circumstances*, which would seem to be the prime candidates for these types of information. As always, when introducing some new functional component, or, as in this case, only a network which should in the end be included in the ideational component, one is inevitably introducing additional complexity into the overall system. It is our present suggestion, though, that the newly introduced complexities, mainly deriving from the interaction with other networks and components, are less than those introduced by extracting the same information from a large number of already existing networks, which, in addition, are set up to handle different phenomena.

Before we start outlining a preliminary system network and operationalizations of the features in it, let us first try to relate the basic distinctions in the Aktionsarten approach to the classification of verbs and clauses in SFG according to transitivity as introduced in section 3.4 of the present study. As is common when approaching a relatively new area, the account is restricted to the more basic distinctions, and it is exploratory, rather than definitive.

At the outset, there would seem to be at least four possible types of relationships between classifications according to Aktionsarten and classifications according to transitivity:

- The two types of classification yield classes with no recognizable rule-governed connection between them. In other words, the relationship between classes of clauses is random, as is the relationship between classes of verb readings obtained by the two approaches. We shall discuss some important arguments against Aktionsart as a lexical phenomenon shortly, thus explaining our use of the notion of *verb reading* in this section in some more detail.
- Both types of classification yield the same classes, which would mean that they should be conflated into one, and that terminological distinctions are merely superficial.
- One of the two types of classifications yields sub-classes of the other.
- The classes of readings and clauses identified by one classification overlap in some lawful way with those identified by the other.

However, what, precisely, is it that we are classifying? To the extent that, as we shall see, the classification into Aktionsart can only be made of a verb plus its valency bound arguments plus its non-valency-bound modifiers, we are classifying clauses, rather than verb readings according to Aktionsarten. To the extent that difference in number and type of semantic arguments and syntactic Complements motivates different lexical entries, though, we are also classifying verbs and verb readings which can be inserted into the clause types which we have identified. There is this systematic, but theoretically motivated ambiguity in our use of the term *classification* here. The same, in principle, is true of SFG classifications according to transitivity, with the difference, though, that classifications in transitivity explicitly do not in any way respect non-valency-bound elements (Modifiers): There is a bi-uniqueness condition between semantic arguments and grammatical Complements in SFG, as there is in Lexical Functional Grammar LFG between semantic arguments and grammatical functions, or in Government and Binding Theory between *theta-roles* and syntactic phrases (cf. Steiner 1988: 138ff.). This bi-uniqueness holds *one-to-one* and *into* from the set of participant roles of some verb into the set of syntactic complements of that same verb, i.e. each semantic role is assigned one and only one syntactic function. In stronger versions of this condition, this also holds from the set of complements into the set of semantic roles. Such a condition has so far not been formulated for Circumstances, although it applies there as well, with the fundamental reservation that neither circumstantial roles, nor syntactic Adjuncts are assigned by the verb. Furthermore, the usual requirements of completeness and coherence of syntactic and semantic structures cannot, by definition, apply to any non-valency-bound structure. Apart from this restriction, though, the same ambiguity in the use of the term *classification* applies in the case of transitivity as in the case of Aktionsarten.

Let us begin, then, with a brief investigation of the relationship between the *stative vs. dynamic* distinction, as used, for example, in Zelinsky-Wibbelt (1988), and semantic classes according to SFG transitivity. The network is given in section 3.10.2 below (cf. Figure 33).

The following classes of verb meanings identified through transitivity would seem to correspond to stative verb readings, given the operationalizations which we shall put forward in the following sections:

(88) [relational, simple attribuant]
(89) [mental process, phenomenon oriented, phenomenon -intention],
to the extent that this class is recognized
(90) [communication, sender -intention]
(91) [mental process, two phenomena]
(92) [mental process, processor oriented, processor -intention]

We give an example of each class below, with classification applying to the superordinate clause:

(88) *The meeting is in Luxembourg.*
(89) *The council's decision surprised everyone.*
(90) *The inscription says: "Never change a winning team."*
(91) *An optimal solution presupposes that no mistakes are made.*
(92) *I understand that you are in some kind of trouble.*

Note that our analysis in (88) implies that we either analyze the *be+ -ing* in cases like (93) below as "not progressive", or else exclude that sub-class from our statement:

(93) *The lamp is hanging down from the ceiling.*

Our account so far does not preclude the possibility of sub-classes of other transitivity classes being stative, too. The following cases come to mind immediately:

Some [affected-centred] verb readings, the so-called *middles*, are exemplified in (94) and (95):

(94) *Cheap books sell well.*
(95) *Synthetics wash easily.*

Interestingly, and also typically, (94) can be made dynamic if we add some *time specification* which introduces some limited temporal space, as shown in (96):

(96) *Cheap books are selling well this summer.*

Examples (94) and (95) possibly exemplify a sub-class [action, affected-centred, affected -intention], which could be added to the cases identified in (88) to (92) above (cf. Steiner 1989, where *ergative* and *middle* are introduced as sub-types of *affected-centred*). This is an illustration of a case where the introduction of an Aktionsarten-network could save us from having to introduce additional sub-networks in transitivity. Moreover, transitivity with its theoretically necessary restriction to valency-bound elements, cannot be extended to cover a distinction like that between (94) and (96) in principle, without violation of the concept as such. Observe, by the way, that there are, indeed, [action, affected-centred, affected+intention] verb readings, as can be seen in (97):

(97) *The boss worked his men very hard.*

The same point we have made with respect to (94) and (96) could be made with respect to (98) and (99):

(98) *Mary walks to work every day.*
(99) *Mary is walking to work at the moment.*

Both readings of *walk* would be [relational, locational], and the difference between (98) and (99) cannot be handled in principle under transitivity. Theoretically, one would therefore want to say that it is a grammatical ("grammatical" in the sense including semantics), rather than a lexical difference, which makes sense for English. That same difference, though, can be realized lexically in different languages, such as Russian, which throws an interesting light on the alleged universality of semantic and syntactic facts even on such a level of generality.

So, when we speak of *reading* in terms of Aktionsarten in this section, we mean precisely "readings having a certain preference for taking feature x in terms of Aktionsart". This is different from the case of transitivity features, which by themselves fully specify certain syntactic realizations positively or negatively, even if the specification is conditioned through paths in other networks and components.

We are not claiming here that differences in Aktionsart are not captured at all within SFG, or other functional models. Indeed, they are at present handled within the networks for *circumstance*. What we are claiming is that if we want to control generation or analysis, without assuming some network for Aktionsarten, we have to formulate a complex interaction between transitivity and Circumstances. The question is whether it would not be more economical to have a separate network for Aktionsarten, which would still involve stating interconnections with transitivity, but, hopefully, in a more efficient way.

Let us, next, move on to the first-level sub-classes of dynamic verbs, those which are *action*, or *process*, or *event*. As above, we shall try to establish correspondences between classes identified by transitivity features and classes identified by Aktionsart features. The following classes of verb readings in terms of transitivity would seem to correspond to *action* readings in terms of Aktionsarten. Observe that our [relational] readings, as implied by the notation, generalize across [locational vs. classificatory vs. identifying, vs. associative] sub-classes.

(100) [action, agent only]
(101) [action, agent-centred, overt agent]
(102) [action, affected-centred, overt causer]
(103) [relational], with an Agent-Attribuant
(104) [relational], with a 3rdpartyagent
(105) [mental,processor oriented, processor +intention]
(106) [mental, phenomenon oriented, phenomenon +intention]
(107) [communication, sender +intention]

All of (100) to (104) may require the additional condition that the agent be [+animate], which would have the same function as a feature [+intention] in (105)–(107). We shall exemplify these selection expressions in sentences (100)–(107) below:

(100) *John was laughing.*
(101) *The parliament expelled the Prime Minister.*
(102) *The IRA blew up the National Assembly.*
(103) *The working group went into the back room.*
(104) *They elected some fool president of the committee.*
(105) *The council observes the current development with concern.*
(106) *The ambassador impressed the council positively.*

(107) *The council declared that they had no time to lose.*

The following classes of transitivity structures, or verb readings, would seem to correspond to *process* or *event* classifications according to Aktionsarten:

(108) [relational], with an Affected-Attribuant
(109) [action, affected only]
(110) [action, affected-centred, (affected -intention), covert causer]
(111) [action, attribuant only]

These classes are exemplified in the following sentences:

(108) *The proposal went to the committee for consideration.*
(109) *The minister died yesterday.*
(110) *The meeting ended late in the afternoon.*
(111) *The gold was melting.*

As we have said above, the presence or absence of certain Circumstances may affect classification according to Aktionsarten. Apart from this fact, which in itself is of importance, it seems to be fairly uncontroversial to assume that all those readings in terms of transitivity, which involve a "wilfull" agent, will receive the categorization *action* in terms of Aktionsarten, whereas all those which

- do not have an agent, and
- are not stative

will receive the features *process* or *event*.

To round off this discussion, let us move on to the subclassification of *action* predicates into *activity, accomplishment, achievement*: The remarks which we shall have to make here are even more tentative than those offered above, mainly because the distinctions between Aktionsarten in this area would seem to be less clear-cut than those on the more general level. Still, we would like to suggest the following correspondences between the transitivity classification and the Aktionsarten classification:

The Aktionsarten sub-class *achievement* corresponds to the following transitivity classes, or sub-classes of them:

- [relational, agent attribuant]
- [action, agent-centred]
- [relational, 3rdpartyagent]

The Aktionsarten sub-class *activity* corresponds to the following transitivity classes, or at least sub-classes of them:

- [action, agent only]
- [action, agent centred]

The Aktionsarten sub-class *accomplishment* corresponds to the following transitivity class, or sub-classes of it:

- [action, agent-centred].

At the beginning of this introductory section, we listed four types of possible relationships between the two classificatory schemes. Our considerations so far seem to indicate that the third and fourth of these relationships obtain:

- in general, the classes of verb readings and clauses identified by the two classifications are partly overlapping in a rule-governed way.
- In parts of the two schemes, the results seem to yield verb readings and clauses in a class to sub-class relationship.

We have already discussed some of the theoretical differences between the two approaches of classification according to transitivity and classification according to Aktionsarten. These differences seem to culminate in the general effect that the classification according to Aktionsarten is oriented more towards *world knowledge* than towards purely formal *linguistic knowledge*, to the extent that the distinction between the two types of knowledge is considered useful. The tendency which we have tried to point out in this section for an assignment of Aktionsarten features, namely that of reliance on knowledge of the world, seems to find its expression methodologically in the admission of non-valency bound elements into the set of criteria accepted for classification. It also points to interesting areas of future research: So-called *linguistic knowledge* may simply be more predictable (even lexically predictable), than so-called *world knowledge* - both types of knowledge, however, ultimately are instances of systems of linguistic, and therefore social, norm. Linguistic norms, as we have tried to show in chapter 2 of this study, are just a special case of norms for human activity in a given society, and thus the sharp distinction between types of knowledge appears as what it is: A justifiable methodological abstraction for a given purpose. From a strict intra-linguistic perspective, the inclusion of world knowledge appears to make distinctions "fuzzy" and vague, but on the other hand often highly relevant and insightful, even if such a formulation only has a pre-theoretical status.

Figure 33 shows a preliminary and simple system network for Aktionsarten, with sample realizations being given in (112) to (117). A fuller realization statement would have to make reference to the insertion or blocking of circumstantial and transitivity functions, to *time* and *time specification* features, to more syntactic features, such as [singular vs. plural], to features in the *mood* systems, and also, partly, to choice of verb readings. All of these realizations will be or have been illustrated informally in this section.

3.10.2 A preliminary system network for Aktionsart

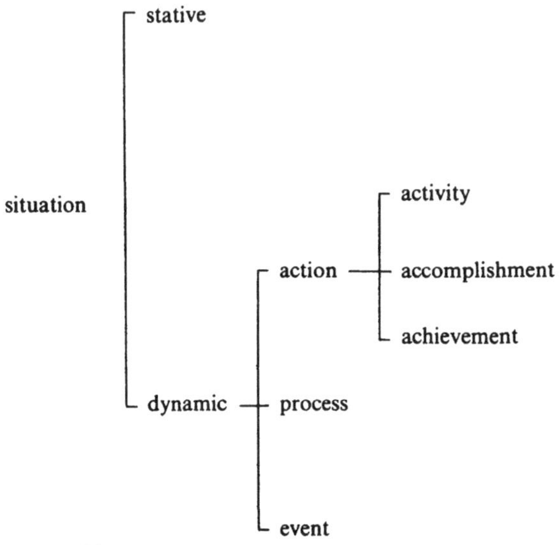

Figure 33.

3.10.3 Operationalization of features for Aktionsarten

The following sequence of steps (Figure 34) is used to assign Aktionsarten features to clauses in our corpus. It will be seen that the operationalizations given are all well-known tests for Aktionsarten features, which are here used in a particular sequence of decisions to yield an unambiguous classification.

The following sample sentences are meant to illustrate the selection expressions which are obtained by assigning features from our system network according to the procedure embodied in our operationalization:

(112) *Peter is the king of France*
[situation, stative]
(113) *Some rocks are rolling down the hill.*
[situation, dynamic, process]
(114) *The charge explodes.*
[situation, dynamic, event]
(115) *Peter is driving around in a circle.*
[situation, dynamic, action, activity]
(116) *Peter reached the top.*
[situation, dynamic, action, achievement]
(117) *Peter is drawing a circle.*
[situation, dynamic, action, accomplishment]

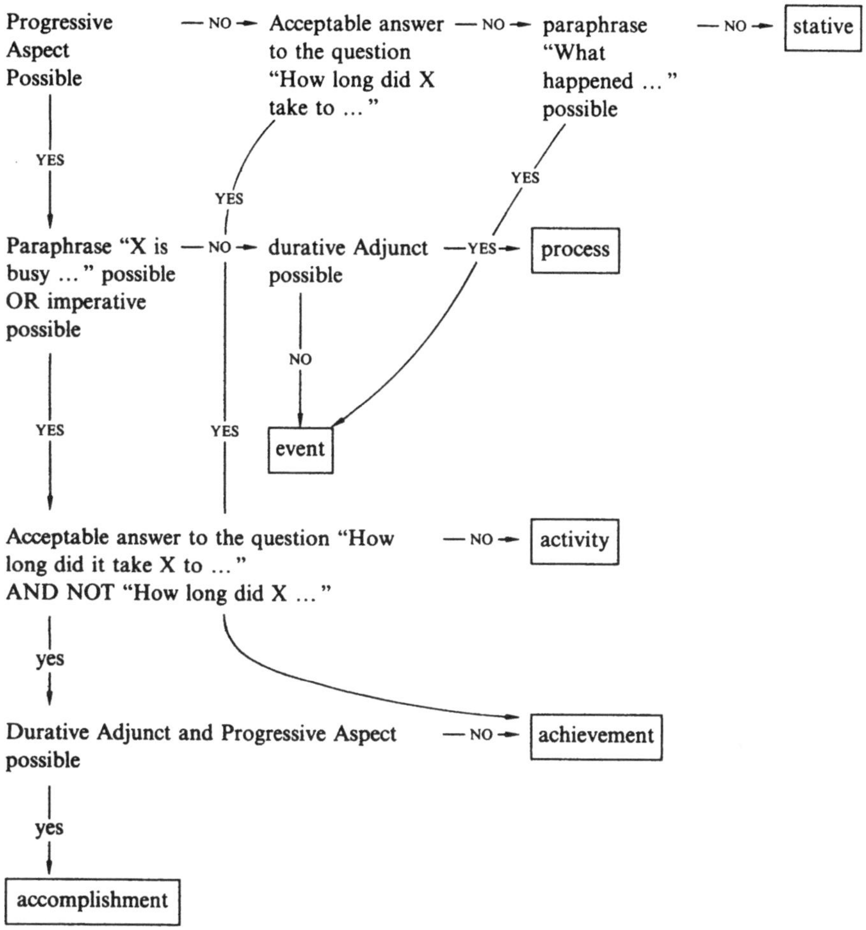

Figure 34. Operationalization of Aktionsart-features

From an overall perspective, the three most important distinction here seem to be

- Whether or not the verbal group admits a *progressive aspect*, or some corresponding lexico-syntactic device;
- Whether or not a clause admits agency;
- Whether or not a clause focuses on the result of the action/ process/ event encoded, and if it does, whether or not it focuses on some duration.

However, it can be seen that these criteria interact with each other in a rather complicated way, which accounts for the somewhat "messy" look of our procedure (Figure 34). Also, judgements on acceptability of sentences under the agency criterion implied in the *imperative* test and the *to be busy-* tests depend crucially on the degree of metaphoricness some hearer is willing to accept. The same applies to tests using questions implying the result of some process (*How long did it take X to..*), or implying some extended duration (*How long did X... / how long was X ...ing...*). A special comment may be in place on the two lines leading from secondary test-questions within the *non-progressive* section of the operationalization chart to *achievement* and *event* respectively: The simple reason for this complication is that there are clauses which cannot take the progressive, but which are not *stative* either. Cf. (118) and (119):

(118) *John smashed the cup.* [dynamic, action, achievement]
(119) *The stone hit the tree.* [dynamic, event]

Both (118) and (119) would be classified as *stative* if we admitted the *progressive* criterion to be sufficient for the assignment of *stative.* Furthermore, classification of the predicate here is clearly influenced by certain features, such as *number*, of valency-bound constituents, cf. (120) and (121):

(120) *John was smashing cups.* [dynamic, action, activity]
(121) *Stones were hitting the tree.* [dynamic, process]

Also, many verbs which may have one preferred Aktionsarten-reading, can take on a different reading given a certain syntactico-semantic context, cf. (122)–(124):

(122) *Stop being a fool!*
(123) *Charges were exploding all through the night.*
(124) *I am thinking bad thoughts all the time.*

The verb in (122) is prototypically [stative], yet can easily acquire agency in a context which enforces agency, like the imperative. The verb in (123) has a preferred [event] reading, yet may acquire a [process] reading due to the durative *time*-Adjunct and the [+plural] Subject, a parallel case to (120) and (121). The verb in (124) has a preferred [achievement] reading when it has a clausal Direct Object, yet has an [activity] reading in cases like in (124). The fact that *to think a thought* might also be analyzed as an *analytical verb construction* is of particular interest, but does not affect our general point here (cf. Steiner in press). On the other hand, there is clear evidence that such distinctions as are made according to Aktionsarten are relevant and theoretically necessary, for example in the fact that different predicate types take different pro-forms in English (stative vs. dynamic), or correspond to different verbs with the same root (Russian), or trigger processes like prefixation, as can be seen in German pairs like *klettern vs. erklettern, blühen vs. erblühen, malen vs. bemalen* etc., although very often what is involved are even finer distinctions within Aktionsarten than the ones we are using here.

3.10.4 Hypotheses

What are likely types of hypotheses that one might derive from the theory of activity which we are using for the structure of linguistic utterances as far as Aktionsarten are concerned?

It should be remembered at this point, that in the PLANNING phases the language realizes the ACTION itself, which, as we have already seen several times, in no way implies that it encodes the ACTION itself. However, whatever individual future or hypothetical events or states of affairs are encoded, they should be in some ways differently encoded from even the same event or state of affairs in the EXECUTION phases, to the extent that they are encoded in the EXECUTION phases at all.

(H1) A higher percentage of *stative* predicates in the PLANNING phases than in the EXECUTION phases is to be expected, if the assumption is correct that stative verbs or verb readings encode abstract relationships rather than changes of state or some kind of action, and if the further assumption is correct that the phase of some ACTION where such relationships are discussed and projected is the PLANNING rather than the EXECUTION phase.

(H2) For the same general reasons as given above, one would expect that, within *dynamic* verbs, the overall percentage of *action* verb readings is higher than the percentage of non-*action* readings in EXECUTION phases than in PLANNING phases, although this expectation is not particularly strong.

(H3) The absolute frequency in percent of *activity* verb readings should be higher in the EXECUTION than in the PLANNING phases, because they express some ongoing process rather than one which implies its own termination in a result. Also, in EXECUTION phases, they should have a higher relative frequency as against *accomplishment* and *achievement* readings, whereas this is not an expectation for the PLANNING phases. Again, the strength of these expectations has to be seen against the fact that, whereas Aktionsarten are less strictly tied to lexicosyntactic realization than transitivity features, and to that extent less metaphorical, they are still metaphorical in some sense if compared to a pure "world knowledge semantics", if such a construct is accepted.

3.10.5 Results and discussion

Table 73 gives us the results obtained by applying our system of classification for Aktionsarten to the data.

(H1) predicts that there will be a higher percentage of stative predicates in PLANNING than in EXECUTION phases. The percentages obtained are 55% to 51%,

Table 73. Aktionsart: results

FEATURE	PLANNING		EXECUTION	
stative	62	(55%)	68	(51%)
activity	7	(6%)	20	(15,5%)
accomplishment	6	(5,5%)	4	(3%)
achievement	30	(27,5%)	33	(24,5%)
process	0		0	
event	7	(6%)	8	(6%)
TOTAL	112	(100%)	133	(100%)

1) Percentages are approximative figures only

and it would clearly require a much greater amount of data to judge if, and on what level these differences are significant.

(H2) predicts that within *dynamic* predicates, the percentage of *action* predicates should be higher than the percentage of non-*action* readings in EXECUTION phases than in PLANNING phases. This, however, has to be regarded as disconfirmed.

(H3) predicts that the frequency of *activity* predicates should be higher in EXECUTION than in PLANNING phases. This is, indeed, confirmed, the respective figures being 15,5% and 6%. The relative frequency for *activity* vs. non-*activity* predicates within *action* predicates is, for the PLANNING phases 7:36, i.e. roughly 1:5, and for the EXECUTION phases 20:37, i.e. roughly 1:1,8, which means that this part of (H3) is strongly confirmed.

Probably the main point, which is illustrated once more in our figures here, is that linguistic categories should not be seen in a one-to-one correspondence with categories of some non- linguistic semantics, such as the one embedded in our theory of ACTIVITY. The realization relationships between the two levels of representation are complex and, as yet, not very well understood. We commented on this fact in some more detail in our section on transitivity, and in other places in this study. There is, of course, the additional fact that our hypotheses may be incorrectly derived from the theory of ACTIVITY, which is, indeed, a possibility, especially as our expectations in this chapter are somewhat weaker than those in other chapters anyway. Altogether, though, we hope that we have been able to demonstrate that it is possible, and even desirable, to include some account of Aktionsarten in SFG semantics, and this claim would stand with or without the particular empirical motivation which we have been trying to give through our empirical investigation here.

Chapter 4
Conclusion

At the end of this study, where do we stand with respect to the goals which we outlined in the introduction (chapter 1)?

Essentially, what we have presented consists of two complementary parts: Chapter 2 is primarily theoretical, developing a theory of human goal-directed action in a Systemic perspective from the sources we have given. Chapter 3 is primarily applied in character, investigating certain variables in semantic complexity in English child language under the guidelines of hypotheses generated from the theoretical framework developed in chapter 2.

However, just as the theoretical chapter has applied parts which are designed to serve as the background for discussions of relatively specific theoretical questions, so, conversely, the applied chapter has theoretical parts where certain key notions of Systemic semantics are discussed against the background of the specific requirements inherent in our data. The structure of our study, considered on this general level, thus expresses what Systemicists frequently refer to as "the interrelationship between theory and application".

Very briefly, then, let us critically evaluate what has been achieved and what is the potential for future development:

The present study develops a certain approach to the analysis of human goal-directed action, to the point where it can be applied to natural language texts of the type it is designed to handle (chapters 2.3. and 2.4.). Key fragments of a grammar of activity are introduced (2.3., 2.4.), approaching the level of explicitness and detail as in Halliday (1961), which, in this respect, is still seen as a kind of standard in SFG. To achieve the level of detail and breadth of coverage of Halliday's (1985a) *Introduction to Functional Grammar* clearly is a goal for the future - yet in order to achieve this goal, a phase of extensive application would be required. There is, after all, no a priori reason to assume that the structure of human goal-directed action is isomorphic to the structure of language. Indeed, there is every reason to assume that such a strong claim would be false. It should also be emphasized that for a presentation of the overall theoretical framework of Systemic Functional Grammar, or any part of Systemic theory, the model probably still is Halliday's (1961) *Categories of the theory of grammar*, or Fawcett's (1980) *Cognitive linguistics and social interaction* for his own version of SFG, rather than the more recent *Introduction to functional grammar*, which is explicitly not an introduction to Systemic theory (Halliday 1985a: x).

Next, we have formulated hypotheses generated from our theory of human goal-directed action for some variables in semantic complexity in English child language - on a general level in 2.5., and more specific hypotheses in the sub-sections of chapter 3. Quite clearly, there is a considerable potential here to exploit the structure of SFG theory in terms of its components, networks, and realizational rules much more fully in the future, the result of which should be a larger number of more specific research hypotheses. As we hope to have indicated, this kind of work would submit the "tools" of SFG to one of the most productive ways of testing a theory, and of developing it further.

We have also attempted to link our approach to human goal-directed action, and specifically the representations it generates, to techniques of knowledge representation in artificial intelligence (chapter 2.6.), and the more extensive exploitation of SFG within artificial intelligence can be seen as one of the most promising areas of future development, a development, though, which began years ago but which has gained momentum in recent years: The recent past has seen several attempts at formalizations of SFG, a component for SFG has been outlined which would seem to form an almost ideal interface with the terminal elements of our theory of goal-directed action (*Rhetorical Structure Theory*, as represented in Mann and Thompson 1987, and elsewhere), and implementations of SFG, either in part, or rather comprehensive, have shown what the model can achieve in an artificial intelligence context. In Kasper (1987) in particular, SFG itself is described as a formalism which is essentially an extension of Functional Unification Grammar, as we have indicated in our more detailed comments in 2.3. This direction of work, along with such contributions as in Patten & Ritchie (1987), points to important clarifications and extensions of SFG concepts in the immediate future (categories and scales of the theory, relationships between and within ranks and levels etc.). Quite clearly, though, most of the ideas presented in the present study, which derives its interest from the very fact that it is exploratory in the areas of *context* and *situation*, are formulated on the level of linguistic theory or even on the level of description according to the models generated, rather than on the level of some implementation language, or on the level of formalization. At several points, we have made brief excursions into the area of formalization, but a full formalization of the theory requires more theoretical clarity than we have now - and some of this clarity will have to be the result of analytical practice, rather than formal deduction. A number of relevant questions for further development in that connection are addressed in 2.3., 2.4., and 3.2. Implementations of the clause semantics which we are using in 2.4. and in large parts of chapter 3 are described in Steiner et al (1988), Steiner (1989), (Steiner et al 1990), and Steiner (1990).

In chapter 3, finally, we presented a pilot study of certain variables of semantic complexity in English child language. It is the main function of this part of our study to show the potential for this type of investigation of the particular notions of human goal-directed action which we have developed, as well as the particular suitability of SFG theory, models, and tools, for precisely this type of task. There is the further claim that looking at data from child language development from the perspective of language as human goal-directed action, with SFG as a linguistic model, opens up new perspectives on key notions such as *context dependency*, or, indeed, *semantic complexity*. However, it is crucial to remember that we presented a pilot study with the aim of stimulating full-scale studies in the future - hence the size of our particular corpus is small, with no claim to statistical significance attached to our figures. A full study with the broad range of variables investigated here would clearly go far beyond the limits which were set for the present study.

We have come a long way, then, starting from theories of human goal-directed action, going through different texts from different genres, investigating techniques of knowledge representation in artificial intelligence, finally entering the wide area of semantic complexity in child language. There is, though, an overall perspective holding all of these topics together and determining the type and specificity of questions raised at each particular point:

It is the perspective on human language as a form of activity, a perspective, we believe, which is adopted in Systemic Functional Grammar more consistently than in any other school of modern linguistics.

Appendix 1[1]

Page - 1 -
12 A Boys Play Sessign
Children: A.W. 25.7.66
P.G. 19.3.66 Date of Recording: 3.7.78
S.M. 26.3.66 Length: 10mins.
Positions of Children:

	P.G.
A.W.	S.M.
	M.

S now what shall we use/
M what shall we build I mean/
A well/what d'you wanna build/
S build a house man/
be easy enough/
come on then/ easy enough/
A well/ just make the outside/first/
S no/not going to use these for it mun/
P why/what's the point/
you put those on/for windows/
A you d don have to/
S won't be long/
P it's easiest mind/.
A I know something easy/
build a garage/
P oh/fantastic/
S or somethink (=thing) like a skyscraper/
P this worked out/
it won't fit/
S go on/we can always.
move it along/can't we/
P ((sniffs))
A ooof/
P will that one fit in by there/
come on/let's (get going/put a door in?)/
A can't fit any this/this very big one/for that matter/ laughing

[1] For brackets indicating simultaneity of turns cf. the published transcripts Fawcett & Perkins (1980: pp. 1-18)

Page - 2 -

P	((sniffs)) (I can't even?)	
S	little one/you want a little one/	
	do you/	
	a little small thing/	
?A	here you are/	
S	correct/oh/here we are./	(untwist/another person?)
P	how come./	
	won't fit/down there/now/((sniffs))	
A	hold on/d'y want	
P	it's got weird/ well um/	
P	oh/we've done this wrong/	
A	no we haven't/	
P	yes we have/	
S	wit/	
A	hang on/lets go have a look./ooof/	
S	th just add a bit now/	
	add a bit here/-	
A	mm/	
P	doesn't fit/	
A	it has gone a bit weird/hasn't it/	
P	hang on/	
P	we'll start again/	
S	wait a minute/I got it/	
A	we'll have to	
A	hey/I tell you what/	
A	we can move this like	enthusiastically in charge
?S	I got it/	
A	we can move this up a bit./or down/or	
P	hang on/bung that brick in by there/-	
S	hang on/hang on/	
	let's push the door out one/	
A	ooof./	

Page - 3 -

S yeah/hang on/
A what are you missing now then/—
P oh/– (-? -? -)
A oh/this is getting wrong/this is/
S hang on/
A they don't have to be the same size/do they/
P yeah/we'll have corners and things/
hang on/
A it doesn't have to be square/
P oh/let's have a dinp/by there/
damp/oh/I don't know it is/
A oh hang on/ I I uh
I see what you mean/
P a bump/or a bunb in there/
hang on/
it has to be square/doesn't it/
yeah/
A alright/- -
S good idea/
A try to get one of them. big ones/now/
?P have you got one/- - - -
S you can do that thing by there/
A we'll have to use
S I got it/
P I got it/
S an I have/
A try and find one with. uh
hang on/how many spaces are there/-
two three four   counting quietly
S there's ten/
? six upon/
S well/that's it/

Page - 4 -

	there's twelve then/	
A	hang on/pass pass that one here	
	for a minute/ooof/	
	oh/I can't get this flippin thing off/	quietly to self
S	I've got it/	
A	come on/you naughty thing/	talking to Lego
P	have you got what/	
A	oh/you are/(=here you are)	
S	hey/the uh uh uh	
A	oh dear/another one of those/	
S	and/know what we want/	putting on a voice
	I've got it/	
	I've got the complete answer/	
	if I can find one/	
P	have a dip in/	
A	- - ?	
P	let's have a dip in/to match/	
	I've got it/	
A	right/	
S	I've done it/-	
P	hang on/((sniffs))	
S	we've done it/-	
A	right then/now/we build/the walls/	
P	come out my dear/	talking to Lego
A	ooh/	
P	hang on/	
S	I got a little house/in there/	
	little house/in the house by there/	
A	little house in the house/((laughs))	
S	I got Lego/	
	can't remember how to build it - though/	
P	don't match/	
A	put a few wheels on/	
S	a few wheels/((laughs)) few	

Page - 5 -

P	it's sticking off the end/	
A	I'm enjoying this/I am/	
	and I/	in a funny voice
A	hold on/oj aye/that's right/	
S	I bet you all go wrong/	
A	oh/never mind/	
S	it's not overlapping/	
P	we got most of it/	
	hang on/that's not enough/	
A	alright/-	
S	that is not overlapping neither/	
A	what d'you mean/overlapping/	
	oh aye/I see what you mean/	
S	that is not overlapping/	
A	it's it's stronger/in it/	
P	((sniffs)) (- ?) that (- - - ?)	
	it fits down there/	
A	that one/ that one/	
	that one was overlapping/	
S	was not/	
A	oh/	
P	((sniffs)) lets just build in units/	
	it's easier/((laughs))	
A	hang on/ right/now hold on/	
A	try an get a four one/right/	
	try an get a four/	
	if we get. a small four one in/	
	it it'll be alright/then/	
P	I/	
S	here's a four one/	
P	hang on/	
	let's just play with these ones/	
S	here's a four one/-	
	d'y want a four/	

Page - 6 -

A	oh/th they all overlap/now./	
	just about/ I hope/	
P	((sniffs))	
S	now we gotta get (some more/small ones?)/- -	
P	that's not overlapping/-	
A	that's right/	
P	((sniffs)) (good/go on?)	
S	it's fantastic/it's coming shape/	a whispering crescendo
	hey we built a mansion/	
P	((sniffs)) let's bung two two of these/in there/-	
	((sniffs))	
?S	peekaboo	wispering comically
P	((sniffs))	
A	((laughs quietly)) -	
A	can build it too high/	
A	otherwise we won't have enough stuff/	
P	hey./let's have a	
P	'ave an 'ouse/with a lift in it/	
	a lift in it an' things/	
A	no/	
S	we're doooing it/	
A	you have to build anoth another storey/	
S	that's alright/	
A	to get it right/	
P	hay 'ave we got corners/	
P	no/	
P	wouldn't be no help/anyway/ - -	
S	have to build another/	
P	(hey look at them (- - ?) box/can I have the small box)	
S	what/ (-7.sec - pause)	
S	it's tipping down/outside/	
P	hang on/ you can't build/on there/	

Page - 7 -

A	I know it is/
P	it's a square/it's awkward/
P	that one by there/
	that one by there/and wait for - ((sniffs))
A	oy/got any uh more of those
	little small ones/-
	need one/in there/ - -
S	((makes 4 unintelligible sound effects))
	I just found it/
	ha ha ha/rock bottom/
A	that's right/brainy/Jock/
P	'an that's/wrong/
S?	they haven't got no chimney things/yere/(=herc)
A	chimney/((laughs))
	well/(- - ?)
A	oh we can put all the fancy bits/here/to do after/
?	(- - ?)
?	(- - ?)
?	(- - ?)
?	I got a few/-5-
S	((whistles for 3 secs))
P	hey/can you/
	have we got a long one/of those/
S	what/
P	half one/
S	((sniffs)) no/
P	we got enough of them/
?	?
S	oy/we'll have to use two of them
P	(- - ?)
S	smaller half things/now/
P	oh alright then/
S	just dig a few up/

Page - 8 -

S	there's a couple in there/	
	I saw a few/	
A	ah./yes/well I	
P	they're kind of not overlapping Jock/	
A	hey/shutters/((titters))	
S	here/lets have some shutters/	
P	put one of these in/	
	now it'll shut/	
S	what/	
P	see/((sniffs))	
S	lets put a few windows in/	
P	((sniffs)) oh oh we forgot the windows/	
S	they're shutters dear/-	
A	I've just found them/haven't I/	
S	we'll put them in/when we've finished/	
?A	I dunno/	
P	too high/	
	it's supposed to be down on that level/	
	to to to come up to the heighth of.	
	that's right/((sniffs))	
A	na./they are supposed to be	
	on that level/	
S	mine was right/	in larking about goon voice
A	oh	
P	oh I don't care/	
S	have we got a finishing time/	
	oh/never mind/	
P	oh/I never do anything right/	
A	mm/	
S	doesn't matter if they're not overlapping/	
P	oh/they fall apart/	
A	I know/ it's like they're stronger/	

Page - 9 -

A	that's the only reason/	
P	yeah/they go whee donk/	
S	oh lets do one of these/	
S	modern houses/	
	flat roofs/- lot easier/((laughs)) c	
P	mm we haven't got no spikey ones/	
	have we/	
	oh yeah/those/	
A	oh here's/a here's a/here's a -	
S	grreat/	
A	((laughs))	
S	yeah/oh/look at this/this is fantastic/	laughing
A	got a tree/- a tree/	laughing
P	oh great/	
S	one of these modern houses/	
A	a tree/	
S	a couple of trees/	
A	windows/	exclaiming
P	you don't put windows in/shutters/do you/	
A	course you do/	
S	could/if you want to/	
A	now then/	
P	can you/- haven't got shutters/	
	so wouldn't know/- -	
S	can't you use anyother colours/but oh	
P	we haven't got a back door/	
S	haven't you/we have/	
P	that's the front door/	
A	that's the front door/	
A	we we'll think about oh/yes/well/	
	((laughs)) come on/	
S	well it can bo our. oh	
	well/you know/you do have these	

Page - 10 -

S	houses with a funny front door/((laughs))	
?	we got (a?) window/	
A	painful/	
P	whaat/	
S	never mind/-	
	what are you missing now then/ Gregory/	
P	English/uggh	
S	who with/	
P	um.	
S	Jones/is it/	
	no/you don't have her/do you/him/	
A	Howells/	
P	Anderson/	
S	oh Anderson/	
	I don't like her much/	
P	I hate her/ugh/	
A	she's al she's alright for a free lesson/	
A	but lessons/ well I'm not sure she's	
	particularly good/	
S	oh that's what I thought/	
	I don't know what she's like though/	
	for lessons/	
P	I don't like her/anyway/	
S	don't have her/-	
A	who do you have for English then/	
P	me/	
A	no you/	
S	Dinosaur/	
A	d'y/her/oh/your form teacher/	in surprised tone
S	bad/isn't it/ -4-	
	((sniggering))	
A	oh/uh mm	
P	((laughs)) hey/	
S	((laughs hilariously))	

Page - 11 -

P	let's see if they got any people/		
S	oh/dear dear/		
P	hey/they got people/		
S	they haven't/		
P	they have/		
S	where/		
P	here/in there/		
A	oh	ahem	clearing throat
S	yes/well/		
A	I usu lly put it I (- - ?)		
S	you're gonna cop it/you are my dear boy/		
P	yes/		
A	((laughs)) when's that G. plane/		
P	I've got a persons head/		
S	'ang on/		
P	haven't got no body/		
A	look at Mrs Walker/Miss Walker/in it/		
A	what are they doing/oh rounders/		
S	rounders/aye/		
P	'aven't got no body/ 'aven't got no bodies/		
S	L Louise Evans/just fallen over/		
P	ah/here's a body/- there's a body/		
A	her/oh/I don't like her/much/		
A	I don't like Louise Evans/I don't/		
S	what school did she go to/		
P	ah		
S	I don't know/don't particularly care/		
P	she went to w she went to my old school/		

Appendix 2

Page - 55 -
12 B Boys Play Session

Children: G.W. 8.8.66
M.N. 3.7.66 Date of recording: 3.7.78
M.B. 24.4.66 Length: 10 mins.

Position of Children: M.N.
G.W. M.B.
M

MN	((breath in)) solved/ there you are/	
G	ah/	
MN	who said you 'ad a window backward/going backwards/	
MB	((laughs))	
MN	((nonsense sounds three secs.)) ((3 secs. biulding noises))	
G	three/	
MN	oh/you beaten me to it look/ ((4 secs. building))	surprised
MB	this is the sort of thing that we'd need for roads/because it's the only black one we got/	slurred
G	yeah/	
MN	yeah/I know/but we're not going to make a road/are we/	
MB	na we can ha/	
G	no/it's not worth it/really/	
MB	we can use this/as a path/going from the door/	
G	yeah/	
MN	yeah/	
G	oh/it's a bit big/in it	isn't
MN	nh . no/	

Page - 56 -

	ah/I got an idea/I got an idea/	excitedly
	uh try and get me a flat one/	
	a flat one/	
G	a flat what/	
MN	just a flat brick/	
G	a flat brick/	
MB	there's plenty of them there/	
MN	a flat brick/	
	sor/	
G	a red flat one/	
MN	no no/we can't have that/	
G	I got a red flat one/if you want	
	a red flat one/	
MN	no/not like that/a little one/	
G	ah/	
MN	look/that one/that thick/	quickly
G	ooh/	
MB	hey/who wanted a double four/	
MN	and this it's got a flat and square/ - -	
	oh look/now we've put the other	
	ones in/I've found another brick .	
	a flat one/	
MB	oh that's too thick (in it?)/	
G	we didn't need red ones/anyway/	
	we were look	
MB	an there's another red one/	
MN	oh/come on/	
G	we wasn't looking for red ones/we	
	had blue ones anyway/	
MB	I got another yellow one/as well/	

Page - 57 -

G	oh/I see what you mean/	
G	oh/we don't need yellow though/	
MN	don't need yellow/now/	
MB	yeah/that's true/	drawn out
	((5 secs. building))	
MB	I got a good idea/for the roof/	enthusiastically
G	what/	
MB	we could have blue ones of these/all the way around/	
MN	no/	
MB	and then a flat/jn we're going to have to have a little ledge/to show	
MN	no/	
MB	that it's the roof/	confidently
MN	no/	
	I got	
	I I I start/	
MB	like that/	emphatically
MN	no/	
MB	look's alright/	
G	I know I know what type of roof you mean/	
	I think/	
MN	I got it look/((breath in))	
	you put the bricks on top of one another/like that/	
G	yeah/	
	yeah/that's how I do it/	
MN	and you put them all the way round/	
	and they are up like that/	
G	yeah/	
MB	I don't think we got enough red/	

Page - 58 -

MN	we're not going to use red for the white/	
G	we're going we don't have to use red/	
MN	we're going to make a multi-coloured/	
	yellow white and blue/	
MB	we'll do a white	
	we'll do a white bottom/	
G	yeah/	
MB	then a different colour next/	
	then a different colour next/ then a	
	different colour next/	
MN	yeah/	
	exactallally/	drawn out
MB	exactly/((sigh))	
MN	right/got a three Gwynf/	
G	not a three/	
	if you can find a square/you're ok/	
MB	this is a thingy/for an elect	
	from an electric label (=cable?)	
	that is/	
G	huh/	
MN	don't matter/- -	
		to himself
G	a square/	
MB	um ((3 secs. pause))	
	you want a square/	
G	here's a little one/	
MB	square red/I gotta square blue/	
G	hang on/	
MN	I haven't got a square blue one/	
G	wait a minute/did you have another	
	small one/like that/	
MB	oh here's one one red too short/	

Page - 59 -

MB	I can see one/	high-pitched excited
	I think/	
G	did you have one like this/	
MN	got one/	
MB	that's small is it/	mumbled
	((2 secs. banging))	
	bang it in now/	
	((banging))	
G	yeah/press it that looks/look by there/	
MN	((breath in)) ah/that'll tho'll go joined together/when the bricks/	
G	m	
MN	the bricks go brica brac/a see/all the way along/	
G	right/	
	((banging))	
	bang bang bang	v. quietly
MN	this is what is known as (ivy?) shutters/	
G	((laughs))	
MB	((laugh aloud)) come on/	
MN	right/we got (- - ?)	
	we put that like that/	
G	right/	
MB	and widen it/slowly/	
MN	no/-	
	like this look/	
	let me show you/no/	
MB	it'll sort of like a wall/for the fencing/	
MN	no/	
G	oh/	

Page - 60 -

MB	yeah/	enthusiastically
MN	no/	
G	it'll be good/	
MB	it'll be good/	excitedly
MN	no/	
G	oh/	
MB	use it as a wall/for the fencing/ it'll go down 'ere/	hig-pitched
MN	no/	
MB	what/	
G	oh alright then/	
MN	it's going to be the pavement/like that/and the road's going to be in the middle/ ((2 sec. pause))	
MB	makes sense/	
G	we'll put a little bit for fencing then/ or something/	
MB	we're going to have some fencing/	emphatically
MN	oh aye/we can have some/	
MB	and a gate/what do we want a ga/ what d'you want a gate for/	
G	yeah I got gates/ well/. what do you usually have a gate for/	
MB	'cose we haven't got a garage/so we won't need a gate/	
G	no I know that/	
MN	I got an idea/	
MB	we can we can s blonk it by 'ere/	
G	it's too big/ it's too big/	

Page - 61 -

MN	no/	
MB	((belch)) it's too big/	
	let's get the fencing done/	
G	((cough))	
MN	oh/I can smell your dinner Bo/	disgust
MB	ah/((laugh))	
MN	I can smell your dinner/	
MB	I just done a ((belches))/	
MN	I know/	
MB	yes/but I gotta/	
MN	it's not going to fit/	
	it's not going to fit/	
MB	what/	
G	what's not going to fit/	
MN	that black/it's not going to fit/	
MB	let's start putting the fencing on then/	
G	oh/	
MN	no/	
MB	why couldn't we have it as a	
	country house/'cos usually/you only	
	have one side/as a pavement/- -	
	in the country/	
MN	yeah/let's have a tree/	
G	yeah/I gotta a tree there/	
MN	Gwynf/you gotta tree/	
	two trees/	
MB	and usually/they have to one sort of	
	we'll put the fen	
MN	and one bar as well/	
G	yeah (we can put it up there?)/	
MB	oi/we'll put	

Page - 62 -

	I know what/I gotta an idea/	
	we can put all/we can	
MN	look/look/	
MB	what you do/	
	what you sticking that/in the middle	
	of the road for/	
MN	because country lanes/have	
	country ((2 secs. Lego)) trees/	
MB	yeah/but they don't stick it in	
	the middle of the road/	
MN	they do/	
G	((laughs))	
MN	each side/in it/that's the road/	isn't
	like that/	
	that's the rest of the road/over 'ere/	
MB	no/I got a better idea/	
	put these by yere/and then	excitedly
	put all put all	
G	line the path with them or something/	
MB	the pavemement put the path on	
	this side of the road/then we can	
	shove fencing all along yere/	
MN	oh ai/	
G	yeah/	
MB	see/	
MN	just move the bricks across in	
	their proper positions/	
	don't take them off like that/	
G	right/	
MN	can you	
	proper position/. just move them/	

Page - 63 -

G	where's the fencing then/	
	((8 secs. moving Lego))	
MB	yeah/	
	now then/	
	we'll we'll have the trees by yere/	
	and put the the fencing in front/	
	get this in line/	
	that's going in/	
MN	the easier	
	the easier way/count one four up	
	from eight block/	
G	right/I got it/I got it/	
MN	look/	
	like that/((breath in))	
MB	now then/	
	now put the fencing one line in front/	
MN	like that/-	
G	yeah/	
MB	yeah/	
	that's two lines in front of the tree/	high-pitched
G	it isn't/	
MN	it isn't/	
	it's exactly the same as yours/	
G	that's right/it's the same as yours/	
MB	m	
MN	Gwynfor/where's your double gate/	
G	(where/and the?) double gate/	
MB	what do you want the double gate	
	for/	
	oh/I'll shove it in the front/	
G	that's right/	

Page - 64 -

MB	here's fencing Nash/
	I've got tons of it/here/
G	oh/that's not in the middle/
MN	it is/
G	it isn't/it's in . that's - -
	you have to move that one along one/
	that's it/
MB	Nash/(here/there's?) plenty of fencing/in there/
	((3 sec. pause))
MB	aha/we want a three fence/
G	we haven't got three fence/
MN	we haven't got a three fence/
	look/if we put that/like that/-
	there you are/
G	yeah/
MN	nice little path/
G	yeah/
	((5 secs. building))
MN	right/
	we can start building a roof/now/
	white bricks/clear everything else/
	back in the box/
G	oh/what about these/
MN	((deep breath in))(we'll?)keep
G	are you going to keep these out for a
	bus stop or something/
MB	yeah/
	'cose they'll we'll have the odd bus stop/
	in the country/
G	m/
	((4 secs. playing with Lego person))

Page - 65 -

MN	right/we could have we could have we could have him/coming down the path/	
G	m/	
MB	make sure he's facing the right way/	
MN	his cap's alright/	
G	he'll now/that's right/	
MN	right/this one this one's coming along the road/	
G	yeah/	
MB	there we are/	
MN	coming along the road/right/	
	there's a bus stop/	
G	there's another one there/	
	there's a bus stop/there/	
	here's a bus stop/	
MN	ta/	
	bus stop 'ere/	
G	have one in the queue/	
MB	she's in the middle of the road/	excitedly
MN	she isn't/	
G	isn't/	
MB	well/	
G	that's the pavement/	
MB	put her walking along the pavement then/	
MN	alright/	
	walking along the pavement/	
	this one is in the queue/	
	any more Lego people/	
G	I don't know/	
	I don't	v. quietly

Page - 66 -

MN	none in the box/	
	ah/I got the bottom of one/	
G	oh ai/	
MN	the bottom of one/	
MB	so this must be the top of one/	
MN	just a minute/just a minute/	
	gimme the ladder/gimme the	
	ladder/	
G	ah/(- - ?)	
MN	hey/here's another one/	singing
	well (then/done?)/right/((breath in))	
	we need a bloke going up the ladder/see/	
MB	why/	
G	what for/((laughs))	
MN	fixing the roof/	
MB	((breath in)) but a bungalow only has	breath humorously
	a flat roof/	
G	doesn't/	
MN	doesn't/	
G	a bungalow's the same/	
MN	you still need a	
	you still need a res a ladder/	
	out/don't you/	
G	m/	
MB	let's put the ladder on/after we've	
	done the roof/	
G	yeah/	
MB	so keep him out just/	
	not all the white bricks/	
	get all the red bricks off/	
G	all the black and	

Page - 67 -

MB	hang on now/	loudly
	if we're going to put the roof/	
	how we going to divide inside up	
	into sections/	
MN	we're not going to divide it up into	
	sections/	
	that's the wh	
MB	that's a waste of bricks/	
G	m/yeah/	
MB	you start doing it/Nash/and I'll	
	me and me and Warlow'll get	
	all the white bricks out/	
	d'you want them ones/or have they gotta	
	be double/	
MN	na/they gotta be double/	
	double lines/	
G	oh/	
MB	oh/	
	((3 sec. pause))	
MN	gimme all the fours you can first	
	and three's after/	
G	fours/	
MB	which count as fours/	
	these/	
MN	drat/-	crossly
	it won't fit on/	
MB	won't it/I've just knocked a cheese sandwich/	
G	why/	
	oh/because it's too big/	
MN	((breath in))	
G	that's it/	

Page - 68 -

MN	you know what I'm doing now Gwynf/	
G	yeah/I know what you're doing now/	
MB	I know what you're doing/	
G	hey/come to think of it/we haven't got all that many whites/over here/	
MN	(that's what?) I said/	
MB	we're only doing one layer/	
MN	we're only doing one layer of white/	
G	oh/	
MN	then we're doing a yellow or blue/ this won't fit/either/	
G	what/	
MN	it's gotta fit on to the corner/ 'ave you got an 'alf/ just an 'alf of a square/	
MB	yeah/there's plenty in there/	
G	I've gto one/	
MN	great/ see/. watch this/now/	
G	yeah/I know what you mean/	
MN	right/and you want a window in the roof/do you/	
MB	yeah/we'd better have a window in the roof/	
MN	get me two yellow shutters then/	
G	two yellow shutters/	
MN	please/	
MB	two yellow shutters/two yellow shutters/	singing
G	please s s s/	

Page - 69 -

MB	I got one/	
G	I got one/	
	and I got one/-	
MN	right/	
MB	where are you going to put it/by 'ere/	
MN	gimme three brick/	
	no no no a three brick/	
	gimme a three brick/	
G	((clears throat)) three brick/	
MB	what sort of three brick/	
G	white/blue/green/	
MB	white preferably/	
MN	white three brick/	
G	white/	slowly
MB	it's all singles/in 'ere/	
	((3 secs. sorting Lego))	
	here's a four/	
MN	's not/a two/	
MB	two/	
MN	((breath in)) right/watch this now/right/	
	a window/now/	
G	shutter/	
MN	window/	to himself
	and a shutter/right/	
G	((clears throat))	
MB	we've got a white window/in here/	
	wouldn't we better if we had a white window/	
MN	I have got a white window/	emphasised
G	he's gotta white window/	
MB	oh/	

Page - 70 -

	let's have it at the back/	
MN	no/	
MB	it'd look better/	
MN	it . better at the front/won't it/	
MB	oh/be careful/	loudly
MN	but the shutters won't go on/then/	
MB	put it on first/in it/	isn't
	and then stick it aa bit on/	
	it'd be easier/	
MN	wait a minute/	
	tell me how did I do it in the house/	
	I done it like that/	to himself
G	m/ - -	
MN	then I had some ste/some roofing	
	coming up there/	
	and then I had them like that/ - -	swallowing
	like that/like/-	
	like then/like that/	
	yes I did/yeah/	
	I had them like that/	
	so/- - like the one here putting	
	that obove a door like/'cose they	
	usually have them above a door/	
	right/	
G	yeah/	
MB	yeah/	
MN	right/a . any colour bricks now/	
MB	any colour/	questioning
	what'd you mean/	
MN	why that's/	
MB	blue/we got plenty of blue (-?)/no/	

Page - 71 -

	yellow/get all yellow/	
MN	'cos that's nearest to white/in it/	isn't
MB	yeah/ ((6 secs. sorting Lego))	
MN	(you know/Dew?) if I'ad all these Lego	Dew is anglicised Duw= Welsh for God
	bricks/I think	
MB	I'm enjoying this/I am/	
MN	you know/if 'ad all/	
MB	it's a laugh/	
G	m	
MB	'ere there's plenty of yellow/	

Bibliography

Ackoff, R.L. & Emery, F.E.
1972 *On purposeful systems*. Chicago: Aldine.

Anders, Karl
1982 *Von Worten zur Syntax: Spracherwerb im Dialog*. Berlin: Max-Planck-Institut.

Appelt, Douglas
1985 *Planning English sentences*. Cambridge: Cambridge University Press.

Bache, Carl
1985 *Verbal aspect: A general theory and its application to present day English*. Odense: Odense University Press.

Ballmer, Thomas T. & Waltraud Brennenstuhl
1981 *Speech act classification. A study in the lexical analysis of English speech activity verbs*. Berlin: de Gruyter.

Barwise, John & John Perry
1983 *Situations and attitudes*. Cambridge,Mass.: The M.I.T-Press.

Bateman, John A.
1985 Utterances in context: Towards a systemic theory of the intersubjective achievement of discourse. Unpublished Ph.D. Thesis Edinburgh: Department of Artificial Intelligence/ School of Epistemics University of Edinburgh.
1987 Designing a computational systemic grammar of Japanese for text generation: A progress report. [Unpublished MS]. Kyoto University: Dept. of Electrical Engineering.
1988 "Conversation generation – a theoretical watershed?" in: Benson, Jim and William S. Greaves (eds.)1988. 263-286.
1989 "Upper modelling for machine translation. A level of abstraction for preserving meaning", in: IAI Working Papers No. 12. 1-51. Saarbrücken.

Bateman, John A. & Cecile L. Paris
1989 "Phrasing a text in terms the user can understand", in: Proceedings of the Eleventh International Joint Conference on Artificial Intelligence. Detroit: University of Michigan.

Bateman, John A, Robert T. Kasper, Jörg Schütz & Erich Steiner
1989 "A new view on the process of translation", in: Proceedings of the conference of the Association for Computational Linguistics, European Chapter. 1989 , 282-290. Manchester: University of Manchester Institute of Science and Technology.

Bateman, John A, Robert T. Kasper, Johanna Moore & Robert Whitney
1989 "The PENMAN Upper Model". Marina del Rey: University of Southern California Information Sciences Institut. ISI Report

Bateman, John A., Robert T. Kasper, Jörg Schütz & Erich Steiner
1990 "Interfacing an English text generator with a German MT-analysis". in: Brigitte Endres-Niggemeyer, Dietmar Rösner & Alfred Kobsa (eds.) 1990 *Interaktion und Kommunikation mit dem Computer*. Fachberichte Informatik 238 Heidelberg: Springer. 155-163.

Bateman, John A. & Leo Wanner
1990 "Towards a lexicon for German organized by communicative function: An application of 'lexical functions'". in: Marburger (ed.) 1990 Proceedings of the German Workshop on Artificial Intelligence 1990, Heidelberg: Springer, 196-205.

Beaugrande, Robert de
1982 "Story of grammars and a grammar of stories", in: Coots, James H. (ed) 1982. 383-422

Benson, James D & William S. Greaves (eds.)
1985 *Systemic perspectives on discourse*, Vol. 1 and 2. Norwood, N.J.: Ablex.
1988 *Systemic Functional approaches to discourse*, Norwood, N.J.: Ablex.

Berko, Jean
1958 "The child's learning of English morphology", *Word* 14: 150-177.

Bernstein, Basil
1980 "Codes, modalities and the process of cultural reproduction", Pedagogical Bulletin No.7 University of Lund Department of Education.

Bernstein, Basil (ed.)
1971 *Class, codes, and control*. Vol.1. London: Routledge & Kegan Paul.

Berry, Margaret
1975 *Introduction to Systemic Linguistics. 1 Structures and systems*. London: Batsford.
1977 *Introduction to Systemic Linguistics. 2 Levels and links*. London: Batsford.

Bierwisch, Manfred
1983 "Psychologische Aspekte der Semantik", in: Wolfgang Motsch & Dieter Viehweger (eds.) *Richtungen der modernen Semantikforschung*. Berlin: Akademie Verlag. 1983. 15-64.

Block, Russel L.
1986 *Revolution und Revision in der Generativen Theoriebildung*, Tübingen: Narr.

Bobrow, Daniel G & Collins (eds)
1975 *Representation and understanding. Studies in Cognitive Science*. New York: Academic Press.

Brachman, Ronald J. & James G. Schmolze
1985 "An overview of the KL-ONE knowledge representation system", *Cognitive Science* 9.2: 171-216. 1985

Bresnan, Joan
1982 "Polyadicity", in: Joan Bresnan (ed.), 149-172.

Bresnan, Joan (ed.)
1982 *The mental representation of grammatical relations*. Cambridge,Mass.: The M.I.T. Press.

Brew, Chris
1990 "Partial descriptions and systemic grammar", in: Hans Karlgren (ed.) 1990, Proceedings of Coling Helsinki: University of Helsinki, Vol.3, 36-41

Brown, Gillian & George Yule
1983 *Discourse analysis*. Cambridge: Cambridge University Press.

Brown, Roger
1973 *A first language: The early stages*. Cambridge, Mass.: Harvard University Press.

Busemann, Stephan & Wolfgang Hoeppner & Marburger H. & Katharina Morik
n.d. States and events: Representing and processing verbs in HAM-ANS. [unpublished manuscript]

Butler, Christopher
1985 *Systemic linguistics: Theory and application*. London: Batsford.

Charlton, Roger
1988 English verb-particle colligations. Unpublished PhD thesis, Saarbruecken: University of the Saarland.

Chomsky, Noam
1981 *Lectures on government and binding*. Dordrecht: Foris.

Clahsen, Harald
1984 Der Erwerb von Kasusmarkierungen in der deutschen Kindersprache. [manuscript].

Clark, Eve & Herbert Clark
1977 *Psychology and language*. New York: Harcourt Brace Inc.

Colby, Benjamin N.
1982 "Notes on the transmission and evolution of stories", in: James H. Coots (ed.), 463-472.

Comrie, Bernhard
1976 *Aspect*. Cambridge: Cambridge University Press.

Conrad, Rudi (ed)
1985 *Lexikon sprachwissenschaftlicher Termini*. Leipzig: VEB Bibliographisches Institut.

Coots, James H. (ed.)
1982 *Journal of Pragmatics*, Vol.6. No.5/6.

Cranach, Mario von
1982 "The psychological study of goal directed action", in: Mario v. Cranach & Romano Harré (eds.). 35-74.

Cranach, Mario von & Romano Harré (eds.)
1982 *The analysis of action*. Cambridge: Cambridge University Press.

Cranach, Mario von & Urs Kalbermatten
1982 "Ordinary interactive action: Theory, methods and some empirical findings", in: Mario v. Cranach & Romano Harré (eds.). 115-160.

Crystal, David
1966 "Specification and English tenses", *Journal of Linguistics*, 2.1. 1-34.

Cummings, Michael
1987 "Backward and forward chaining in a Prolog simulation of linguistic models", in: L.T. McCranck, (ed.) 1987 *Data bases in the humanities and social sciences.* New York: Paradigm Press.

Danlos, Laurence
1987 *The linguistic basis of text generation.* Cambridge: Cambridge University Press.

Davey, Anthoney
1978 *Discourse production.* Edinburgh: Edinburgh University Press.

Davidson, Donald
1967 "The logical form of action sentences", in: Norbert Rescher (ed.) 1967 *The logic of decision and action.* Pittsburgh: University of Pittsburgh Press.

Davies, Eirean
1979 *On the semantics of syntax: Mood and condition in English.* Atlantic Heights, N.J.: Croom Helm and Humanities Press.

Dijk, Teun A. van
1976 "The philosophy of action and the theory of the narrative", *Poetics*, 5: 287-338.
1979 *Macro-structures.* Hillsdale, N.J.: Erlbaum.

Eckensberger Lutz H. & Peter Burgard
1985 Abschlußbericht an die Stiftung Volkswagenwerk über das Projekt "Entwicklung von Konfliktlösungsvorstellungen", Saarbrücken: Fachrichtung Psychologie der Universität des Saarlandes.

Eckensberger Lutz H. & Rainer Karl Silbereisen (eds.)
1980 *Entwicklung sozialer Kognition, Modelle, Theorien, Anwendung.* Stuttgart: Klett-Cotta.

Eckert, Ursula & Ulrich Heid
1988 "Semantic relations in Eurotra-D and LFG: A comparison in the context of lexical transfer in machine translation", in: Erich Steiner, Paul Schmidt & Cornelia Zelinsky-Wibbelt (eds.), 178-185.

Elliot, Alison J.
1981 *Child language.* Cambridge: Cambridge University Press.

Engelberg.K.J./Knöpfler.S.
1982 Dokumentation über Wissensrepräsentationen in der KI-Forschung unter linguistischen Aspekten, Universität Konstanz: Sonderforschungsbereich 99.

Engelkamp Jürgen
1980 "Some studies on the internal structure of propositions", *Psychological Research* 41: 355-371.

Engelkamp Jürgen, Kuno Lorenz & Barbara Sandig (eds.)
1987 *Wissensrepräsentation und Wissensaustausch. Interdisziplinäres Kolloquium der Niederländischen Tage in Saarbrücken, April 1986*. St Ingbert: Werner Röhrig Verlag.

Erdmann Peter
1990 *Discourse and grammar. Focussing and defocussing in English.* Tübingen: Niemeyer.

Fahlman, S. E.
1979 *NETL. A system for representing and using real-world knowledge.* Cambridge.Mass.: M.I.T-Press.

Fawcett, Robin P.
1974 "Some proposals for systemic syntax. Part 1", *MALS Journal*, 1: 1-15.
1975 "Some proposals for systemic syntax. Part 2", *MALS Journal*, 2(1): 43-68.
1976 "Some proposals for systemic syntax. Part 3", *MALS Journal*, 2(2): 35-68.
1980 *Cognitive linguistics and social interaction.* Heidelberg: Groos.
1987 "The semantics of clause and verb for relational processes in English", in: Michael A.K. Halliday & Robin Fawcett (eds.). 130-183 .
1988 "Language generation as choice in social interaction", in: Michael Zock & Gerard Sabah (eds.) 1988, *Advances in natural language generation.* London: Frances Pinter, Vol.2: 37-50.

Fawcett, Robin P. & Michael Perkins (eds.)
1980 *Child language transcripts.* Pontypridd: The Polytechnic of Wales.

Fawcett, Robin P. & Michael Perkins
1981 "Project report: Language development in 6-12 year-old children", *Foundations of Language*, 2: 75-79.

Fawcett, Robin P. & Michael Alexander Kirkwood Halliday & Sydney Lamb & Adam Makkai (eds.)
1984 *The semiotics of culture and language.* Vols. 1 and 2. London: Frances Pinter.

Fawcett, Robin P. & David Young (eds.)
1988 *New developments in Systemic Linguistics, Vol.2: Theory and application.* London: Frances Pinter.

Fillmore, Charles F.
1968 "The case for case", in: Emmon Bach & Robert T. Harms (eds.) 1968 *Universals in linguistic theory.* New York: Holt, Rinehart & Winston, 1-88.
1977 "The case for case re-opened", in: Peter Cole & Jerrold M. Saddock, (eds.) 1977 *Syntax and Semantics.* Vol.8. New York: Academic Press. 59-82.

Fine, Jonathan
1988 "Cognitive processes in context: A systemic approach to problems in oral language use", in: Erich Steiner & Robert Veltman (eds.), 171-182.

Firth, John Rupert
1950 "Personality and language in society", in: John Rupert Firth, 1957, 177-189.
1957 *Papers in linguistics 1934-1951.* London: Oxford University Press.

Fletcher, Paul
1985 *A child's learning of English*. Oxford: Basil Blackwell.

Fletcher, Paul & Michael Garman (eds.)
1985 Child language seminar papers, Reading: University of Reading, Dept. of Linguistic Science.

Ford-Meyer, Cynthia & Barbara Paskay & William Spruiell
1988 "An analysis of child language as a test of the Systemic theory of Circumstantials", Sheila Embleton (ed.) *The fourteenth Lacus Forum*, Columbia: Hornbeam Press. 467-478.

Gazdar, Gerald
1979 *Pragmatics*. New York: Academic Press.

Gazdar, Gerald & Ewan Klein & Geoffrey Pullum & Ivan Sag
1985 *Generalized Phrase Structure Grammar*. Oxford: Basil Blackwell.

Gentner, Dedre & Albert L. Stevens (eds.)
1983 *Mental models*. Hillsdale, N.J.: Lawrence Erlbaum Associates.

Ghadessi, Michael (ed.)
1988 *Registers of written English*. London: Frances Pinter.

Goldmann-Eisler, Frida
1958 "The predictability of words in context and the length of pauses in speech", *Language and Speech*, Vol.1.

Gregory, Michael
1985 "Towards 'Communication' Linguistics: A framework", in: Jim Benson & William Greaves (eds.) 1985 Vol.1, 119-134

Grice, Paul
1975 "Logic and conversation", in: P. Cole and Jerrold M. Morgan (eds.) 1975 *Syntax and Semantics*. Vol.3. 41-58. New York: Academic Press.

Grishman, Ralph
1986 *Computational linguistics*. Cambridge: Cambridge University Press.

Grimes, Joseph E.
1975 *The thread of discourse*. The Hague: Mouton.
1985 The structures of discourse structure, Technical note 369, SRI International. Menlo Park. California.

Grosz, Barbara J. & Candace L. Sidner
1986 "Attention, intentions, and the structure of discourse", *Computational Linguistics*. Vol.12. 3: 175-204.

Hacker, Wilfried (ed.)
1976 *Psychische Regulation von Arbeitstätigkeiten*. Berlin: VEB Deutscher Verlag der Wissenschaften.
1982 "Objective and subjective organisation of work activities", in: Marion v. Cranach & Romano Harré (eds.). 81-98.

Halliday, Michael Alexander Kirkwood
1961 "Categories of the theory of grammar", *Word* 17: 241-292.
1967-68 "Notes on transitivity and theme in English, Parts 1,2 & 3", *Journal of Linguistics* 3.1.: 37-81, 3.2: 199-244, 4.2: 179-215.
1974 *Language and social man*. London: Longman.
1975 *Learning how to mean*. London: Edward Arnold.
1978 *Language as social semiotic*. London: Edward Arnold.
1984 "Language as code and language as behaviour", in: Robin P. Fawcett & Michael A.K. Halliday & Sydney Lamb & Adam Makkai (eds.) Vol.1.: 3-36.
1985a *An introduction to functional grammar*. London: Edward Arnold.
1985b "Systemic background", in: James D. Benson & William S. Greaves (eds.) Vol.1, 1-15.

Halliday, Michael Alexander Kirkwood, & Raquaia Hasan
1976 *Cohesion in English*. London: Longman.
1980 *Text and context: Aspects of language in a social semiotic perspective*. (Sophia Linguistica 6) Tokyo: Sophia University Linguistic Institute for International Communication

Halliday, Michael Alexander Kirkwood, & Jim R. Martin (eds.)
1981 *Readings in Systemic Linguistics*. London: Batsford.

Halliday, Michael Alexander Kirkwood, & Robin P. Fawcett (eds.)
1987 *New developments in Systemic Linguistics. Vol.1: Theory and description*. London: Frances Pinter.

Harras, Gisela
1983 *Handlungssprache und Sprechhandlung*. Berlin: de Gruyter.

Harré, Romano
1982 "Theoretical preliminaries to the study of action", in: Marion v. Cranach & Romano Harré (eds.). 5-34.

Hartung, Wolfgang
1982 "Tätigkeitsorientierte Konzepte in der Linguistik. Ergebnisse, Grenzen, Perspektiven", *Zeitschrift für Germanistik* 4: 389-401.

Hasan, Raquaia
1977 "Text in the systemic-functional model", in: Wolfgang U. Dressler (ed.) *Current trends in textlinguistics*. Berlin, New York: de Gruyter. 228-246.
1985 "Meaning, context and text: Fifty years after Malinowski", in: James Benson & William Greaves (eds.) 1985 Vol.1: 16-49.

Hayes, J.R. (ed.)
1970 *Cognition and the development of language*. New York: Wiley.

Heid, Ulrich & Dittmar Rösner & Birgit Weck
1987 "Das EUROTRA-D/SEMSYN Experiment: Generierung deutscher Sätze aus semantischen Repräsentationen", in: Hans Georg Tillmann& Gerd Willée (eds.) 1987 *Analyse und Synthese gesprochener Sprache*. Hildesheim, Zürich, New York: Olms. 172-179. Updated English version in: Steiner et al. (eds.) 1988.

Hoeppner, Wolfgang
1982 "ATN-Steuerung durch Kasusrahmen", in: Wolfgang Wahlster, (ed.) 1982. *GWAI-82. German Workshop on Artificial Intelligence.* Heidelberg: Springer.

Hoeppner, Wolfgang & Katharina Morik
1983 "Das Dialogsystem HAM-ANS: Worauf basiert es, wie funktioniert es und wem antwortet es", *Linguistische Berichte* 83: 3-37.

Houghton, George & Stephen Isard
1987 "Why to speak, what to say, and how to say it: Modelling language production in discourse", in: P. Morris (ed.) 1987 *Models of cognition.* New York: Wiley.

Hovy, Eduard
1988 *Generating natural language under pragmatic constraints.* Englewood Cliffs, N.J.: Lawrence Erlbaum.

Huddleston, Rodney
1988 "Constituency, multi-functionality and grammaticalization in Halliday's Functional Grammar, review article", *Journal of Linguistics* 24: 137-174.

Hudson, Richard A.
1971 *English complex sentences: An introduction to systemic grammar.* Amsterdam: North Holland.
1976 *Arguments for a non-transformational grammar.* Chicago & London: University of Chicago Press.
1984 *Word Grammar.* Oxford: Basil Blackwell.
1986 "Systemic grammar, review article", *Linguistics* 24: 791-815.

Ikegami, Y.
1981 "Activity", "Accomplishment", "Achievement". A language that can't say "I burned it but it didn't burn" and one that can. Trier: Linguistic Agency University of Trier papers in Linguistics.

Jackendoff, Ray S.
1983 *Semantics and cognition.* Cambridge, Mass.: The M.I.T.-Press.
1987 "The status of Thematic Relations in linguistic theory", *Linguistic Inquiry* 18.3: 369-412.

Jakobson, Roman
1941 *Child language, aphasia, and phonological universals.* The Hague: Mouton. Translation 1968.

Johnson-Laird, Philip N.
1983 *Mental models.* Cambridge: Cambridge University Press.

Jones, Linda K.
1977 *Theme in English expository discourse.* Lake Bluff, Ill.: Jupiter Press.

Kaplan, Ronald M. & Joan Bresnan
1982 "Lexical-Functional Grammar: A formal system for grammatical representation", in: Joan Bresnan (ed.) 173-281.

Kasper, Robert T.

1987 Feature structures: A logical theory with application to language analysis. [Ph.D. thesis University of Michigan. Available through University of Michigan Microfilms].

1988a "Systemic Grammar and Functional Unification Grammar", in: James Benson & William S. Greaves (eds.) 1988: 176-199.

1988b "An experimental parser for Systemic Grammars", in: Denes Varga (ed.) 1988 Proceedings of COLING 1988, 309-312 Budapest: John von Neumann Society

1989 Unification and classification: An experiment in information-based parsing, Proceedings of the International Workshop on Parsing Technologies. Pittsburgh: Carnegie Mellon University.

Kay, Martin

1985 "Parsing in Functional Unification Grammar". in: David R. Dowty & Lauri Karttunen & Arnold Zwicky, (eds.) 1985 *Natural language parsing*. Cambridge: Cambridge University Press. 251-277.

Kempen, Gerard (ed.)

1987 *Natural language generation.* Dordrecht: Martinus Nighoff Publishers.

Kintsch, Walter

1977 *Memory and cognition.* New York: Wiley. Klann-Delius, Gisela & Klaus Blaschko & Heiko Hausendorf & Horst Kock & Jürgen Richter-Johanningmeier & Gerlinde Salzmann

1985 Untersuchungen zur Entwicklung von Diskursfähigkeit am Beispiel von Spielerklärungen. Abschlußbericht des DFG-Projektes. Fachbereich 16. FU Berlin Linguistische Arbeiten und Berichte Heft 21.

Kress, Gunther (ed.)

1978 *M.A.K. Halliday: System and function in language.* Oxford: Oxford University Press.

Langacker, Ronald

1983 Foundations of Cognitive Grammar. I + II. Trier: Linguistic Agency University of Trier (LAUT) Papers in Linguistics.

Lakoff, George & Mark Johnson

1980 *Metaphors we live by.* Chicago: University of Chicago Press.

Lemke Jay L.

1983 "Thematic analysis: Systems, structure, and strategy", *Recherches Semiotiques/Semiotic inquiry* 3.2: 160-187.

1984 *Semiotics and education.* (Toronto Semiotic Circle Monographs 2) Toronto

1985 "Ideology, intertextuality, and the notion of register", in: James Benson & William Greaves (eds.) 1985. Vol.1. 275-294.

Lenk, Harald (ed.)

1980 *Handlungstheorien – interdisziplinär.* Bd.1-4. München: Fink.

Leont'ev, Alexei A.

1975 *Psycholinguistische Einheiten und die Erzeugung sprachlicher Äußerungen.* Berlin: Akademie Verlag.

1981 *Psychology and the language learning process.* Oxford: Pergamon Press.

1982 *Psychologie des sprachlichen Verkehrs*. Basel: Beltz Verlag.

Leont'ev, Alexei N.
1978 *Activity, consciousness, and personality*. Englewood Cliffs, N.J.: Prentice Hall.
1981 *Problems of the development of the mind*. Moscow: Progress Publishers.

Leont'ev, Alexei A. & Alexei, N. Leont'ev & E. G. Judin
1984 *Grundfragen einer Theorie der sprachlichen Tätigkeit*. Stuttgart: Kohlhammer. Hrsg. Dieter Viehweger.

LePore, Ernest & Brian McLaughlin (eds)
1986 *Actions and events*. Oxford: Basil Blackwell.

Levelt, W.J.M. & A. Mills & A. Karmiloff-Smith
1981 Child language research in ESF countries. An inventory. Strasbourg: European Science Foundation.

Luria, Sergei R.
1973 *The working brain*. Harmondsworth: Penguin.

Lyons, John
1977 *Semantics*. Vols. 1 and 2. Cambridge: Cambridge University Press.

Mac Gregor, Robert & Raymond Bates,
1987 The LOOM knowledge representation language. ISI Technical Report ISI/RS-87-188, USC Information Sciences Institute, Marina del Rey California.

Malinowski, Bronislaw
1935 *Coral gardens and their magic*. London: Allen & Unwin.

Mann, William C. & Christian M.I.M. Matthiessen
1985 "Demonstration of the NIGEL text generation computer program", in: James Benson & William Greaves (eds.) 1985 Vol.1. 50-83.

Mann, William C. & Sandra Thompson
1986 "Relational propositions in discourse", *Discourse Processes* 9.(1): 57-90.
1987a "Rhetorical structure theory: A theory of text organization", in: Livia Polanyi (ed.) *Discourse structure*. Norwood,N.J.: Ablex.
1987b "Rhetorical structure theory: Description and construction of text structures", in: Gerard Kempen, (ed.): 85-97.

Martin, Jim R.
1985 "Process and text: Two aspects of human semiosis", in: James Benson & Willaim Greaves (eds.) 1985. Vol. 1: 248-274.
1987 "The meaning of features in Systemic Linguistics", in: Michael A.K. Halliday & Robin Fawcett (eds.) 14-40.

Matthiessen, Christian M.I.M.
1987 "Notes on the organization of the environment of a text generation grammar", in: Gerard Kempen (ed.): 253-279.
1989 Text generation as a linguistic research task, PhD thesis. University of California Los Angeles.

Matthiessen, Christian M.I.M. & Sandra A. Thompson
1988 "The structure of discourse and subordination", in: John Haiman & Sandra A. Thompson (eds.) 1988 *Clause combining in discourse and grammar*. Amsterdam: John Benjamin.

Matthiessen, Christian M.I.M. & Bateman, John
in press *Text generation and systemic functional linguistics*. London: Frances Pinter.

McClelland, James L. & Alan H. Kawamoto
1986 "Mechanisms of sentence processing: Assigning roles to constituents", in: Rumelhart et al. 1986. Vol.2. 272-326.

McClelland, James L. & David E. Rumelhart & Geoffrey E. Hinton
1986 "The appeal of Parallel Distributed Processing", in: Rumelhart et al. 1986 Vol.1.3-44.

McCord, Michael C.
1977 "Procedural Systemic Grammars", *International Journal of Man-Machine Studies*, 9: 255-286.

McNeill, David
1970 *The acquisition of language: The study of developmental psycholinguistics*. New York: Harper & Row.

McTear, Michael F.
1985 *Children's conversation*. Oxford: Basil Blackwell.

Mellish, Chris
1988 "Implementing systemic classification as unification", *Computational Linguistics* 14

Mellish, Chris & Roger Evans
1989 "Natural language generation from plans", *Computational Linguistics* 15. 4. 233-249.

Metzing, Dieter (ed.)
1980 *Frame conceptions and text understanding*. Berlin: de Gruyter.

Miller, George A. & Eugene Galanter & Karl Pribram
1960 *Plans and the structure of behavior*. New York: Holt.

Miller, Max
1976 *Zur Logik der frühkindlichen Sprachentwicklung*. Stuttgart: Klett.

Mills, A. E.
1984 "The acquisition of German", in: Dan I. Slobin (ed.) 1984 *The cross-linguistic study of language acquisition*. Hillsdale, N.J.: Erlbaum.

Minsky, Marvin
1975 "A framework for representing knowledge", in: P.H. Winston (ed.) 1975. *The psychology of computer vision*. McCraw-Hill.

Moore, Robert C.
1986 A formal theory of knowledge and action. Centre for the study of Language and information (CSLI) report No.31. Stanford

Moore, Johanna D. & Cecile L. Paris
1989 "Planning text for advisory dialogues", in: Proceedings of the Association for Computational Linguistics American Chapter Conference. Vancouver. 1989.

Nikolaus, Kurt & Uta Quasthoff & Michael Repp
1984 "Der Erwerb kommunikativer Fähigkeiten am Beispiel des kindlichen Erzählens", in: Linguistische Arbeiten und Berichte. Berlin/West: LAB 20.

Nirenburg, Sergei (ed.)
1987 *Machine Translation.* Cambridge: Cambridge University Press.

Nuyts, Jan
1989 "On the functionality of language", Papers in Pragmatics. 3.1. 88-128.

Painter, Claire
1984 *Into the mother tongue.* London: Frances Pinter.

Patten, Terry
1988 *Systemic text generation as problem solving.* Cambridge: Cambridge University Press.

Patten, Terry & Graeme Ritchie
1987 "A formal model of Systemic Grammar", in: Gerard Kempen (ed.) 279-301.

Pause, Peter
1988 "Anaphern im Text", Arbeitspapier 4. Fachgruppe Sprachwissenschaft. Konstanz: Universität Konstanz.

Pawelzig, Gerd
1970 *Dialektik der Entwicklung objektiver Systeme.* Berlin: VEB Deutscher Verlag der Wissenschaften.

Polenz, Peter von
1985 *Deutsche Satzsemantik.* Berlin, New York: de Gruyter.

Pollard, Carl & Ivan Sag
1987 *Information-based syntax and semantics.* Stanford: CSLI lecture notes.

Postal, Paul
1967 *Constituent structure.* Bloomington: Indiana University.

Pribram, Karl
1971 *Languages of the brain.* Englewood Cliffs, N.J.: Prentice Hall.

Quillian, M. R.
1968 "Semantic memory", in: Marvin Minsky (ed.) 1968 *Semantic information processing.* Cambridge, Mass.: M.I.T. Press.

Quirk, Randolph & Sydney Greenbaum & Geoffrey Leech & Jan Svartvik
1972 *A grammar of contemporary English.* London: Longman.
1985 *A comprehensive grammar of the English language.* London: Longman.

Rath, Rainer
1979 *Konversationspraxis.* Göttingen: Vandenhoeck & Ruprecht.

Reed, A.
1984 The CLOC users guide, Birmingham: University of Birmingham Computer Centre.

Rehbein, Jochen
1976a "Planen I: Elemente des Handlungsplans", Trier: Linguistic Angency University of Trier (LAUT) papers in linguistics.
1976b "Planen II: Planbildung in Sprechhandlungssequenzen", Trier: LAUT papers in linguistics.
1979 "Handlungstheorien", *Studium Linguistik.* 7.1-25.

Reich, Peter A.
1986 *Language development.* Englewood Cliffs.N.J.: Prentice Hall.

Reichenbach, H.
1966 *Elements of symbolic logic*, New York: The Free Press.

Robins, R. H.
1979 *A short history of linguistics*, 2nd. edition. London: Longman.

Rochemont, Michael S.
1986 *Focus in generative grammar*, Amsterdam: John Benjamin.

Rohrer, Christian
1985 "Indirect discourse and consecutio temporum", in: Lo Cascio & Vet (eds.) *Temporal structure in discourse.* Dordrecht: Foris.

Romaine, Suzanne
1984 *The language of children and adolescents.* Oxford: Basil Blackwell.

Rosch, Eleanor & C. Mervis
1975 "Family resemblances: studies in the internal structure of categories", *Cognitive psychology* 7: 573-605.

Rühl, P.G.
1983 *Tätigkeit – Einstellung – Fremdsprachenunterricht. Zum Verhältnis von Psychologie, Psycholinguistik und gesteuertem Fremdsprachenerwerb in der Sowjetunion.* (Tübinger Beiträge zur Linguistik 229.) Tübingen: Gunter Narr Verlag.

Rumelhart, David E. & James L. McClelland & the PDP research group
1986 *Parallel distributed processing*, Vols. 1 and 2. Cambridge, Mass.: M.I.T. Press.

Rumelhart, David E. & Geoffrey E. Hinton & James L. McClelland
1986 "A general framework for parallel distributed processing", in: David Rumelhart et al. Vol.1. 45-76.

Sacerdoti, Earl D.
1975 A structure for plans and behaviour, Technical Report TN-109, SRI.

Schank, Roger C.
1975 *Conceptual information processing.* Amsterdam: North Holland.

Schank, Roger C. & Robert Abelson
1976 *Scripts, plans, goals, and understanding.* Hillsdale, N.J.: Erlbaum.

Schütz, Jörg
1989 "Towards a framework for knowledge-based machine translation", in: *Proceedings of the 1989 German Workshop on Artificial Intelligence.* Berlin: Springer.

Scott, C. M.
1982 Review of Robin Fawcett & Michael Perkins. *Child language transcripts 6-12, Journal of Child Language.* 9: 704-8.
1984 "Adverbial connectivity in conversations of children 6 to 12", *Journal of Child Language* 11: 423-452.

Searle, John R.
1969 *Speech acts: An essay in the philosophy of language.* Cambridge: Cambridge University Press.

Sharp, Randy
1988 "CAT2 – implementing a formalism for multilingual machine translation". in: Proceedings of the Second International Conference in Theoretical and Methodological Issues in Machine Translation of Natural Languages. Pittsburgh: Carnegie Mellon University.

Simmons, R.F.
1973 "Semantic networks: Their computation and use for understanding English sentences", in: Roger Schank & Colby (eds.) 1973 *Computer models of thought and language.* New York: Freeman.

Somers, Harold L.
1983 An investigation into the application of the linguistic theories of valency and case to the automated processing of natural language. [PhD Thesis University of Manchester]
1986 "The need for MT-oriented versions of Case and Valency in machine translation", in: Universität Bonn: COLING proceedings. 1986. 118-123.

Sowa, John F.
1983 "Generating language from conceptual graphs", in: N. Cercone (ed.) 1983 *Computational linguistics.* Oxford: Pergamon Press.

Sperber, Dan & Deidre Wilson
1986 *Relevance: Communication and cognition.* Oxford: Basil Blackwell.

Steiner, Erich
1983 *Die Entwicklung des Britischen Kontextualismus.* (Sammlung Groos Bd.16) Heidelberg: Groos.
1985a "Working with transitivity: System networks in semantico-grammatical descriptions", in: James Benson & William Greaves (eds.) 1985. Vol.1: 163-184.
1985b "The concept of context and the theory of action", in: Paul Chilton (ed.) *Language and the nuclear arms debate.* London: Frances Pinter.
1986 "Generating semantic structures in Eurotra-D. Universität Bonn, Institut für Kommunikationsforschung und Phonetik: Proceedings of COLING 1986. 304-307.

1987d "Extended legislation on Semantic Relations", in: Eurotra Reference Manual, version 4.0 December 1987, Revised version 4.1. February. 1988. Extended version 5.0. June 1988. Luxembourg: Commission of the European Community.
1988a "Semantic Relations in Eurotra-D and LFG – a comparison", in: Erich Steiner et al. (eds.) 1988.
1988b "Language as a form of goal-directed action: The analysis of a moral dilemma", in: James Benson & William Greaves (eds.) 1988: 211-239.
1988c "Describing language as activity – an application to child language", in: Robin Fawcett & David Young (eds.) 1988.
1988d "Language and music as semiotic systems", in: James Benson & William G-reaves & William Cummings (eds.) 1988 *Linguistics in a Systemic perspective*, Amsterdam: John Benjamin.
1989 "Argument structure: Grammatical issues", in: The Eurotra Reference Manual, Version 6.1. Luxembourg: The Commission of the European Community.
1990 "Aspects of a functional grammar for machine translation", in: Proceedings of the Third International Conference on Theoretical and Methodological Issues in Machine Translation, University of Texas at Austin.
in press "Analytical verb constructions in English". in: Margaret Berry & Christopher Butler & Robin Fawcett (eds.) in press. *Meaning and choice. Essays in honour of Michael Halliday*. Norwood, N.J.: Ablex.

Steiner, Erich & Jutta Winter
1987 "Frames on nouns", *Sprache und Datenverarbeitung*. 1

Steiner, Erich & Jutta Winther-Thielen
1988 "On the semantics of focus phenomena in Eurotra", in: Denes Varga (ed.) 1988 Proceedings of COLING 1988. 630-635, Budapest: John von Neumann Society

Steiner, Erich & Ursula Eckert & Birgit Roth & Jutta Winter-Thielen
1988 "The development of the Eurotra-D system of Semantic Relations", in: Steiner et al. (eds.) 1988.

Steiner, Erich & Paul Schmidt & Cornelia Zelinsky-Wibbelt (eds.)
1988 *From syntax to semantics – insights from machine translation*. London: Frances Pinter and Norwood. N.J.: Ablex.

Steiner, Erich & Robert Veltman (eds.)
1988 *Pragmatics, discourse, and text: Some systemically oriented approaches to discourse*. London: Frances Pinter.

Steiner, Erich, John Bateman, Elisabeth Maier, Elke Teich, & Leo Wanner
1990 Of hills to climb and ships to sink – generating German within a functional approach to text generation, Gesellschaft für Mathematik und Datenverarbeitung, Institut für Integrierte Publikations- und Informationssysteme: Internal Paper.

Stephany, U.
1976 "Werden sprachliche Relationen in der Zweiwortphase durch die Wortstellung signalisiert?" in: G. Drachman (ed.) 1976 *Salzburger Beiträge zur Linguistik*. 2: 235-246.

Thredgold, Terry & E.A. Grosz & Gunther Kress & Michael A.K. Halliday (eds.)
1986 *Semiotics, Ideology, Language*. Sydney: Sydney association for studies in society and culture.

Van Eynde, Frank
1988 "The analysis of tense and aspect in Eurotra", in: Denes Varga (ed.) Proceedings of COLING 1988 Budapest: John van Neumann Society.

Vendler, Zeno
1967 *Linguistics in Philosophy*. Ithaca, N.Y.: Cornell University Press.

Vermazen, B. & M.B. Hintikka (eds.)
1985 *Essays on Davidson: Action and events*. Oxford: Clarendon, Oxford University Press.

Vygotsky, Lev S.
1962(1934) *Thought and language*. Cambridge, Mass.: The M.I.T. Press.
1978 *Mind in society*. Cambridge, Mass.: Harvard University Press.

Wahlster, Wolfgang
1984a Künstliche Intelligenz I. Vorlesungsskript. Saarbrücken: Fachbereich Informatik. Universität des Saarlandes.
1984b Künstliche Intelligenz II. Vorlesungsskript. Saarbrücken: Fachbereich Informatik. Universität des Saarlandes.
1984/85 Algorithmen zur syntaktischen und semantischen Analyse natürlicher Sprache. Vorlesungsskript. Saarbrücken: Fachbereich Informatik. Universität des Saarlandes.

Wanner, Eric & Lila R. Gleitman (eds.)
1982 *Language acquisition: The state of the art*. Cambridge: Cambridge University Press.

Wanner, Leo & John A. Bateman
1990 "A collocational based approach to salience-sensitive lexical selection", in: Proceedings of the 5th International Natural Language Generation Workshop, Pittsburgh.

Weir, Ruth H.
1962 *Language in the crib*. The Hague: Mouton. Wells, Gordon & Martin Montgomery & Margret MacLure
1979 "Adult-child discourse: outline of a model of analysis", *Journal of Pragmatics* 3: 337-380.

Winograd, Terry
1972 *Understanding natural language*. Edinburgh: Edinburgh University Press.
1983 *Language as a cognitive process*. Vol.1: Syntax. Reading,Mass.: Addison Wesley.

Wright, George H. von
1972 *An essay in deontic logic and the general theory of action*. Amsterdam: North Holland.

Yang, Gijoo
1990 Prediction in generation: Using tree adjoining grammars in the systemic framework. [University of Delaware working paper].

Zelinsky-Wibbelt, Cornelia
1988 "From Cognitive Grammar to the generation of semantic interpretation in Machine Translation", in: Steiner et al. (eds.) 1988.

Zwart, Sinclair de
1973 "Language acquisition and cognitive development", in: T.E. Moore (ed.) 1973. *Cognitive development and the acquisition of language*. New York: Academic Press

Index

Bei Fragen zur Produktsicherheit wenden Sie sich bitte an:
If you have any questions regarding product safety,
please contact:

Walter de Gruyter GmbH
Genthiner Straße 13
10785 Berlin
productsafety@degruyterbrill.com